Narratives of
Black Hawk's War,1832

I0165441

Narratives of
Black Hawk's War, 1832

The Expedition Against the Sauk and Fox
Indians 1832 by Henry Smith

Sac and Fox Indians in Kansas by C. R. Green

The Great Indian Chief of the West: Or,
Life and Adventures of Black Hawk
by Benjamin Drake

Narrative of the Capture and Providential
Escape of Misses Frances and Almira Hall
by William Edwards

LEONAUR

Narratives of Black Hawk's War, 1832
The Expedition Against the Sauk and Fox Indians 1832
by Henry Smith
Sac and Fox Indians in Kansas
by C. R. Green
The Great Indian Chief of the West: Or, Life and Adventures of Black Hawk
by Benjamin Drake
Narrative of the Capture and Providential Escape of Misses Frances and Almira Hall
by William Edwards

FIRST EDITION

First published under the titles
The Expedition Against the Sauk and Fox Indians 1832
Sac and Fox Indians in Kansas
The Great Indian Chief of the West: Or, Life and Adventures of Black Hawk
Narrative of the Capture and Providential Escape of Misses Frances and Almira Hall

Leonaur is an imprint of Oakpast Ltd
Copyright in this form © 2018 Oakpast Ltd

ISBN: 978-1-78282-748-1 (hardcover)
ISBN: 978-1-78282-749-8 (softcover)

http://www.leonaur.com

Publisher's Notes

The views expressed in this book are not necessarily
those of the publisher.

Contents

The Expedition Against
the Sauk and Fox Indians 1832

Contents

Indian Campaign of 1832

The Sauks and Foxes, forming one nation of Indians, occupying, until 1831, more or less of the country on both banks of the Mississippi, for about 150 miles above, and the same distance below, Rock Island, have always manifested, as a people, a hostile feeling towards the people of the United States. During the war with Great Britain, they were active and exceedingly useful allies of the English; repeatedly, and (as they boast) always successfully engaged against us. Several detachments of our army and militia were, previously to 1815, defeated by this warlike people. Since the latter date, the hostile feeling has been *openly* shown, only by a portion of the combined nation (Sauks and Foxes) called the "British Band," of which a chief called Muck-ut-tay Mich-e-kaw-kaik (the celebrated Black Hawk) *was* the head. This band occupied the territory on the east bank of the Mississippi, principally along the Rock River, and ordinarily numbered about 400 warriors

By a treaty, duly signed and ratified, the Sauks and Foxes, previously to 1831, conveyed that portion of their country lying east of the Mississippi, to the United States; and our settlers advanced to the shores of Rock River; the Indians so far acknowledging the treaty as to abandon the country and cross the Mississippi, where the majority (if not all) took up their residence for a time.

In 1831 (the spring) Major General Gaines, commanding the western department, learned, by express, that the Indians in great numbers had re-crossed the river, commenced a system of aggression on the whites, and, by threats, and in some instances by violence, had driven off many families, and bade fair to succeed in their design of breaking up the settlements along the frontier of Illinois. The general promptly moved, with such troops as he could find disposable, (the 6th regiment and a small portion of the 3rd) to the scene of difficulty.

11

Here he found the tone of the Indians so high, and their deportment so insufferably insolent, that, apprehending the necessity of an immediate resort to blows, he called on the Governor of Illinois for an auxiliary force of mounted militia, and made preparations to enforce the demand he had already made of the Indians, to evacuate the ceded territory. After much delay, and an unusual display of reckless audacity on the part of the Sauks and Foxes, they finally crossed again to the west side of the river, and executed a treaty, one article of which solemnly stipulated, that *they never would land again on the east bank of the Mississippi, without the consent of the President of the United States and the Governor of Illinois.*

★★★★★★

The Indians came openly armed into council with the general—a proceeding, it is believed without precedent among them. They used in speech the most violent and threatening language and gestures. Had not the general felt compassion for their infatuation, he would probably have chastised them on the spot.

★★★★★★

Within four months after the signing of this treaty, a numerous war party of this very band ascended the Mississippi, *landed on the east bank,* and within the limits of the American village of Prairie des Chiens, attacked a body of Menominies, (a nation distinguished for their unalterable friendship for the United States) and murdered, it is believed, twenty-eight individuals. It was for the purpose of demanding and obtaining the leaders in this outrage on our flag and laws, that Brigadier General Atkinson was ordered with his regiment (the 6th) to ascend the Mississippi, in the spring of 1832; and although circumstances have shown, that the Secretary of War, with the acuteness of judgment for which he is distinguished, aided by a thorough knowledge of the Indian character, clearly foresaw the result to which the disposition of the Indians would lead; yet very few others anticipated any occurrences more bloody than those of the preceding spring.

On the 8th April, '32, the force under General Atkinson,—six companies of the 6th regiment, with an aggregate of about 280, embarked at Jefferson Barracks, and proceeded up the river, in obedience to the orders before mentioned. At the Des Moines Rapids (200 miles above) it was first learned by the detachment, that the Indians meditated, not only resistance to the demand for the surrender of the murderers, (which *talks* with some of the frontier commanders had taught them to expect), but of the seizing and holding the territory, "the debateable land," which they had already twice or thrice ceded to the United States. Accounts here gave the number of warriors at between 600 and 800, who had already ascended the river towards Rock Island. The detachment of General Atkinson arrived at Rock Island about the 12th April, and there ascertained that on that day, or the day before or after, the Indians had entered the mouth of Rock River, and were ascending it.

The general also received correct and undoubted information of their numbers and condition. Different traders and others had carefully counted them, and reported the number of efficient warriors to be about 650, consisting of the British band (the Black Hawk's) the friends of the war party who had committed the murders at Prairie des Chiens, and about 120 Kickapoos. They were subsequently joined, on Rock River, by the Prophet's band. About 450 of this force was mounted: and it is but doing them justice to say, that they were very efficient cavalry, armed with good guns, spears, and tomahawks, on well trained horses; they never, it is believed, came in contact with our mounted force (*both parties mounted*) that the Indians did not come off the victors, whatever might be the disparity of numbers.

Under their intention of holding the country, the Indians had brought with them their families, and their moveables of every description. They had said to many traders, that they were "going to keep possession of their old hunting grounds, and would never turn their faces to the west again; that they would not strike the first blow, but that if the Americans attempted to drive them back, they were *able and willing* to give the whites *war to their hearts' content*" Accordingly, their course up the Mississippi and Rock River was, for some time, marked with great forbearance and moderation.

General Atkinson immediately summoned such of the chiefs of the nation as had not participated in the movement—at the head of whom was Pask-e-paw-ko, Waw-pel-to, and Ke-o-kuck, demanded of them such of the murderers as were within their power, and warned them of the consequences which would result to them on their joining or aiding the invading bands. The murderers (three being all within the control of these chiefs) were promptly surrendered, and the general was assured of the fidelity of the chiefs towards the government of the United States. The conference was ended by an order from the general for the friendly Indians to return to their homes west of the Mississippi, and remain there.

Two messengers, one a friendly Sauk chief, the son of Tay-e-mah,

13

and the other a half-breed, whose father was a Frenchman, and his mother a Sauk woman, were despatched to the Black Hawk, by General Atkinson not only officially ordering him and his people (in the name of the president) to return, but individually advising him of the consequences of his persisting in his present enterprise. The demand for the surrender of the murderers was also made.

Up to this time it appeared to have been the general belief among the officers of the army, as it certainly was the opinion of the writer of this, that the Indians, almost always "*more sinned against than sinning,*" would, under the forbearing, dignified and determined course pursued by the general, be brought to a sense of their conduct and situation, and induced to comply with the demands of the government. But we were soon undeceived; the messengers returned, greatly alarmed, after having been abused and insulted, and compelled to escape at the risk of their lives. They brought from the Indians the most insolent and bullying replies to the general's message—generally, in amount, ridiculing his demands, and challenging the Americans to come against them.

About this time, also, Henry Gratiot, Esq., the sub-agent for the Winnebagoes of the mining country, obeying the impulse of his duty, intrepidly proceeded to the Black Hawk's camp, (near the Prophet's village) for the purpose of holding a council with the chiefs, to ascertain their object, and to warn them to return. The Indians not only refused to hear him, but tore down his American flag, erected the British flag, and took Mr. Gratiot prisoner. There is little doubt that his fate would have been sealed, but for the interposition of the Winnebagoes, who *purchased* him of the Sauks, and restored him to liberty. We also learned, that the Sauks and Foxes had been instigated to their present course by the Prophet, (Waw-be-ka-s chick) or the "white cloud," a half Winnebagoe and half Sauk, and possessing much influence with both nations from his assumption of the sacred character, from his talents, his inveterate hostility to the Americans, and his cold-blooded cruelty.

General Atkinson, an officer possessing all the requisites for command—military skill, undaunted courage and perseverance, together with a knowledge of the Indian character, now commenced vigorous preparations for a campaign. He ordered such troops as could, with safety, be called from Forts Crawford and Leavenworth, to reinforce him; and was, in consequence, joined at Rock Island by four companies of the 1st Infantry, and subsequently at Dixon's Ferry, by two more companies of the 6th regiment from Fort Leavenworth. He took measures for collecting provisions and stores, and means for their transportation; a work of exceeding difficulty under all the circumstances, but in the execution of which he would doubtless have encountered greater delays, but for the efficient assistance derived from the different branches of the general staff. He notified the Governor of Illinois, (Reynolds) that the Indians had ascended Rock River, and entered the territories of the State in a hostile attitude. Lastly, the general took measures to secure the neutrality of the adjoining Indian nations, or should he deem it proper, their assistance. These preparations detained the troops at Rock Island three or four weeks, during much of which period, the weather was unusually cold and rainy, and our tents quite unfit for service, and useless as u shelter.

About the 9th day of May, provisions and boats having been collected, and a force of 1,800 militia (1,500 of whom were mounted) arrived, who had been ordered by Governor Reynolds to report themselves to the commander of the United States' troops; our force moved up Rock River; the regulars and a battalion of militia infantry under the command of Col. Taylor, 1st infantry and the mounted force under Brigadier General Whitesides. Governor Reynolds accompanied this latter corps in person. The mounted brigade was ordered to proceed to the Prophet's village, about 30 or 40 miles by land, and 60 or 70 by water; while the regular force was charged with the severe and unpleasant duty of dragging up the river the provisions and stores for the whole, in boats, one a *keel* of 90 tons, one of 30 tons, and a number of Mackinac boats.

It is unnecessary to describe this duty, further than to say that the weather was cold; and that for many days the troops, so employed, had not a dry thread on them; compelled to wade against a rapid stream, dragging or lifting the boats along, from daybreak until night. On our arrival at the Prophet's village, it was found that the mounted militia had advanced to Dixon's Ferry. About 30 miles below the last named point, an express informed our commander of the defeat of a battalion of the militia, under Major Stillman; and the troops were hastened forward with all possible despatch. At Dixon's Ferry, about 120 miles from the Mississippi, (by water) we learned the particulars of the *first* affair.

Major Stillman, commanding a volunteer battalion of Illinois militia, who had joined Governor Reynolds at Dixon's Ferry, and never been for a moment under the orders of General Atkinson, had been detached by the governor, at his own solicitation, to endeavour to ascertain the position of the Indians. Deceived by some individuals, who assured him that they had reconnoitred the country for 45 miles above Whiteside's camp, and that there were no Indians within that distance, Stillman encamped an hour before sunset, at 25 miles from Dixon's, in a well-chosen position, on a stream, since called *Stillman's run*. Very soon after pitching tents and unsaddling, some Indians were discovered on the open prairie, at a mile or two distance. The camp entirely filled a small open wood, which was on every side surrounded by open and clear prairie, slightly undulating; the strongest fortress could hardly have been more efficiently defended against a savage force than the camp in question, where an hundred men *ought* to have repulsed ten times their numbers of an attacking force.

On the discovery of the Indians, (only two or three in number) the militia sallied out, as all agree, in great confusion—some with saddles, and some without, and pursued and *captured* these Indians. Someone called out that three or four others were in sight; on which another pursuit occurred, in still greater disorder: the last Indians were overtaken, and two of them killed, it is said *unresistingly* and *without provocation*. In a few minutes others were descried advancing; their numbers, no doubt, appeared in the dusk of the evening much greater than they really were, and a panic seized the whites. "*Sauva qui peut*" was the word; or, rendered into backwoods English, "*the devil take the hindmost!*" and the whole corps fled, without firing a well-directed shot.

They passed, running directly through their camp, plunged into the creek, and did not halt until they arrived at Dixon's where they came straggling in for twenty hours. Twelve of the whites and four of the Indians, including those first wantonly slain, were killed. It is asserted by the enemy that this rout was caused by less than one hundred Indians, and the pursuit continued through the night by less than thirty. There were doubtless many gallant fellows in Stillman's corps, and it is difficult to account for this, as well as other similar affairs, between the whites and the Indians, save by attributing it to want of discipline, and of mutual confidence among themselves.

The army continued their advance up Rock River to Stillman's run, having left the defeated corps to guard the sick, wounded and provisions at the depot at Dixon's. At Stillman's run, General Atkinson was overtaken by an express, with intelligence that the corps left to guard the depot had determined to abandon their charge and *return*

16

home. He also ascertained that the enemy had moved rapidly up Syca-more Creek (called by the Indians "*Kish-waw-kee*") towards its head. The mounted force (now about 2,000) was despatched in pursuit, and the regular infantry ordered to occupy the depot at Dixon's Ferry. Whitesides accordingly moved up Sycamore Creek with his com-mand for two or three days pursuing, without, however, being able to get sight of the enemy. The next intelligence from this corps, received by the general gave the information that they had proceeded across the country to the Illinois River, and disbanded themselves, or been discharged. This was said to have been brought about from some cause connected with the local political parties of the State.

The general, with his staff, immediately proceeded across the country, to the Illinois River, and by much exertion succeeded in inducing a few companies of mounted men to volunteer to assist in protecting the settlements.

Within a few hours after the general's departure, intelligence ar-rived at the ferry, by expresses, that the enemy had struck the settle-ments at different points, 80 or 90 miles apart, and committed butch-eries with all the accustomed horrors of Indian warfare. On the same day the report of a few mounted men of the disbanded militia, who arrived, induced the serious apprehension, that the general had been cut off in his journey across the country. Fortunately our fears proved to be without foundation. Among the sufferers, the fate of no one excited more sympathy than that of Felix St. Vrain, Esq., Indian Agent for the Sauks and Foxes, who had accompanied the army to Dixon's Ferry, where he had obtained leave to return and secure his family at Rock Island. On his way to Galena, with a party of seven men, they were attacked by a large party of Indians commanded by the Prophet, and Mr. St. Vrain and three others most barbarously murdered; the others made their escape.

By indefatigable exertions General Atkinson succeeded, in less than three weeks, in calling out a new militia mounted force, (for it was already found that the war could not be successfully prosecuted against a well-mounted enemy, by infantry alone), in organizing it anew, and in procuring provisions and land transportation for a new movement.

In the meantime, however, several little affairs occurred. Two com-panies of regular troops, with a company of mounted men, had been despatched to Kellogg's Grove, for the purpose of occupying the country between Rock and Fever Rivers, and dispersing a party of the enemy known to be lurking therein. While there, the Indians, who daily watched the movements of this detachment and the different portions of it, in their various excursions, carefully avoided the regular troops; but, seizing their opportunity, they attacked the militia on their return to the camp, and beat them, killing three of their number. The Indians lost four.

After remaining at Kellogg's Grove ten days, this party was ordered in, and it was replaced by a battalion of militia 250 strong, commanded by Major Dement. This battalion, the day after their arrival at the position, was attacked and defeated by 130 Indians under command of the Black Hawk, who drove the whites into their stockade, and besieged them, until relieved by General Pozey with the residue of the brigade, when the Indians leisurely withdrew. About this time, also, General Dodge, (now Colonel Dodge of the United States' Dragoons) with a party of 28 mounted men, learned that certain murders had been committed in the neighbourhood of Fort Hamilton, and pursued the murderers. Dodge and his party overtook the enemy, (who they found to be a party of fifteen Sauks), and after a sharp conflict, killed every one of them with loss of three whites.

On the 28th of June, the army again advanced on the enemy. Our force consisted of upwards of 400 regular infantry, and Henry's brigade of 1,000 mounted militia. Brigadier General Brady, of the United States Army, had in the meantime joined, and by order of General Atkinson assumed command of this division of regulars and militia. A company of regulars were left to guard the depot at Dixon's Ferry, and Pozey's and Alexander's brigades detached and disposed so as to protect the settlements. On the third of July we found ourselves in the neighbourhood of the enemy, who, however, occupied an inaccessible position, in a swamp a few miles from us. They had retired before us, and in several instances we found in their camps scalps and *heads* previously taken and left in triumph.

They also for several days, left in their camps a sort of *guide-post*, with a wisp of hay done up, and so fixed as to indicate their direction. This however, was mere bravado, as they avoided a conflict, though it was eagerly sought by the army. The force of the enemy, at this time, could not have been far from 1,000 efficient warriors, nearly all mounted.

Our marching had became exceedingly disagreeable and difficult; wading through swamps and morasses; our provisions and baggage on pack-horses, frequently damaged and falling short by the horses sinking in the swamps. Every exertion had been made to procure guides, but in vain. Such Winnebagoes or Pottawattomies as joined us or could be taken were either ignorant or treacherous.

On the 6th of July we reached a deep and muddy stream, called, most inaptly, *white water*, beyond which, we were informed by the Winnebagoes, we should find the enemy. With much difficulty we forded or swam this stream, or rather the first of its three branches; and after a perplexing march of twelve or fifteen miles, we arrived where the friendly Indians assured the general with one voice, that further advance was impossible, having arrived, as they said, and as it appeared, at a *wilderness* of that description of morass called by the French *terre tremblante*. We had no resource but to retrace our march, for the purpose of reaching and crossing Rock River, to reach the enemy by moving up the other bank. Arrived again at the mouth of White water, the mounted force under Generals Henry and Dodge was despatched with the pack horses to Fort Winnebago for provisions.

Under these vexations and disappointments, we had the satisfaction of knowing that our enemy were completely besieged; cut off from all their resources. General Atkinson knew that they must soon be driven by famine to give us battle or to retreat from their present position, when he had little doubt of overtaking them. He therefore took such measures as prevented their escape. To enable a company to guard our provisions and sick, when we should again advance, a stockade was erected, which was called Fort Kosh-ko-nong.

Here we learned by despatches from Major General Scott to our commander, of the arrival of that officer with his troops at Chicago, and that the "Asiatic cholera" was raging among them—this was the first intimation any individual of our command had received of the existence of this disease on this continent. We also received other disagreeable and mortifying intelligence through the public prints and from *other sources*—the censure conveyed in insinuations and innuendoes by certain prints; the information from private letters; and perhaps the *tone* of official despatches, all gave us too clearly to understand, that thus far for our toil, exposure, and exertions, we had received nothing but censure; how unjustly, every individual of the army knew and felt.

On the arrival of the provisions, a new guide (an Indian chief), was procured, who promised to conduct the army to the enemy's camp; his services were gladly accepted, and the army once more advanced, through the swamps, in the direction of the enemy. When again within a few hours march of them, the night set in with the most tremendous storm of rain and wind, thunder and lightning, that the writer ever witnessed. Before morning, an officer overtook us with information from General Henry, that the enemy had retreated, by crossing Rock River, and that the mounted corps of Henry and Dodge, having fallen on the fresh trail of the retreating Indian army, had taken that trail in pursuit, after despatching the express to General Atkinson. Instantly we commenced our retrograde movement again; that evening arrived at Fort Kosh-ko-nong: the next day passed round Lake Kosh-ko-nong, and forded Rock River below the lake.

Our marches were now forced and severe. One day we marched, it is believed, near twenty miles, during a hot day, without water. Before the arrival of the army at the Wisconsin, we were met by the intelligence that Henry and Dodge had come up with and attacked the rear of the enemy near the river, and defeated it. Rafts were forthwith constructed at the Wisconsin, and the army crossed that river, at a small place called Helena, on the 27th of July; and within two hours afterwards struck the trail of the enemy. Their trail gave evidence that their numbers must be considerable. Their order of march was in three parallel columns. Over the dry prairie, the route of each column was worn from two to six inches in the earth; and where the ground was such as for a moment to interrupt their regular order of march, their trail appeared like an ordinary road which had been travelled for years, wanting only the tracks of wheels.

From this time until we reached the Mississippi, we continued without deviation to follow the trail of the enemy, having no other guide; and it led, doubtless with a view of baffling the army, over such a country as, I venture to say, has seldom been marched over: at one moment ascending hills, which appeared almost perpendicular; through the thickest forest; then plunging through morasses; fording to our necks, creeks and rivers; passing defiles, where a hundred resolute men might repulse thousands, whatever their courage or capacity; next clambering up and down mountains perfectly bald, without so much as a bush to sustain a man. It was in this march that our infantry regained their confidence in their own powers, which (lacking the powers of rapid locomotion to make a dash against the enemy) had been somewhat impaired early in the campaign. They far outmarched the horsemen, nearly all of whose horses were broken down.

The enemy were under the impression that it was impossible for us to follow them; and to that error we probably owe our ultimate success in overtaking them, or at least in bringing them to action, on grounds of equality. We, each day, made two of their day's marches, and passed one or two of their camps. We frequently passed their dead, who, exhausted by wounds or fatigue, had expired, and fallen from their horses: on the 1st of August we passed the bodies of eleven. A little before sunset that day, we learned from a prisoner that the enemy were but a few miles in advance of us. Up to this time, not a man of the army knew where we were, save that we were north of the Wisconsin, and on the enemy's track. We marched until after dark, hastily encamped, slept two or three hours, when reveille beat, and we were again in march before daybreak on the 2nd of August.

At a little after sunrise, we discovered the curtain of mist hanging over the Mississippi, and the scouts in advance (a detachment of Dodge's corps) announced the vicinity of the enemy. We were halted for an instant, our knapsacks and baggage thrown off, and our pack horses left. We then advanced rapidly into the timbered land; and the occasional shots in advance confirmed the report of the scouts. This firing was from a select rear-guard of the enemy, about seventy in number.

Our order of battle was promptly arranged, under the personal supervision of General Atkinson; the centre composed of the regular troops, about 380 in number, and Dodge's corps, about 150; the right, of the remains of Pozey's and Alexander's brigades, probably in all 250 men; the left, of Henry's brigade, in number not far from 400 men. This last was, throughout the campaign, a most excellent militia brigade, and well commanded. The army advanced by heads of companies, over a space of two or three miles. At length, after descending a bluff, almost perpendicular, we entered a bottom thickly and heavily wooded, covered also with much underbrush and fallen timber, and overgrown with rank weeds and grass; plunged through a bayou of stagnant water, our men as usual holding up their arms and cartridge boxes. A moment after, we heard the yells of the enemy; closed with them, and the action commenced.

As I have already been more prolix than I had intended, I refer your readers to the official account of the battle. Suffice it to say, that quarters were in no instance asked or granted. The official reports give the number of killed of the enemy, at 150; though doubtless many were killed in the river and elsewhere, whose bodies were never seen afterwards. Our loss was but 27, among whom was one officer, Lieutenant Bowman, a gallant fellow of Henry's brigade. This disparity of loss was probably owing to the rapid charge made by our troops on the enemy, giving them time to deliver but one confused fire. About 150 horses were taken or killed. The Black Hawk, the Prophet, and some other chiefs escaped from the action, but were brought in by the Winnebagoes, and the friendly portion of the Sauks, and ultimately delivered to the commanding general.

After the action, 100 Sioux warriors presented themselves, and asked leave to pursue on the trail of such of the enemy as had escaped. This was granted, and the Sioux, after two days' pursuit, overtook and killed 50 or 60, mostly, it is feared, women or children.

The afternoon previous to the action, the steamboat *Warrior*, on her return from the Sioux villages above, with some officers and 20 or 30 soldiers of the United States Army, discovered the Indian army on the bank of the Mississippi, (exactly where General Atkinson subsequently attacked them) engaged in constructing rafts and other means of crossing the river. The enemy for some time endeavoured to decoy the steamboat to the shore, assuring those on board that they (the Indians) were Winnebagoes, &c. A sharp skirmish was finally the result, in which several of the Indians were killed, and one soldier wounded. The Indian loss is differently reported by themselves at from 7 to 23. The steamboat returned to Prairie des Chiens, and arrived again opportunely at the close of the action the following day.

The troops moved down the river to Prairie des Chiens, where they were met by Major General Scott, who with his staff had left the brigade at Chicago, prostrated by an enemy far more terrible than the savages—the *cholera*—and was hastening to take part in the campaign. The wounded were left at this place, and the army descended to Rock Island, where they arrived in fine health and spirits on the 9th of August. Indeed, it is astonishing how perfectly healthy the troops had been during much and great exposure to the ordinary causes of disease; up to this time, not a death from disease had occurred during the campaign, among the regular troops. They had borne, without the slightest murmur, their fatigues and privations, and scarcely an occasion for the most trifling punishment had been given, from the time the army took the field. It has never been the fortune of the writer, during a service of twenty years, to witness for a length of time, the conduct of any command so perfectly exemplary.

About the 20th of August the troops from Chicago arrived under the command of Colonel Eustis, and were encamped about four miles from the command of General Atkinson. Poor fellows! we listened with sincere condolence to the tale of their wretched sufferings from disease; few of us imagining that we should call on them, so soon, to reciprocate our sympathy.

About the 26th of August, a case of *cholera* exhibited itself; this was followed by several others, and the ravages of this shocking disease then became truly dreadful. The troops were encamped in wretched tents, in close order of encampment, and for several days of continued cold rain, the pestilence raged. Every man in camp could hear the groans and screams of each individual attacked by spasms, which added greatly to the horrors of the scene. During a very few days, four officers and upwards of fifty rank and file, out of about three hundred infantry, became its victims.

The rangers, also (encamped near them) suffered severely. It is but rendering justice to Major-General Scott (then our commander) to say, that his conduct at Rock Island during the period of horrors, was worthy the hero of Chippewa, Fort George and Niagara, By his example, exciting confidence and courage; fearlessly exposing himself to disease and death, in its most terrible form, in his attentions alike to the officer and the private soldier; while he enforced, with the most vigilant care, the strictest sanitary regulations. At length the troops were moved across the Mississippi (not out of sight of their late camp), and the pestilence ceased.

The Indians sued for peace. A treaty was held at Rock Island, by which the whole country east of the Mississippi, called the mining district, and a large tract on the west bank (probably in the whole about 8,000,000 acres), was ceded to the United States, and all the surviving insurgent chiefs of note were to remain in confinement, as hostages, during the pleasure of the president.

And thus ended the Sauk War!

About the 28th of September, the troops were ordered to their respective stations.

In the foregoing narrative, the writer is aware that he might have more interested his readers by details of individual scenes; but the fear of being insufferably prolix, has induced him to confine himself to a general account of the campaign, leaving the minutiae to some future opportunity. He is aware, that in his views of causes and results, he must necessarily differ from some, but he believes this narrative will be acknowledged to be in the main correct.

Sac and Fox Indians in Kansas

Contents

Some Sauk History for 100 years

At the close of the Revolution the Confederate tribes of Sauk and Foxes, lived on both sides of the Mississippi River; and while their domain on the east side, in what was later, Illinois and Wis., was quite restricted as to size yet I presume from the long continuance of their habitations and cultivated fields that in 1783 one half or more of their population was in the U.S. Ty. But the domain on the west bank that they claimed, extended south to the Missouri River also west to the same river. Over all this vast territory several bands of the Sauk and Foxes hunted annually.

The Sauk tribe from the best authorities numbered in those days, 4500. The Foxes, 2000. The warriors of both tribes were noted for their bravery. The Sauks were great friends of the British, for they encouraged their fur traders to penetrate to these places that the U.S. did not take possession of until after the La. Purchase. Therefore it is a strange circumstance that the Sauk along with many other tribes, are found at Greenville O. in 1789 and again in 1795, where General Wayne enters into a general treaty with all the Indians of the North West Ty.

The Indians of Ohio, Mich. and Ind., many of them emigrant tribes from further east before the revolutionary war, violently and persistently for many years opposed any white settlements north of the Ohio River and west of New York. The British located at Detroit up to the war of 1812, did all they could to stay the settlement of this N.W. Ty. Through it all in spite of bribes and presents from the British to the Sauk and Foxes to harass the early settlers of Ohio, they as a tribe kept away, saying as they did in the Revolution, "that it was the white mans quarrel, and they could fight it out among themselves".

The old Sauk warrior Black Hawk could not stay out, with twenty of his warriors amidst 2000 or more Indians and 250 British soldiers they thought to overpower General Wayne on the Maumee Aug. 20 1794 General Wayne with 900 troops, obtained such a complete victory over the forces opposing him, that the Indians decided after wards that it was folly to listen to the British, and war against such a veteran as General Wayne. This battle which resulted later in the Greenville Treaty, was called the Battle of Fallen Timbers. It is said in history that the Sauks could not stand up to the firearms in the battle, but after seeing how it was going against their Indian allies they pulled out and went home. (Compiled in 1906, from many sources, by C. R. Green, Olathe.)

I now come to a period and transaction in 1804-8 that though more than a century has elapsed since it was done, seems in the light of history to have been very disgraceful on the part of our government. The Louisiana Purchase was in 1803.

After President Jefferson had purchased Louisiana from Napoleon he hastened to establish peaceable relations with the Indians along the Mississippi and Mo. Rivers; and sought to quiet the title to lands held by the Indians east of the Mississippi.

William H. Harrison was then Governor of the Indian Ty. of La. and Superintendent of Indian Affairs for that district, with headquarters at St Louis. To him was delegated in June, 1804, the responsibility of making a treaty with the Sacs who, as Jefferson wrote, own the country in the neighbourhood of our settlements of Kaskaskia and St Louis. The treaty was made Nov. 3rd 1804, and included the Foxes, who were recognised as holding two fifths interest in the possessions ceded east of the Mississippi.

But the remarkable phase of this first and very important treaty with these two tribes is that there is strong probability that not a single Fox or Musquakie was within a hundred miles of St Louis at the time the treaty was made. And that of all the chiefs and warriors of the two tribes the instrument bears the signature of but four Sacs and one half breed, the former of whom, as Black Hawk asserted and as the Sacs and Foxes have always affirmed they had been dispatched to St Louis in the autumn of that year to plead for the freedom of a Sac who was being held at that post on the charge of murder. The account of this treaty, which took from Black Hawk and his band all their villages and cultivated fields on the Illinois side, around the mouth of Rock River, as given by Black Hawk is so representative of the Indian version of the case that it may well be incorporated here to throw light on the first, and perhaps greatest mistake, not to say blunder, made by our government in dealing with these people.

Black Hawk says:

> One of our people killed an American, was taken prisoner and
> confined at St Louis for the offense. We held a council at our
> village to see what could be done for him, and determined that
> Quash-qua-me, Pashepaho, Ouch-e-qua-ka, and Hashe-quar-
> hi-qua should go down to St Louis, see our American father
> and do all they could to have our friend released by paying for
> the person killed, thus covering the blood and satisfying the
> relations of the murdered man. This being the only means with
> us for saving a person who had killed another, and we then
> thought it was the same way with the whites.'

The party started with the good wishes of the whole Nation.
Quash-qua-me and party remained a long time absent. They
at length returned and encamped near the village, and did not
come up that day. They appeared to be dressed in fine coats and
had medals. Early the next morning the Council Lodge was
crowded. Quash-qua-me and party came up and gave an account of their mission. On our arrival at St Louis we met our
American father and explained to him our business, urging the
release of our friend. The American chief told us he wanted
land. We agreed to give him some on the west side of the Mississippi, likewise more on the Illinois side opposite Jefferson.
When the business was all arranged we expected to have our
friend released to come with us. About the time we were ready
to start, our brother was let out of the prison. He started and ran
a short distance when *he was shot dead.*
This was all they could remember of what had been said and
done. It subsequently appeared that they had been drunk the
greater part of the time while at S Louis.—*Autobiography of
Black Hawk.*

It is incredible to believe that these two tribes and the government in four months time settled this treaty affair by which the Sacs
disposed of their almost undisputed possession of the rich valleys and
prolific hunting grounds between the Illinois and Wisconsin rivers,
containing 50 million acres, for the paltry sum of $1000. a year annu-
ity. When the other tribes of this particular section had been treated
with, Governor Harrison sent the treaty to Congress to be ratified,
with this terrible wrong in it, and the tribes ignorant of its binding

terms.

This was what made the Black Hawk War 25 years later. The fatal error of Governor Harrison in driving a sharp bargain with a few drunken and irresponsible members of one band, was sure to cost his nation dearly afterwards. When the treaty was proclaimed both tribes repudiated it. In these days was Mokohoko growing up in the Sauk camp drinking in the hatred to the white civilization that made him such a fateful ally of Black Hawk in his war.

Now I do not want the reader to think there were no further treaties with the Sac and Fox before the Black Hawk War. There were several. But one concluded May 13 1816 at St Louis in which the Sac and Foxes of the Rock River band took part, confirmed the 1804 Treaty. To this treaty Black Hawk's name was signed, and he took pay, treacherously years afterwards trying to crawl out of it.

There was a great difference in the make up of these Sac and Fox chiefs even in 1845, when they came onto their new reservation on the "Head Waters of the Osage River." Mokohoko with a respectable following went off by themselves beyond the Mo. River with the Sauk and Iowa Indians, on the Great Nemaha reserve. He was jealous of the Keokuks, yet in the late Fifties he came and joined our Kansas band and as we see at the close of this work in 1862 was hatching a lot of mutiny for Agent Martin.

The Indian agent's reports, for the years succeeding their arrival in Kansas all speak of Keokuk's farming operations, 500 acres of those rich Marias des Cygne bottoms in Franklin Co. put into corn before 1850. A log school built and Senator Benton's son installed as teacher a couple of years later. One of the bands reported to be a teetotallers band of Indians. All this before Kansas was ever heard of.

Take the matter of signing the final treaty of Oct 14 1868. The first one signed some months before had come back from Washington with amendments and new articles, to be submitted to the Nation again. The common Indians told Keokuk to keep out of it the second time he promised; only to be coaxed over to Ottawa where designing white men dosed him with liquor until they got him into the mood to sign the treaty. The paper being all signed then but Mokohoko's name, the bearers rushed off to Washington, while Keokuk had a year of contempt from his followers as his portion.

C. R. Green. Oct. 1914.

JOHN AND JULIA GOODELL.

John Goodell was a native of N. Y. who enlisted in the U. S. A. in the 30's and did service among the Indians. I have his Record. When discharged he became Agent Streets Interpreter with the Sac & Fox Indians there in IOWA. Julia the Indian wife of a Lt. Mitchell before the BLACK HAWK war, after many vicisitudes returned to live with her friend Agt. Street. John and her were married 4th July 1840. He died at Quenemo 1868. The grave up in the old Mission grave yard is lost. Julia died June 4 1879 in Okla.

REV. ISAAC McCoY, WIFE AND BOY. MISSIONARY TO THE SAC
AND FOX INDIANS, THESE 20 YEARS OR MORE.
HE IS AN OTTOWA INDIAN WHILE HIS WIFE, WHO WAS MARY
THORP, IS A HALF BREED SAUK INDIAN.

Mokohoko's Home,
and Date of Death

CYRUS CASE'S NARRATIVE.—MOKOHOKO.

Cyrus Case was born Dec. 1st 1838,
in Farmington Franklin Co. Maine.

I lived there until I moved to Kansas. I had a good academy school education, as the noted Abbott Schools were there before the war.

CIVIL WAR SERVICE.

I enlisted Sep. 10 1862 for 9 months in Co. E 24 Me. V. I. Then I served a few months in 1st D. C. Cav. there in Washington. I was transferred about Oct. 1864, to Co. C 1st Maine Cav. I was an orderly sergeant in all three regiments. We were in the siege of Port Hudson. I was slightly wounded three times. We were let out of the service Aug. 1st 1865, and I went home to Farmington.

Jan. 14 1869, I was married to Faustina McClure of same place. We started west pretty soon, and arrived in Ottawa Feb. 28 1869. I came out from the East with E. M. Kalloch, now of Ottawa and we took claims near each other. I laid claim on the S. W. ¼ Sec 31 17 17. while he took Wing's claim. I am in Lincoln township, three miles east and one mile north of Melvern, The Marais des Cygne and Rock Creek both flow in on my farm.

We settled in the midst of the Indians. We built the first house on this side, we lived a few weeks in an Indian house along with John Tracy. I cut and hauled logs for my lumber to Henderson's sawmill over on Tequas, near Jerry Hussey's present home. I built my house using native shingles. I had 50 acres all heavy bottom timber which I cleared all off. I paid $1.50 per acre, the patent being signed by U. S. Grant.

Some of my neighbours in those early years were; E. M. Kalloch, now dead, Dr. Floyd, dead, Wm Fleak, Joe McMillen, Wm H. Connelly, Jabez Adams Sr. and boys, R. L. Graham, T. L. and Joe Marshall, and others.

I had a good team and did hauling for others. I use to haul goods from Lawrence for Rankin & Co. Quenemo, and for Dr. A. Wiley.

They use to ask me to drink, but being born and raised anti-liquor, I was a well known Temperance man before Kansas made it a law. We generally did our trading in Ottawa. Once I killed and dressed a load of fat hogs and marketed them way down in Sumner Co. where I received 10 cts per lb. I went once down into Lynn Co to work on a R. R., but never got my wages.

Kalloch and I owned the two quarters in partnership. I had 65 acres of prairie up on the wing quarter. I belong to the Baptist Society. I have been S. S. Superintendent of two Union Schools in this section as well as our own church school.

The Mo-Ko-Ho-Ko-Band of Indians.

As I have said in another place we settled in the midst of the Indians. When they were removed Nov. 1869, many were soon back here living along the river. Mokohoko's favourite camping place was on my timber bottom near where Rock Creek empties into the Marias de Cygne. He came there with about 100 of his followers in the fall of 1869. He was a peaceable chief that a white seldom saw unless they went to his hut. He wanted nothing to do with white men. Occasionally a family would pull off, go south and join their tribe. In fact it was quite a practice of many of his band to generally go south in the winter, to hunt, fish, and seek warmer climate. Some times they managed to enrol and draw annuities. But Mokohoko and family always staid. In October 1875 my team went along with others to haul Mokohoko and others down there the second time.

Mokohoko a trespasser in law.
Date of death never revealed by Indians

He was soon back. I went to law to get them off my place and to show Chief Mokohoko that if he didn't sign the Indian Treaty of 1868, giving the Sac and Fox Diminished Reserve back to the government, that there were all the other chiefs who did and thus he was a trespasser. Mokohoko and his band set up a good defence, for they had Geo Powers as their lawyer, while Judge Blake was ours about 1874. He only moved a dozen rods to get on another man. I never knew when he died. It might have been in 1880 or before. He charged his followers to never reveal the time of his death or place of burial, and that his successor in office should never willingly leave the reserve.

Next in rank to Mokohoko was Ke-aqua, A fine specimen of an Indian about 45. He died about 1880, and I was down at the burial on the river bank on my land. They made quite a display, the coffin being hewed out of a hollow basswood.

I hired the Indians much. There were about thirty or forty male adults. Quite a large proportion of the band were women and children. They never would have any missionary among them, so their children the 16 years they continued here got no schooling. They were determined to stick to their wild tribal customs. They had good moral virtues, and when they sat at my table adopted our ways. Kelly was a half breed and Interpreter, he went off long before the last did. Old Co-to-pa, one of the councillors was a fat jovial old fellow well known by the whites. Captain Sam, who was chief after Mokohoko, was lame, of medium height and heavy set.

LIEUTENANT HAYES REMOVES THE INDIANS NOV. 1886.

It was in Nov. 1886 that a young man, Lieutenant Hayes of the 4th U. S. Cav. and about twenty privates, came from Fort Riley with orders to gather all the Indians together and remove them by wagons to their reservation in Okla. where dwelt the Sac and Fox tribe My team went again to help haul them. They were treated kindly but had to be watched closely. They had ponies, and the first day or two out raced with the soldiers to get away.

This was virtually Cyrus Case's talk one pleasant day about 1905 after they had sold their farm and were packing up to leave for Ceres, Stanislaus Co. Calif. However bad Mr. Case hated to break up and leave, he had for months been at the point of death from Brights Disease. The move has helped him. Their son Cyrus Walter Case born there on the Osage Co. farm May 3rd 1870, married Oct. 26 1898 to a Haverell Mass. lady, has brought two fine grandsons, Clifford Dwight, and Albert Fernald Case, into the family before they moved. And I hear nothing otherwise than that Cyrus Case and his family who for 36 years laboured to make their neighbourhood in Kansas better, now enjoy the richest of life's blessings in their California home.

C. R. G. Sep. 1914.

Mokohoko's Noted Speech

NARRATIVE OF JABEZ ADAMS JR. OF AGENCY TWP,
EX-COUNTY SUPERINTENDENT OF PUBLIC SCHOOLS.

Early in the spring of 1869, my father Jabez Adams Sr., 4 brothers John C, Wm. H., Isaac Adams and myself, moved from Douglas Co. Kan. and settled on Tequas Creek, five miles south of Quenemo, then called Sac and Fox agency.

We soon learned that the treaty with said Indians was not complete and much doubt existed among the new settlers about the Treaty standing the "test" at Washington City. (So much fraud used to get the treaty signed, and protests stopped.)

Several weeks after our settlement there, I learned that a "Council" of Indian chiefs and Government officials would be held in the agency (now Quenemo) for the purpose of completing the Treaty and arranging for the removal of the Indians. In company with many of the white settlers, I attended that council.

THE SAC AND FOX INDIAN COUNCIL SUMMER OF 1869.

I cannot remember the date; but shall never forget some of the important business decided that day. The council was held in an enclosed greensward—embellished by fine shade trees. Besides the chiefs and braves whose business it was to be there, It seemed that every Indian living on the reserve was there. Indians formed an inner circle around the officials; whites the outer circle. The ground was covered with people for many rods.

My first surprise that day was the intelligent features of many of the noted Indians. In this brief account only two chiefs Keokuk and Mokohoko will be mentioned. In symmetry and physique they were perfect. Keokuk fair, almost like a white man Mokohoko, dark. Their physiognomies beamed with intellectuality and showed strong marks of philanthropy. They were neatly dressed and made a fine appearance before the vast audience

When the officials had explained to the interpreter the object of the meeting and he had rehearsed the same to the chiefs, they were called by turn.

The Indian Council of 1869.

Keokuk and Mokohoko were the principal orators, and responded promptly when called. With the Sac and Fox Tribe they were Clay and Webster. For, like them they were noted for their eloquence, and esteemed for their untiring efforts for right. Their eloquence run in the same channel, but their finals reversed.

Keokuk delivered with impressive pathos, the oration; "The Treachery of the Paleface" in driving the Indians from one reservation to another for the last hundred years. After settlement in each instance promising to let them alone forever. And now again we are to be driven from this lovely home we all love so well. When the paleface put us here he said, this is yours as long as the sun bedecks the Heavens. "In conclusion my dear people the last thing I say is *the* saddest of all, we must go; they *will not* let us stay". Half the audience seemed to be crying.

Mokohoko's Speech.

Chief Mokohoko then arose and delivered an address that would do honour to any statesman. His closing remarks were even more pathetic than those of Keokuk, and when interpreted were about as follows:

Now my dear people, our noble Keokuk has been persuaded to put his hand to a "Paleface" paper; and they say it gives away our Kansas home. O, tell me not such sad words! We cannot give up this happy home we have loved so long. I'll *never never*, never put my hand to the paper that says that we must leave here!

My own people who follow me shall live here in peace with these good paleface people so long as the moon and stars shine by night and the sun illumes the day. When my life is out,—wrap me in my blanket,—gently consign my soul to the Great Spirit of all,—in that quiet nook on Tequas,—circle around my grave and let my friends and brothers say the last words for Mokohoko.

★★★★★★

Soon after this council. Chief Keokuk and all his followers migrated to their new home in the Ty. But Chief Mokohoko and his band of followers, erected their wigwams at the mouth of Rock Creek on the Marias des Cygne River, and lived there many years in peace with the white settlers. Mokohoko true to his word lived there until he died. (Of course Mr. Adams knows all about the forced removals of Mokohoko and his band, who always as soon as they could, returned to this their true home. C. R. G)

The Sac and Fox Indians have been friendly to the whites many years. In the spring of 1870, I attended an Indian dance two miles from my homestead at their village; and learned many interesting things about their lives and peculiar habits.

★★★★★★

A Sac and Pox Indian Dance, as seen by Mr. Adams.

Many white people think the "Indian dance" rude and queer, so it is; but compared with our *fandangos* the behaviour and etiquette is about equal. Early in the day, before beginning the dance, the best food obtainable is put on to cook. Every dance is attended with a banquet. The dance continues all day by intervals.

While dancers move in a circle they chant, the dogs bark, and the musicians blow horns and beat the drums.

As I have attended but one Indian dance I can only tell from that how they performed. They first dress up in their best, putting on all their beads, animal claw necklaces, and jewellery they posses. They dance in a circle—single file. The tallest "Buck" is put in the lead, next the tallest is second, and so on until all the men and big boys are in. Then came the squaws and big girls in the same order, and after them the children. They had a swinging motion from side to side as they stepped forward and chanted.

They ate three times during the day and rested a long time after each meal. The leader was supplied with a pair of buffalo horns which he wore on his head. A little fellow who carried water for the dancers all day wore nothing but a common shirt. I learned that he was a Cheyenne Indian whom they had captured and kept in slavery.

A Sac and Pox Indian Funeral about 1871

There are two or three cemeteries on Tequas Creek. I attended an Indian burial at the one a half a mile east of our residence This was in 1871. The deceased was a noted brave, I do not remember his name now. Long before the funeral procession arrived two squaws had come and dug the grave about four feet deep. The body was brought to the grave by a little wagon drawn by two ponies. The funeral procession— in which many whites participated, was somewhat similar to ours on such occasions, and the ceremony at the grave was carried out much as our fraternal orders carry out theirs. The corpse was wrapped in his blanket and with head to the east placed in the grave.

The braves and chiefs marched around the grave three times, Mo-kohoko in the lead, uttering apparently, some sad ceremony. Each one in the circle deposited something in the grave as they marched around. Tobacco I saw dropped in. At the end of the 3rd round the leader stopped at the head of the grave, the others completing the cir-cle. In this position all stood still while the chief delivered the funeral sermon.

During the exercises at the grave two bucks appointed for that purpose, divided the property of the deceased, (except ponies and gun) into two heaps of equal value. After the two squaws mentioned had filled the grave, each received one of the piles of property in pay-ment for their services. After stones were piled on the grave, a signal was given and all dispersed.

Mo-Ko-Ho-Ko's Band Always Friendly

Although these Indians lived here among the whites several years after Keokuks followers were in the Ty. I never knew or heard of their disturbing the settlers. They were peaceable, obliging and friendly all these years. Government soldiers took them by force to the Ty. several times; but most of them returned each time. Yet the few who did re-main there gradually reduced the 150 in the 16 years to less than 80 Indians when in 1886 the soldiers took them and all they possessed down to their people in the territory, and induced them to stay.

They presented a sad scene when compelled to leave their old home for the last time. Their crying and weeping could be heard by many neighbours whose sympathy they had won.

J. Adams, Quenemo Kan. March 1905

Odds and Ends About the Sac and
Fox Indians in Kansas

As gathered up the last twenty years by C. R. Green

Mo-Ko-Ho-Ko, "He who floats visible near the surface of the water". A chief of the band of Sauk that took the lead in supporting Black Hawk in their war of 1832. He was of the Sturgeon clan. The ruling clan of the Sauk, and was a bitter enemy of Keokuk. The band still retains its identity. It refused to leave Kansas when the rest of the tribe went to the Ind. Ty, and had to be removed thither by the military.   Wm Jones, son of Henry Clay Jones

In handbook of American Indians, Part First.

★★★★★★

May 18 1854, certain chiefs and others of the Iowa and Missouri Band of Sac and Fox tribe of the Great Nemaha Reserve, made a treaty at Washington with the government by which they ceded part of their reservation, keeping 50 sections in Kansas next the Mo. River and Neb. line that they proposed taking in severalty. This tract of country they had received by cession in 1836. Some of the Sauk had already left and joined the Mississippi band on the Osage. And in four or five years Mokohoko came down.

> Signers;   Petookemah. or Hard Fish.
>
> Wah-pe-mem-mah, Moles or Sturgeon.
>
> Neson-quoit or Bear.
>
> Mo-ko-ho-ko, Jumping Pish.
>
> No-ko-what, or Fox,

I presume it was on this occasion in 1854, while there in Washington, that the two pictures of Mokohoko I present in this book were taken, for on application to the Bureau of Ethnology, they were sent me free. See *U. S. Book of Indian Land Cessions* Part 2 18th Report, page 792, and its references.

★★★★★★

Albert Wiley U. S. Indian Agt. taking charge at the Sac and Fox Agency, March 1867, in his report the 30th of July of that says;

> The wild band under Mokohoto, is peaceable docile and will-
> ing to assist in carrying out the wishes of the government. He
> is a good man to his band, which comprises more than half of
> the tribe. He says that he has not been recognised as a man and
> may have done some things not altogether right.

Indian Agents Reports Published by the U. S. in 1868.

★★★★★★

A BUCKEYE SCHOOL TEACHERS CONTRIBUTION.

In the winter of 1885-86, when the river was frozen, a young man, a cousin of mine Charles H. Shelton of Wakeman, Ohio was teaching school in the Wing District, near Mokohoko's old camp.

One moonlight night desiring to mail a letter at Maxon Post Office two or three miles distant, he struck a bee line, which took him down thro' some timber along the river. Here he run on to a larger sized hut in which appeared some thing was going on, but with closed doors Charlie quietly proceeded to investigate the Indian question. But before he could much more than get a "peek", the guard was out and he was motioned off. Some secret council work was on.

Mr Shelton dismissed his school long enough the day the soldiers started with the Indians, to go and see them off. Captain Sam, the fat old chief had to be bound and lifted like a struggling hog into the wagon.

WHAT ONE OF SHELTON'S PUPILS OBSERVED.

Mrs. —— Clarke, formerly Mississippi Connely of Lincoln twp; and a large girl of the school, knew some of these Indians quite well. They were Register of Deeds about 1905 at Lyndon. I showed her my Indian photos. She said the one I had marked as Con-a-pak a was Kanope, a great friend of hers, who staid in Mokohoko's camp and hunted the prairie chickens around. Kanope was very friendly to children and to the whites. Mr. Cross living near thought Kanope the same as Capt Sam chief of the band. Mrs. Clark said not. Cross said they had the use of five acres from someone down along the river. They had quite a herd of ponies, that at the last run in the Riggs pasture. I am able to present Kanope's picture.

43

A Petition to Congress For some Restoration of Annuities.—

Doc. 690 H. R. March 22 1892. Spelling as given;

Number of In Mo-kaw-ho-ko's Band when removed to the Ty. in Nov. 1886; 93. Total number of Sac and Fox of the Miss. band 830.

Mo-kaw-ho-ko and his band would not sign the Treaty of Oct. 14 1868, wherein provision was made for their removal. Mokawhoko and band were allowed to stay by the government in Kansas until 1886, where they got no funds they claim. $71045.40 has accrued to them, and they want it back out of the general Sac and Fox fund in $7000 yearly instalments.

(They never got this. When I visited the tribe in 1903, this band lived aloof from the tribe over north of Stroude Okla, on Euchee Creek. I got several pictures of them from the Stroude Photographer. There they were known as the "Kansas Band", and were drawing their annuities the same as the rest, C R. G.)

Sac and Fox history, as seen in 1903

AN ARTICLE IN THE *OTTAWA WEEKLY HERALD* OF OCT. 22 1903

To The Old Home.—Indian Delegation Arrives From the Ty.
A Story of Homesickness. A band of Sac and Foxes, contends
that it has never parted with its rights to the reservation lands.

I am only giving extracts of this long article, The writer makes it
appear that Franklin County contained the Sac & Fox Reservation,
whereas it only had one fifth. Osage Co having the balance.

A pathetic story of homesickness is told in the arrival in Ottawa
Saturday of a band of three Sac and Fox Indians, who came to
assert their rights to their old home land . . . . .
All the passionate longing for old scenes and surroundings that
are supposed to go with the instincts of civilization, seems to
have actuated the Indians in their efforts to regain the land
which the government took from them. The coming of the
Indians, is announced in a letter to Hon. J. P. (Jack) Harris, from
the Sac and Fox Agency. And the letter expresses the hope that
the Indians will be kindly received here, and humoured in their
almost childish belief that some day the powers may return
their old home to them.
The names of the delegation are Alex Connelly, a half breed
who acts as guide and interpreter, Kaw-to-pe, Mat-tan-an-ne
and an Indian described as the son of Geo Chaw-ka-no-me. . . .

(Some skipped, too long for my pages. . . . . We have skipped a half
column of interesting literature about the tribes history, all of which
crops out in some one or other of my books.) . . .

Mr. Harris often met the old Chief Mo-ko-ho-ko on his
homesick wanderings back to the old camp, and heard his pa-

thetic protest that he wished to live on the lands that the spirit had given him; and where his children were buried.

The chief died contending that he and his fellow tribesmen had never parted with their right to the lands in Franklin County.

. . . . .The writer goes on further to say in this and another article later;

> That the band after the tribe left, terrorised the early settlers, committing depredations, and stealing supplies to keep themselves alive. The government would pay no annuities unless the Indians went to the reservation. The acts of the Indians became so aggravating that a move was finally started to wipe out the band, and an organisation was actually started among the settlers, having for its object the extinction of the band.
>
> Before the move could be carried out, the government sent a detachment of cavalry under General Sheridan, to round the Indians up and move them to the Indian Ty. General Sheridan was in Ottawa for some time and made many acquaintances here. He knew Colonel Mason and made the latter's law office his headquarters.
>
> The troops got the Indians herded together, and marched them overland to the Ty., as a band of cattle is driven, and nothing more been heard of their claims here until the arrival of the party Sunday.

Extracts from *Ottawa Herald*; later.

> The Indian *powwow*. "The Indians arrived Saturday noon. Two Indians Kaw-to-pe and Mat-tan-an-ne, are quite old. The third full blood in the party is a young fellow. The Indians talked through their interpreter to Mr. Harris in his office.
>
> The chief talked first. Staring straight before them with great solemnity, and his countenance expressing never a change he talked. When he sat down, the next arose and endorsed what the chief said. Mr. Harris advised them not to go on to Washington, but to go to Quenemo, visit the landmarks and George Logan.

The *Ottawa Herald* piece, concluded.

> The delegation still cherish the old belief that the government will return the tribe to the former reservation, as soon as the

story can be told to the Press of how the chief of their Band refused to sign the treaty. The letter from the post trader in the Ty. to Mr Harris, mentions the fact that the Indians rely on the friendship of a one legged man who formerly showed them great kindness. The man referred to is the late H.P. Welch.

End

Copied by C. R. Green at the Kansas Historical Rooms, Dec 7, 1904

★★★★★★

The writer of the above articles by not signing his name has left the responsibility to fall on the *Herald* staff for the truth of some of those statements. I take the following exceptions.

1st When the tribe was removed Nov. 26 1869, which was in a peaceable manner, they were treated with great indulgence and three fourths of the tribe left their diminished reserve in Osage County and went willingly to the nation.

2nd; There had been no trouble of any great consequence, the whites crowded in a year ahead of time to take claims, This irritated the Indians much, but the Indian Agent had a sergeant and squad of soldiers sent there that drove the 'Sooners' out and satisfied the Indians that the government would protect them.

3rd; General Sheridan had the Kan. Mo. Military Dpt. as commander Sep. 12 1867 to March 4 1869, with headquarters at Leavenworth when not out at Fort Hayes aiding General Custer fight the Plains Indians. After Mar. '69, Sheridan went to Chicago.

4th It is the testimony of hundreds of settlers that the Sac and Fox Indians were honest, and well behaved, especially Mo-ko-ho-ko's band that staid 16 years longer.

C. R. Green. 1914.

The U. S. Heeding Complaints of Their Indian Wards on Kan. Reservation, in Agent Martin's Time; 1866

Lawrence, Kansas, October 9, 1866.

Sir; I have the honor to report that in accordance with your instructions of the 14th of August last, I proceeded to the Sac and Fox Agency on the 5th inst. Upon my arrival at the agency on the afternoon of the 5th, Antoine Gokey, the interpreter who accompanied Mokohoko to Washington last spring, was sent out to notify all the Indians that an agent of the department had arrived from Washington to investigate the charges against Major Martin, and to tell all of them to come to the Council House early in the morning.

They came on the next day (the 6th) about 12 o'clock: also Mr George Powers of Centropolis, and an attorney from Ottawa, H. P. Welch, esq., who appeared in the interests of the dissatisfied Indians. When all the parties were ready, the investigation was commenced, the interpreter and witnesses being duly sworn. The investigation continued on the 6th, both parties being permitted to examine and cross-examine. At dark there was an adjournment until the next day.

At 12 o'clock the next day the Indians again assembled, and when I was about to proceed with the investigation, I was informed by Atty. Welch and Mr. Powers that the Indians desired to hold a council; that they thought they could settle their difficulties among themselves. To this I consented, and after several hr's delay they came into the council room. The chiefs made speeches and a paper setting forth the basis of their agreement was drawn up, interpreted to the chiefs and councillors, and signed by them, in this paper it is stated that Mokohoko shall hereafter be considered as a chief by blood; that all other relations in the tribe shall remain as heretofore; that Mokohoko and other disaffected Indians withdraw all charges against Major Martin, and state that they have no further cause for complaint against him. and agree that the expenses incurred by Mokohoko and his band, including $600 attorney's fees shall be paid from the annuities of the tribe. Although Attorney Welch declined to proceed any further with the investigation, and the Indians had declared themselves satisfied, yet, as I had been sent by the department to investigate in regard to the charges preferred against Major Martin, and as he expressed a desire to have the investigation continue. I proceeded to examine all the witnesses that were available during the afternoon and evening of the 7th, and the forenoon of the 8th instant.

All the testimony was carefully written down by a clerk employed by me for that purpose, and the same, together with the agreement signed by the Indians, is herewith transmitted for your consideration.

The testimony taken is not of the best character that could be desired. Nearly all the witnesses being connected with the agency. It was all that was available, and shows as follows in reference to the charges preferred against Major Martin.

1st, In reference to collusion with and receiving gratuities from traders, the witnesses, when interrogated upon this point, answered that they knew nothing about it.

2nd, In reference to favouring one trading-house, resulting in the exaction of exorbitant prices from the Indians, the testimony shows that one house has been patronized, but the fact that exorbitant prices have been exacted is not established.

3rd, In reference to the failure to properly enrol certain Indians, and the detention of annuities rightfully belonging to them. This charge relates to So-kah-nut and his band, whom the testimony shows to have been absent in the Osage country, and who were not enrolled at that time by order of the chiefs and council, but who have since returned to the tribe and have had the annuities lost by their absence made good to them.

4th, In reference to the combination of the agent and Keokuk to oppress that part of the tribe, who do not agree with his policy and the charge that Keokuk and his abettors have grown rich out of the funds of the tribe. The testimony shows that three of the chiefs, Keokuk, Che-kus-kuk, and Pat-a-quaw, are those who have made some advancement towards civilization by living in houses and cultivating land; that Mokohoko who was, during the term of office of your predecessor, Commissioner Dole, removed from office by Agent Martin, probably with the approval of the commissioner and who. according to the agreement of the Indians of the 7th inst was reinstated, represents that portion of the tribe who prefer the Indian mode of life, and who do not desire to adopt the ways of the white man. These I am satisfied, from the testimony, comprise a majority of the tribe. While the testimony shows that Major Martin has encouraged those who have made efforts in the way of civilization, it does not show that the property which Keokuk possesses has been acquired since Major Martin has been agent, except such as may have been derived from his efforts at agriculture.

5th, In reference to the charge that Major Martin has wrongfully appointed certain Indians "sheriffs and councillors", and paid them from the funds of the tribe, it appears that these officials were appointed and their salaries fixed by the chiefs.

6th, In reference to driving away of one Tesson by the agent, the testimony shows that this was done by order of chiefs and council, Tesson being a Menomonee, and that his son, who married a Sac woman and was adopted by the tribe has occupied the farm vacated by his father and has cultivated as much of it as desired.

7th, In reference to the charge that the agent has exerted his influence to divide the tribe, it appears to me from all the testimony that any effort the agent has made to advance the Indians in civilization has been opposed by a majority of the tribe.

The maintenance of the sheriffs and councillors, who the agent, Keokuk, Che-ko-skuck and Pah-teck-quah claim are necessary for the preservation of order and the transaction of business, will probably be opposed by that portion of the tribe who desire to retain their old tribal customs, and it will be a question for the department to decide whether what appears to me to be a minority will be sustained. This minority all, or nearly all, wear the blanket, are unable to speak English, and differ only from the remainder of the tribe in this that they live in houses, make some advancement toward farming, are disposed to send their children to school, and to transact their business in a manner approaching that of the white man. It is proper to state that those favouring wild life raise small patches of corn.

8th, In reference to the interpreter, Mr. Goodell, the majority of the Indians seem to be very dissatisfied with him. The testimony shows no specific cause. That he was not a half breed was the principal ground advanced by Mokohoko. The testimony shows nothing against his character as a man, but, on the contrary, represents that he has set a good example to the Indians. Although there are other parties in the reservation qualified to interpret, I am not prepared to recommend that a change be directed, as I do not feel satisfied from observation that the position could be better filled.

9th, The testimony shows that the administration of Agent Martin has tended to the improvement of the Indians, that there is less drunkenness and theft than there was prior to his term of office, and that he has been uniform in his treatment.

While I was there, the Indians were quiet and orderly. I visited the shops and school. The former seems well conducted, and the children in the latter will compare favourably in advancement and deportment with those of the same age in any white school. I also visited the trading house and examined their books, making copy of some of the Indian accounts, which are submitted herewith.

There are other points brought out by the testimony, which, for the sake of brevity, I will omit, and for which you are respectfully referred to the accompanying record of testimony.

As I promised the Indians, I call your attention to the protest of Keokuk against the division of annuities in favour of members of the tribe of Iowa, and the request of all, for the early payment of their annuities.

The papers accompanying your instructions to me are herewith returned.

I am, very respectfully, your obedient servant.

W. R. Irwin.
Special United States Agent.
To Hon. D. N. Cooley, Commissioner of Indian Affairs,
Washington, D. C.

The Great Indian Chief of the West: Or,
Life and Adventures of Black Hawk.

BLACK HAWK

Contents

Preface

In presenting to the public the life and adventures of Black Hawk, some account of the Sac and Fox Indians—of Keokuk, their distinguished chief—and of the causes which led to the late contest between these tribes and the United States, was necessarily involved. The introduction of these collateral subjects, may possibly impart additional interest to this volume.

In speaking of the policy of the government towards the fragment of Sacs and Foxes, with whom Black Hawk was associated, it has been necessary to censure some of its acts, and to comment with freedom upon the official conduct of a few public officers.

The Indians are frequently denounced as faithless, ferocious and untameable. Without going into the inquiry, how far this charge is founded in truth, the question may be asked, has not the policy of our government contributed, essentially, to impart to them that character? Have we not more frequently met them in bad faith, than in a Christian spirit? and sustained our relations with them, more by the power of the sword than the law of kindness? In the inscrutable ways of Providence, the Indians are walking in ignorance and moral darkness. It is the solemn duty, and should be the highest glory of this nation, to bring them out of that condition, and elevate them in the scale of social and intellectual being.

But, how is this duty performed? We gravely recognise them as an independent people, and treat them as vassals: We make solemn compacts with them, which we interpret as our interest dictates, but punish them if they follow the example: We admit their title to the land which they occupy, and at the same time literally compel them to sell it to us upon our own terms: We send agents and missionaries to reclaim them from the error of their ways—to bring them from the hunter to the pastoral life; and yet permit our citizens to debase them by spirituous liquors, and cheat them out of their property: We make war upon them without any adequate cause—pursue them without mercy—and put them to death, without regard to age, sex or condition: And, then deliberately proclaim to the world, that they are savages—cruel and untameable—degraded and faithless.

If the present volume shall, in any degree, contribute to awaken the public mind to a sense of the wrongs inflicted upon the Indians, and to arouse the Christian statesmen of this land, to the adoption of a more liberal, upright and benevolent course of policy towards them, something will have been gained to the cause of humanity and of national honour.

The author takes this opportunity of acknowledging his obligations to James Hall, Esq., for the valuable assistance received from him, in the preparation of this volume. In collecting the materials for that magnificent work, on which he is now engaged, *The History of the Indians of North America*, this gentleman has become possessed of much interesting matter, in regard to the Sacs and Foxes, and especially the chief Keokuk; to all of which he has kindly permitted the author to have access.

Cincinnati, May, 1838.

HISTORY OF THE SAUKEE AND MUSQUAKEE NATIONS, USUALLY CALLED THE SAC AND FOX INDIANS.

CHAPTER 1

Origin of the Sac and Fox Indians

The word Saukee, or O-sau-kee, now written Sauk or more commonly Sac, is derived from a compound in the Algonquin or Chippeway language, *a-saw-we-kee*, which means "yellow earth." Mus-qua-kee, the name of the Fox Indians, signifies "red earth." These two tribes have long resided together, and now constitute one people, although there are some internal regulations among them which tend to preserve a distinctive name and lineage. The chiefs, on ceremonial occasions, claim to be representatives of independent tribes, but this distinction is nominal. For many years past the principal chief of the Sacs, has been, in fact, the chief of the Foxes likewise. They are united in peace and war, speak the same language, claim the same territory, have similar manners and customs, and possess traditions which represent them as descended from the one common origin—the great Chippeway nation.

Both tribes originally resided upon the waters of the St. Lawrence. The Foxes removed first to the west, and established themselves in the region of Green Bay. Upon a river bearing their name, which empties into the head of this Bay, they suffered a signal defeat by a combined body of French and Indians, at a place, since known as La Butte de Mort, or the Hill of the Dead. (Schoolcraft's *Travels.*) Subsequently to this battle, they were joined by the Sacs, who having become involved in a war with the Iroquois or Six Nations, were also driven to the westward. They found their relatives, the Foxes, upon Green Bay, but so far reduced in numbers, by the attacks of other tribes, that they were no longer able to sustain themselves as an independent people. The union between these two tribes, which then took place, and continues to this day, was as much a matter of necessity as of feeling. The period of their migration from the St. Lawrence to the Upper Lakes cannot be satisfactorily ascertained. La Hontan speaks of a Sac village on Fox River, as early as 1689; and Father Hennepin, in 1680, mentions the Ontagamies or Fox Indians, as residents on the bay of Puants, now Green Bay.

From this place, the Sauks and Foxes, crossed over to the eastern bank of the Mississippi, and combining with other tribes, began to act on the offensive. The period of this irruption from the north, it is not easy to determine. Major Thomas Forsyth, who resided for near twenty years among the Sauks and Foxes, in a manuscript account of those tribes, now before us, says:

> More than a century ago, all the country, commencing above Rock River, and running down the Mississippi to the mouth of the Ohio, up that river to the mouth of the Wabash, thence up that river to Fort Wayne, thence down the Miami of the lake some distance, thence north to the St. Joseph's and Chicago; also the country lying south of the Des Moines, down perhaps, to the Mississippi, was inhabited by a numerous nation of Indians, who called themselves Linneway, and were called by others, Minneway, signifying "men." This great nation was divided into several bands, and inhabited different parts of this extensive region, as follows: The Michigamies, the country south of the Des Moines; the Cohakias that east of the present village of Cohokia in Illinois; the Kaskaskias that east of the town of that name; the Tamarois had their village nearly central between Cahokia and Kaskaskia; the Piankeshaws near Vincennes; the Weas up the Wabash; the Miamies on the headwaters of the Miami of the Lakes, on St. Joseph's River and at Chicago.
> The Piankeshaws, Weas and Miamies, must at this time have hunted south towards and on the Ohio. The Peorias, another band of the same nation, lived and hunted on the Illinois River: The Mascos or Mascontins, called by the French *gens des prairies*, lived and hunted on the great prairies, between the Wabash and Illinois Rivers. All these different bands of the Minneway nation, spoke the language of the present Miamies, and the whole considered themselves as one and the same people; yet from their local situation, and having no standard to go by, their language became broken up into different dialects. These Indians, the Minneways, were attacked by a general confederacy of oth-

er nations, such as the Sauks and Foxes, resident at Green Bay and on the Ouisconsin; the Sioux, whose frontiers extended south to the River des Moines: the Chippeways, Ottoways, and Potawatimies from the lakes, and also the Cherokees and Choctaws from the south.

The war continued for a great many years and until that great nation the Minneways were destroyed, except a few Miamies and Weas on the Wabash, and a few who are scattered among strangers. Of the Kaskaskias, owing to their wars and their fondness for spirituous liquors, there now (1826) remain but thirty or forty souls;—of the Peorias near St. Genevieve ten or fifteen; of the Piankeshaws forty or fifty. The Miamies are the most numerous; a few years ago they consisted of about four hundred souls. There do not exist at the present day (1826) more than five hundred souls of the once great and powerful Minneway or Illini nation. These Indians, the Minneways, are said to have been very cruel to their prisoners, not infrequently burning them. I have heard of a certain family among the Miamies who were called maneaters, as they were accustomed to make a feast of human flesh when a prisoner was killed.

For these enormities, the Sauks and Foxes, when they took any of the Minneways prisoners, gave them up to their women to be buffeted to death. They speak also of the Mascontins with abhorrence, on account of their cruelties. The Sauks and Foxes have a historical legend of a severe battle having been fought opposite the mouth of the Iowa River, about fifty or sixty miles above the mouth of Rock River. The Sauks and Foxes descended the Mississippi in canoes, and landing at the place above described, started east, towards the enemy: they had not gone far before they were attacked by a party of the Mascontins.

The battle continued nearly all day; the Sauks and Foxes, for want of ammunition, finally gave way and fled to their canoes; the Mascontins pursued them and fought desperately, and left but few of the Sauks and Foxes to carry home the story of their defeat. Some forty or fifty years ago, the Sauks and Foxes attacked a small village of Peorias, about a mile below St. Louis and were there defeated. At a place on the Illinois River, called Little Rock, there were formerly killed by the Chippeways and Ottowas, a number of men, women and children of the Minneway nation.

In 1800 the Kickapoos made a great slaughter of the Kaskaskia Indians. The Main-Pogue, or Potawatimie juggler, in 1801, killed a great many of the Piankeshaws on the Wabash.

The land on which St. Louis stands, as well as the surrounding country, was claimed by the Illini confederacy, which had acquiesced in the intrusion of the whites. This circumstance, it is supposed, led the northern confederacy to the attempt, which they made in 1779, to destroy the village of St. Louis, then occupied by the Spaniards. As the Sacs and Foxes were active participators in this attack, no apology is necessary for introducing the following graphic account of it, from the pen of Wilson Primm, Esqr. of St. Louis. (Published in the *Illinois Magazine* under the head of "History of St. Louis.")

In the meantime numerous bands of the Indians living on the lakes and the Mississippi—the Ojibeways, Menomonies, Winnebagoes, Sioux, Sacs, &c. together with a large number of Canadians, amounting in all to upwards of fourteen hundred, had assembled on the eastern shore of the Mississippi, a little above St. Louis, awaiting the sixth of May, the day fixed for the attack. The fifth of May was the feast of *Corpus Christi*, a day highly venerated by the inhabitants, who were all Catholics. Had the assault taken place then, it would have been fatal to them, for, after divine service, all the men, women and children had flocked to the prairie to gather strawberries, which were that season very abundant and fine.

The town being left perfectly unguarded, could have been taken with ease, and the unsuspecting inhabitants, who were roaming about in search of fruit, have been massacred without resistance. Fortunately, however, a few only of the enemy had crossed the river and ambushed themselves in the prairie. The villagers, frequently came so near them, in the course of the day, that the Indians from their places of concealment, could have reached them with their hands. But they knew not how many of the whites were still remaining in the town, and in the absence of their coadjutors, feared to attack, lest their preconcerted plan might be defeated.

On the sixth, the main body of the Indians crossed, and marched directly towards the fields, expecting to find the greater part of the villagers there; but in this they were disappointed, a few only having gone out to view their crops. These perceived the approach of the savage foe, and immediately commenced a retreat towards the town, the most of them taking the road that led to the upper gate, nearly through the mass of Indians, and followed by a shower of bullets. The firing alarmed those who were in town, and the cry "to arms! to arms!" was heard in every direction. They rushed towards the works and threw open the gates to their brethren. The Indians advanced slowly but steadily towards the town, and the inhabitants, though almost deprived of hope, by the vast superiority in number of the assailants, determined to defend themselves to the last.

In expectation of an attack, Silvio Francisco Cartabona, a governmental officer, had gone to St. Genevieve for a company of militia to aid in defending the town, in case of necessity, and had at the beginning of the month returned with sixty men, who were quartered on the citizens. As soon as the attack commenced, however, neither Cartabona nor his men could be seen. Either through fear or treachery, they concealed themselves in a garret, and there remained until the Indians had retired. The assailed being deprived of a considerable force, by this shameful defection, were still resolute and determined. About fifteen men were posted at each gate; the rest were scattered along the line of defence, in the most advantageous manner.

When within a proper distance, the Indians began an irregular fire, which was answered with showers of grape shot from the artillery. The firing, for a while, was warm; but the Indians perceived that all their efforts would be ineffectual on account of the entrenchments, and deterred by the cannon, to which they were unaccustomed, from making a nearer approach, suffered their zeal to abate, and deliberately retired. At this stage of affairs, the lieutenant governor made his appearance. The first intimation that he received of what was going on, was by the discharge of artillery, on the part of the inhabitants. He immediately ordered several pieces of cannon, which were posted in front of the government house, to be spiked and filled with sand, and went, or rather was rolled in a wheelbarrow, to the scene of action.

In a very peremptory tone, he commanded the inhabitants to cease firing and return to their houses. Those posted at the lower gate, did not receive the order, and consequently kept their stations. The commandant perceived this and ordered a cannon to be fired at them. They had barely time to throw themselves on the ground, when the volley passed over them, and struck the wall, tearing a great part of it down. These proceedings, as well as the whole tenor of his conduct, since the first rumour of an attack, gave rise to suspicions very unfavourable to the lieutenant governor. It was bruited about, that he was the cause of the attack, that he was connected with the British, and that he had been bribed into a dereliction of duty, which, had not providence averted, would have doomed them to destruction.

Under pretext of proving to them that there was no danger of an attack, he had a few days before it occurred, sold to the traders, all the ammunition belonging to the government; and they would have been left perfectly destitute and defenceless, had they not found, in a private house, eight barrels of powder, belonging to a trader, which they seized in the name of the king, upon the first alarm. Colonel George Rogers Clark, who was at this time at Kaskaskia, with a few men under his command, understanding that an attack was meditated on the town, offered all the assistance in his power, to aid in the defence.

This offer was rejected by the lieutenant governor. All these circumstances gave birth to a strong aversion to the commandant, which evinces itself, at this day, in execrations of his character, whenever his name is mentioned to those who have known him. Representations of his conduct, together with a detailed account of the attack, were sent to New Orleans by a special messenger, and the result was that the governor general appointed Mr. Francisco Cruzat, to the office of lieutenant governor.

As soon as it was ascertained that the Indians had retired from the neighbourhood, the inhabitants proceeded to gather the dead, that lay scattered in all parts of the prairie. Seven were at first found and buried in one grave. Ten or twelve others, in the course of a fortnight, were discovered in the long grass that bordered the marshes. The acts of the Indians were accompanied by their characteristic ferocity. Some of their victims were horribly mangled. With the exception of one individual, the whites who accompanied the Indians, did not take part in the butcheries that were committed. A young man by the name of Calve, was found dead, his skull split open, and a tomahawk, on the blade of which was written the word Calve, sticking in his brain. He was supposed to have fallen by the hand of his uncle. Had those who discovered the Indians in the prairie, fled to the lower gate, they would have escaped; but the greater part of them took the road that led to the upper gate, through the very ranks of the enemy, and were thus exposed to the whole of their fire.

About twenty persons, it is computed, met their death in endeavouring to get within the entrenchments. None of those within were injured, and none of the Indians were killed, at least none of them were found. Their object was not plunder, for they did not attempt, in their retreat, to take away with them any of the cattle or the horses that were in the prairie, and that they might have taken; nor did they attack any of the neighbouring towns, where danger would have been less, and the prospect of success greater. The only object they had in view was the destruction of St. Louis; and this would seem to favour the idea that they were instigated by the English, and gives good ground, when connected with other circumstances, to believe that Leyba was their aider and abettor.

A Mr. Chancellier had gone on the day of attack, to the prairie for strawberries, with his wife, two daughters and an American, the first that had ever been in the country, in a cart drawn by two horses. When they perceived the Indians, they immediately fled towards the town in the cart; Mr. Chancellier being seated before, and the American behind, in order to protect the women, who were in the middle. In their flight the American was mortally wounded. As he was falling out, Mr. Chancellier seized him and threw him into the midst of the women, exclaiming, "they shan't get the scalp of my American." He was at the same time struck by two balls, which broke his arm in as many places, above the elbow. His wife received a bullet through the middle of her hand, the elder daughter was shot through the shoulder, immediately above the breast, and the younger was struck on the forehead, but the ball glanced aside and merely stunned her. The moment Mr. Chancellier arrived at the gate, his horses dropped dead, pierced with a hundred wounds, but his family was saved.

Mr. Primm, the writer of this interesting narrative, has probably not been fully informed in regard to the extent of Colonel George

Rogers Clark's participation in this affair. In a written memorandum now before us, made on the authority of his brother, General William Clark of St. Louis, who it is presumed has possession of his father's official papers, it is stated, in reference to this affair, that although the Spanish governor could not be made to believe that an attack was intended, the principal inhabitants sent over an express to Colonel Clark, who was then at Kaskaskia with five hundred men, to come and protect them. He accordingly marched his force up opposite the town and encamped a little distance from the river. He did not send over any troops, but was to do so, in case of an attack; when it was actually made Colonel Clark crossed the river; and upon seeing the "long knives," as the Indians called his troops, they hastily retreated, having killed seventy-two or seventy-three of the Spaniards, before his arrival.

This sudden appearance of Colonel Clark, upon the scene of action, explains the conduct of the Indians. So large a body of warriors, making a preconcerted attack, upon a town but badly protected, would not, it is thought, have given up the assault so suddenly and before they had lost a single man, unless alarmed by the presence of a superior force. On the supposition that Colonel Clark actually crossed the river with his troops, the flight of the Indians is easily explained. They were probably apprised of Colonel Clark's being at Kaskaskia, and his name was everywhere a terror to the Indians. As an evidence of this, a short time afterwards, he sent a detachment of one hundred and fifty men, as far up the country as Prairie des Chiens, and from thence across Rock and Illinois Rivers and down to Kaskaskia, meeting with no molestation from the Indians, who were struck with terror at the boldness of the enterprise, saying that if so few dared to come, they "would fight like devils."

General William H. Harrison, long familiar with the North West Indians, in an official letter to the Secretary at War, dated H.Q. Cincinnati, March 22nd, 1814, giving an able view of the Indian tribes, makes the following remarks on the descent of this northern confederacy, upon the great Illini nation.

The Miamies have their principal settlements on the forks of the Wabash, thirty miles from fort Wayne; and at Mississineway, thirty miles lower down. A band of them, under the name of Weas, have resided on the Wabash, sixty miles above Vincennes; and another under the Turtle, on Eel River, a branch of the

Wabash, twenty miles north west of Fort Wayne. By an artifice of the Little Turtle, these three bands were passed on General Wayne as distinct tribes, and an annuity was granted to each. The Eel River and Weas however to this day call themselves Miamies, and are recognised as such by the Mississineway band. The Miamies, Maumees, or Tewicktovies are the undoubted proprietors of all that beautiful country which is watered by the Wabash and its branches; and there is as little doubt, that their claim extended as far east as the Sciota. They have no tradition of removing from any other quarter of the country; whereas all the neighbouring tribes, the Piankeshaws excepted, who are a branch of the Miamies, are either intruders upon them, or have been permitted to settle in their country.

The Wyandots emigrated first from Lake Ontario and subsequently from lake Huron, the Delawares from Pennsylvania and Maryland, the Shawanies from Georgia, the Kickapoos and Pottawatamies from the country between lake Michigan and the Mississippi, and the Ottawas and Chippeways, from the peninsula formed by lakes Michigan, Huron and St. Clair, and the strait connecting the latter with Erie. The claims of the Miamies were bounded on the north and west by those of the Illinois confederacy, consisting originally of five tribes, called Kaskaskias, Cahokias, Peorians, Michiganians, and Temorias speaking the Miami language, and no doubt branches of that nation.

When I was first appointed governor of Indiana Territory, these once powerful tribes were reduced to about thirty warriors, of whom twenty five were Kaskaskias, four Peorians, and a single Michiganian. There was an individual lately alive at St. Louis, who saw the enumeration of them made by the Jesuits in 1745, making the number of their warriors four thousand.

A furious war between them and the Sacs and Kickapoos reduced them to that miserable remnant, which had taken refuge amongst the white people of Kaskaskia and St. Genevieve. The Kickapoos had fixed their principal village at Peoria, upon the south bank of the Illinois River, whilst the Sacks remained masters of the country to the north.

These historical facts are interesting, as showing the manner in which the Sauks and Foxes obtained possession of the fertile plains of Illinois; and, as adding another to the many instances on record, in which hordes of northern invaders have overrun and subjugated the people of more southern regions. The causes are obvious for this descent of the Sauks and Foxes, upon their southern neighbors. They reached a more genial climate, a country where game was more abundant than in the region they left behind, and in which they could, with greater facility, raise their corn, beans and pumpkins. Other causes than these might have had their influence. The Illini confederacy may have provoked the descent of the northern tribes upon them. On this point, Lieutenant Pike in his travels to the sources of the Mississippi, has the following remark.

By killing the celebrated Sauk chief, Pontiac, the Illinois, Cahokias, Kaskaskias and Peorias, kindled a war with the allied nations of the Sauks and Reynards, which has been the cause of the almost entire destruction of the former nations.

The death of Pontiac may have been the immediate exciting cause of the war, but it is more than probable that the love of conquest and the hope of obtaining a more fruitful and genial country, than is to be found upon the shore of the lakes, were the principal reasons which impelled the northern confederacy to the subjugation of the Illini.

The principal village of the Sacs and Foxes, for a long period of time, was on the north side of Rock River, near its junction with the Mississippi. It contained at one time upwards of sixty lodges, and was among the largest and most populous Indian villages on the continent. The country around it is fertile and picturesque, finely watered, and studded with groves and prairies. It is described in the following graphic manner, by a gentleman who travelled over it in 1829, (James Hall, Esqr.)

The Mississippi, which below its junction with the Missouri, is a troubled stream, meandering through low grounds, and margined by muddy banks, is here a clear and rapid river, flowing over beds of rock and gravel, and bordered by the most lovely shores. Nothing of the kind can be more attractive, than the scenery at the upper rapids. On the western shore, a series of slopes are seen, commencing at the gravelly margin of the water, and rising one above another, with a barely perceptible acclivity, for a considerable distance, until the back ground is terminated by a chain of beautifully rounded hills, over which trees are thinly scattered, as if planted to embellish the scene.

This is the singular charm of prairie scenery. Although it is a wilderness, just as nature made it, the verdant carpet, the gracefully waving outline of the surface, the clumps and groves and scattered trees, give it the appearance of a noble park, boundless in extent, and adorned with exquisite taste.

It is a wild but not a savage wild, that awes by its gloom. It is a gay and cheerful wilderness, winning by its social aspect as well as its variety and intrinsic gracefulness. The eastern shore is not less beautiful: a broad flat plain of rich alluvion, extending from the water's edge, is terminated by a range of wooded hills. A small collection of the lodges of the Saukies and Foxes stood on this plain when the writer last saw it, but their chief village was about three miles distant. In the front of the landscape, and presenting its most prominent feature, is Rock Island, on the southern point of which, elevated upon a parapet of rock, is Fort Armstrong.

The region around is healthy and amazingly fruitful. The grape, the plum, the gooseberry and various other native fruits abound,—the wild honeysuckle gives its perfume to the air, and a thousand indigenous flowers mingle their diversified hues with the verdure of the plain. But all this fertility of soil and scenic beauty has produced no ameliorating effect upon the savages. The Sauks of Illinois, when first visited by the French missionaries were as they are now. They are still savages, as much so as the Osages, Comanches and Seminoles, and not superior to the wandering Chippeways.

The civil polity of these two tribes bears much resemblance to that of the north western Indians generally. The peace chiefs are partly elective and partly hereditary. The son succeeds the father by the assent of the tribe, if worthy of the office, and if not, a successor, of a more meritorious character, is chosen by them from some collateral branch of the family. There is a legend among them relating to the relative rank of their chiefs, which, although perhaps purely figurative, may not be uninteresting to the reader. They say that a great while ago, their fathers had a long lodge, in the centre of which were ranged four fires. By the first fire stood two chiefs, one on the right, who was called the Great Bear, and one on the left, called the Little Bear: these were the village or peace chiefs: they were the rulers of the band, and held the authority corresponding to that of the chief magistrate.

At the second fire stood two chiefs: one on the right, called the Great Fox, and one on the left, called the Little Fox: these were the war chiefs or generals. At the third fire stood two warriors, who were called respectively the Wolf and the Owl. And at the other fire, two others who were the Eagle and the Tortoise. These four last named were not chiefs but braves of distinction, who held honourable places in the council, and were persons of influence in peace and in war. This lodge of four fires may have existed among these tribes. It is true that their chiefs remain as described in the legend.

The peace chief or headman presides in council, and all important public acts are done in his name; but unless he be a man of popular talents and great energy of character his place confers more of honour than power. If a weak or irresolute man, although he nominally retain his authority, the war chiefs actually exercise it. It is very seldom that he acquires property, for he is expected to make feasts and presents, and is compelled to be hospitable and liberal as a means of sustaining his power among his people.

The office of war chief is never hereditary, but results from skill and intrepidity in battle, and is held so long as those qualities are successfully retained. It may readily be conceived that among such a race the war chiefs, having the braves and young men of the nation under their command, would generally maintain a controlling influence. The leading war chief is always better known than the principal peace chief, is often confounded with him, and still oftener exercises his authority.

The Sauks are, at the present time, divided into twelve families, and the Foxes into eight, each known by the name of some animal. Among the Sauks there is another division peculiar to it. The males are all classed in two parties or bands—one called Kish-ko-guis, or long hairs; the other Osh-cushis or braves, the former being considered something more than brave. In 1819 each party numbered about four hundred members, and in 1826, the number was increased to five hundred in each. The standard of the Kish-ko-guis or long hairs, is red, and that of the Osh-cushis or braves, blue.

Every male child, soon after its birth, is marked with white or black paint, and is classed in one of these two parties, the mother being careful to apply the two colours alternately, so that if the number of males in a family be even, each band will receive an equal number of members, and the whole nation will thus be nearly equally divided into the two colours of black and white. These distinctive marks are

70

permanently retained through life, and in painting themselves for any ceremonies or public occasions, those of one party use white, the others black paint, in addition to other colours which may suit their fancy. The reason of this singular custom is for the purpose of creating and keeping alive a spirit of emulation in the tribe. In their games, sham-battles and other pastimes, the whites and blacks are opposed to each other; and in war, each party is ambitious of bringing home a greater number of scalps than the other.

The chiefs have the management of public affairs, but as we have already seen are more or less influenced, especially in matters of war or peace, by the braves. In their councils, questions are not considered, generally, as decided, unless there be unanimity of opinion. Their laws are few and simple. Debts are but seldom contracted by them, and there is no mode of enforcing their collection. For redress of civil injuries, an appeal is usually made to some of the old men of the tribe, mutually selected by the parties concerned; and their decision is considered as binding. A murder among them is seldom punished capitally. The relatives of the deceased may take revenge in that way, but it is much more common to receive compensation in property. If the relatives cannot agree upon the amount of the compensation, the old men of the tribe interfere and settle it.

The kinsfolk of the deceased say, that by killing the murderer, it will not bring the dead to life, and that it is better to take the customary presents, which often amount in value to a considerable sum. Occasionally the murderer arranges the whole matter, by marrying the widow of the man he has killed. There is but one offence that is considered of a national character, and that is of rare occurrence. It consists in aiding the enemies of the tribe, in times of war, and is punishable with death. A sentinel who has been placed on duty by a chief, but who neglects it, is publicly whipped by the women.

The Sauks and Foxes have no established mode of declaring war. If injured by a neighbouring tribe they wait a reasonable time for reparation to be made, and if it is not, they avail themselves of the first fitting opportunity of taking revenge. The young Indians manifest, at an early age, a love of war. They hear the old warriors recounting their exploits, and as the battlefield is the only road to distinction, they embrace the first chance of killing an enemy. When the question of going to war is under consideration, some one or a number of them, undertake to consult the Great Spirit by fasting and dreams.

These latter are related by them in public, and often have their influence, being generally so interpreted as to inspire confidence in those who may join the war party. If a party is victorious in battle, the individual who killed the first enemy, leads them back, and on the way, if they have prisoners with them, it is not uncommon to kill those who are old. The young ones are generally adopted into the families of such as have lost relatives in the battle, or whose children have died a natural death.

Upon the return of the victorious party to their village, a war dance is held round their captives by way of celebrating their triumph. Prisoners are sometimes held as slaves, and as such are bought and sold. If they go to war, which they are encouraged to do, and succeed in killing one of the enemy, the slave changes his name and from that time becomes a freeman. The Sauks and Foxes treat their prisoners with humanity, and if they succeed in getting to the village alive, they are safe, and their persons are held sacred. But one instance is known of their having burned a prisoner, and that was in a war with the Menominies, and in retaliation for a similar act, first committed by that tribe.

The young Indians go to war generally between the age of seventeen and twenty, but sometimes as early as fifteen. Many of them at the age of forty and forty-five, look old and are broken down in their physical constitution, in consequence of the hardships which they have endured in war and the chase. In old age they are usually provided for, and live in peace at their villages. When one of them is sick, and thinks he is about to go to the land of spirits, he not infrequently directs the manner in which he wishes to be buried, and his instructions are complied with.

The Sauks and Foxes bury their dead in the ground, and have preferences for particular places of interment. The graves are not dug to any great depth, and a little bark from a tree is made to answer the purpose of a coffin. The body is usually carried to the grave by old women, who howl at intervals, during the ceremony, most piteously. Before closing the grave, one of the Indians present at the funeral will wave a stick or war-club, called *"puc-ca waw-gun,"* saying in an audible voice, "I have killed many men in war, and I give their spirits to my dead friend who lies here, to serve him as slaves in the other world:" after which the grave is filled up with earth, and in a day or two a rude cabin or shed is made over it of rough boards or bark. If the deceased was a brave, a post is planted at the head of the grave, on which, in a rude manner, the number of scalps and prisoners he has taken in war, is represented by red paint.

Upon the death of an adult, his property is usually distributed among his relatives, and his widow returns to her own family or nearest kinfolks. The widow is the principal mourner for the deceased and her grief seems to be sincere. Her countenance becomes dejected—she seldom smiles—clothes herself in rags, and with dishevelled hair and spots of black paint on her cheeks, wanders about in a pensive mood, seldom shedding tears, except when alone in the woods. They generally cease mourning at the suggestion of some friend, wash, paint themselves red and put on their best clothes and ornaments. Some of the Sauks and Foxes entertain the opinion that the spirit of the deceased hovers about the village or lodge, for a few days, and then takes its flight to the land of repose.

On its way, they suppose it passes over an extensive prairie, beyond which the woods appear like a blue cloud. Between this woodland and the prairie, there is a deep and rapid stream of water, across which there is a pole, kept in continual motion by the force of the current. This stream, the spirit must cross on the pole, and if it has belonged to a good person, it will get over safe and find all its good relations that have gone before it. In this woodland, game of all kinds is abundant, and there the spirits of the good live in everlasting happiness.

If on the contrary, the spirit has belonged to a bad or wicked person in this world, it will fall off the pole into the stream, and the current will sweep it down to the land of evil spirits, where it will forever remain in poverty and misery. There is nothing very peculiar in the religious opinions of the Sauks and Foxes, to distinguish them from the aborigines of this country, generally. They believe in one Great and Good Spirit, who controls and governs all things, and in supernatural agents who are permitted to interfere in their concerns. They are of opinion that there is also a bad spirit, subordinate, however, to the great Manito, who is permitted to annoy and perplex the Indians, by means of bad medicines, by poisonous reptiles, and by killing their horses and sinking their canoes. All their misfortunes are attributed to the influence of this bad spirit, but they have some vague idea that it is in part permitted as a punishment for their bad deeds.

They all believe in ghosts, and when they fancy that they have seen one, the friends of the deceased give a feast and hang up some clothing as an offering to appease the troubled spirit. So far as the ceremonials are concerned, the Sauks and Foxes may be called a religious people. They rarely pass any extraordinary cave, rock, hill or other object, with out leaving behind them some tobacco for the use of the spirit who they suppose lives there. They have some kind of prayers, consisting of words which they sing over in the evening and at sunrise in the morning.

Their tradition in regard to the creation of the world, the deluge and the re-peopling of the earth, is a singular mixture of truth and fiction. If anterior in its origin, to the arrival of the whites on this continent, it presents matter of curious speculation. The following account of it, entitled the *Cosmogony of the Saukee and Musquakee Indians*, is taken from Doctor Galland's *Chronicles of the North American Savages.*

In the beginning the Gods created every living being which was intended to have life upon the face of the whole earth; and then were formed every species of living animal. After this the gods also formed man, whom they perceived to be both cruel and foolish: they then put into man the heart of the best beast they had created; but they beheld that man still continued cruel and foolish. After this it came to pass that the Almighty took a piece of himself, of which he made a heart for the man; and when the man received it, he immediately became wise above every other animal on the earth.

And it came to pass in the process of much time, that the earth produced its first fruits in abundance, and all the living beasts were greatly multiplied. The earth about this time, was also inhabited by an innumerable host of *I-am-woi* (giants) and gods. And the gods whose habitation is under the seas, made war upon *We-suk-kah*, (the chief god upon the earth) and leagued themselves with the I-*am-woi* upon the earth, against him. Nevertheless, they were still afraid of *We-suk-kah* and his immense host of gods; therefore they called a council upon the earth; and when they were assembled upon the earth, at the council, both the *I-am-woi* and the gods from under the seas, after much debate, and long consultation, they resolved to make a great feast upon the earth, and to invite *We-suk-kah*, that they might thus beguile him, and at the feast lay hands upon him and slay him. And when the council had appointed a delegate to visit *We-suk-kah,* and commanded him to invite *We-suk-kah* to the great feast, which they were preparing upon the earth for him; behold, the younger brother of *We-suk-kah*, was in the midst of the council, and being confused in the whole assembly, they said unto him, "Where is thy brother *We-suk-kah*." And he answering said unto them "I know not; am I my brother's keeper?" And the council perceiving that all their devices were known unto him, they were sorely vexed; therefore, with one accord, the whole assembly rushed violently upon him and slew him: and thus was slain the younger brother of *We-suk-kah*.

Now when *We-suk-kah* had heard of the death of his younger brother, he was extremely sorrowful and wept aloud; and the gods whose habitations are above the clouds, heard the voice of his lamentations, and they leagued with him to avenge the blood of his brother. At this time the lower gods had fled from the face of the earth, to their own habitations under the seas; and the *I-am-woi* were thus forsaken, and left alone to defend themselves against *We-suk-kah* and his allies.

Now the scene of battle, where *We-suk-kah* and his allies fought the *I-am-woi*, was in a flame of fire; and the whole race of the *I-am-woi* were destroyed with a great slaughter, that there was not one left upon the face of the whole earth. And when the gods under the sea, knew the dreadful fate of their allies, the *I-am-woi*, whom they had deserted, they were sore afraid and they cried aloud to *Na-nam-a-keh* (god of thunder) to come to their assistance. And *Na-nam-a-keh* heard their cry and accepted their request, and sent his subaltern, *No-tah-tes-se-ah*, (god of the wind) to *Pa-poan-a-tesse-ah*, (god of the cold) to invite him to come with all his dreadful host of frost, snow, hail, ice and north-wind, to their relief.

When this destroying army came from the north, they smote the whole earth with frost, converting the waters of every river, lake, and sea into solid masses of ice, and covering the whole earth with an immense sheet of snow and hail. Thus perished all the first inhabitants of the earth both men, beasts and gods, except a few choice ones of each kind, which *We-suk-kah* preserved with himself upon the earth.

And again it came to pass in the process of a long time, that the gods under the sea came forth again, upon the earth; and when they saw *We-suk-kah*, that he was almost alone on the earth, they rejoiced in assurance of being able to destroy him. But when they had exhausted every scheme, attempted every plan, and executed every effort to no effect, perceiving that all their councils and designs were well known to *We-suk-kah* as soon as they were formed, they became mad with despair, and resolved to destroy *We-suk-kah,* by spoiling forever the whole face of the earth, which they so much desired to inhabit. To this end, therefore, they retired to their former habitations under the sea and entreated *Na-nam-a-keh* (the god of thunder) to drown the whole earth with a flood.

And *Na-nam-a-ke*h again hearkened to their cries, and calling all the clouds to gather themselves together, they obeyed his voice and came; and when all the clouds were assembled, he commanded them and they poured down water upon the earth, a tremendous torrent, until the whole surface of the earth, even the tops of the highest mountains were covered with water. But it came to pass, when *We-suk-k*ah saw the water coming upon the earth, he took some air, and made an *o-pes-quie,* (vessel, boat or shell) and getting into it himself, he took with him all sorts of living beasts, and man; and when the waters rose upon the earth the *o-pes-quie* was lifted up and floated upon the surface, until the tops of the highest mountains were covered with the flood.

And when the *o-pes-quie* had remained for a long time upon the surface of the flood, *We-suk-kah* called one of the animals, which was with him in the *o-pes-quie,* and commanded it to go down through the water to the earth, to bring from thence some earth; and after many repeated efforts and with great difficulty, the animal at length returned, bringing in its mouth, some earth; of which, when *We-suk-kah* had received it, he formed this earth, and spread it forth upon the surface of the water; and went forth himself and all that were with him in the *o-pes-quie,* and occupied the dry land.

In the social or family relations of the Sauks and Foxes, it is considered the duty of the men to hunt and clothe their wives and children—to purchase arms and the implements of husbandry so far as they use them—to make canoes and assist in rowing them—to hunt and drive their horses, make saddles, &c. &c. The duties of the women, are to skin the game when brought home and prepare the skins for market, to cook, to make the camp, cut and carry wood, make *moccasins*, plant and gather the corn, beans and pumpkins, and do all the drudgery connected with the domestic affairs. It is the commonly received opinion among the whites that the female Indians are the slaves of their husbands. This is not literally true. The men seldom make their wives feel their authority: as a general rule among the Sauks and Foxes, they live happily together.

The wives take the liberty of scolding their husbands, very frequently, and it is considered by both parties that everything in the family, except the war and hunting implements, belongs to the wife, and she may do with it as she pleases. The men may each have two or three, or even more wives. They generally prefer to take sisters, as they agree better together in the same lodge: the eldest usually regulates all the domestic affairs of the family and has charge of the property belonging to it. The men turn off their wives and the latter leave their husbands whenever they become discontented. While living together, the women are generally faithful to their husbands. The daughters seldom leave their mothers until they are married, which usually occurs when they are about fourteen or fifteen years of age.

The parents of an Indian girl are generally conciliated by presents from her lover, but they may insist upon servitude from him, which sometimes runs throughout one, two or three years. There is no particular marriage ceremony among them, beyond that of the contract between the parents or parties. A young Sauk lover is represented as a silly looking fellow, who can neither eat, drink or sleep—he appears to be deranged, and with all the pains he takes to conceal his passion, his malady is still apparent to his friends. The faithfulness of this sketch, will hardly be questioned, when the close analogy which it bears to a pale-faced lover, is recalled to mind. The Sauks and Foxes, when pinched with hunger, will eat almost any kind of meat, but prefer venison and bear's meat to all other; they never eat it unless cooked. They make much use of corn, beans and pumpkins, and annually raise considerable quantities. They are not fond of fish and seldom eat them if they can procure other kinds of food.

There are but three kinds of musical instruments used among these tribes. The drum, which is beat at their feasts, dances and games, the tambourine, and a kind of flageolet, made of cane or two pieces of soft wood hollowed out and fastened together with strips of leather. Their tunes are always on a flat key, have but few variations and are mostly of a melancholy character. According to Mr. Atwater, who visited those residing near Rock Island, in 1829, the Sacs and Foxes have:

Tunes evidently of French origin, and some songs of considerable length.

These Indians have among them, what answers to the Italian *Improvisatori* who make songs for particular occasions.

The Sauks and Foxes have a considerable number of songs, suited to a great many occasions in their own language.

Among the Indians of the Upper Mississippi, the Sauks and Foxes are decidedly the best actors, and have the greatest variety of plays among them.

In common with the Indian tribes generally, they have a variety of athletic games, in which both the men and women join. They are addicted to cards and other games of chance, and often bet very high.

Touching the condition of these tribes in 1805, Lieutenant Pike, in his travels to the sources of the Mississippi, says, "The first nation of Indians whom we met with, were the Sauks, who principally reside in four villages. The first at the head of the Rapids des Moyens, on the west shore, containing thirteen lodges. The second on a prairie on the east shore about sixty miles above. The third on the river De Roche (Rock River) about three miles from the entrance, and the last on the river Iowa. They hunt on the Mississippi and its confluent streams from the Illinois to the River Des Iowa; and on the plains west of them which border the Mississippi. They are so perfectly consolidated with the Reynards (the Foxes) that they can scarcely be termed a distinct nation; but recently there appears to be a schism between the two nations: the latter not approving of the insolence and ill-will, which has marked the conduct of the former towards the United States, on many late occurrences.

They have for many years past made war (under the auspices of the Sioux) on the Santeaux, Osages and Missouries; but as recently a peace has been (through the influence of the United States) made between them and the nations of the Missouri, and by the same means between the Sioux and the Santeaux (their principal allies) it appears it would be by no means a difficult matter to induce them to make a general peace, and pay still greater attention to the cultivation of the earth: as they now raise a considerable quantity of corn, beans and melons. The character which they bear with their savage brethren, is, that they are much more to be dreaded for their deceit and inclination for stratagem, than for open courage

The Reynards reside in three villages. The first on the west side of the Mississippi six miles above the rapids of the River de Roche. The second about twelve miles in the rear of the lead

78

mines, and the third on Turkey river, half a league from its entrance. They are engaged in the same wars, and have the same alliances as the Sauks, with whom they must be considered as indissoluble in war and peace. They hunt on both sides of the Mississippi, from the River Iowa (below the prairie des Chiens) to a river of that name, above said village. They raise a great quantity of corn, beans and melons; the former of those articles in such quantities, as to sell many hundred bushels *per annum*.

At this period, 1805, according to Lieutenant Pike, the total number of souls in the Sauk nation was 2850, of whom 1400 were children, seven hundred and fifty women, and seven hundred warriors. They resided in their villages and had about seven hundred stand of arms. Their trade was principally in deer skins, with some bear and a few otter, beaver and raccoon skins. The total number of the Foxes was 1750, of whom eight hundred and fifty were children, five hundred women and four hundred warriors, with about four hundred stand of arms. Their number of villages and their trade being the same with the Sauks.

Some further items of information about these tribes may be gleaned from the statistical view of the Indian nations furnished by Lewis and Clark's Expedition. It is there stated that the Saukee, or *O-sau-kee*, speak a primitive language, dwell principally in two villages, have about five hundred warriors and 2000 souls in the tribe, were at war with the Osage, Chippeway and Sioux. The Foxes or *Ot-tar-gar-me*, in the Saukee language, number not more than 1200 souls, and about three hundred warriors. Mr. Lewis says:

These nations, the Sauks and Foxes, are so perfectly consolidated that they may in fact be considered as one nation only: they are extremely friendly to the whites and seldom injure their traders; but they are the most implacable enemies to the Indian nations with whom they are at war; to them is justly attributed the almost entire destruction of the Missouries, the Illinois, the Cahokias, Kaskaskias, and Peorias.

In 1825, the Secretary at War, estimated the entire number of Sacs and Foxes at 4,600 souls, and in 1826, the warriors were supposed to amount to between twelve and fourteen hundred. Supposing these estimates to approximate the truth, it appears that during the twenty years between 1805 and 1825, these tribes had increased very considerably in numbers.

The traders generally and those who have had most intercourse with the Sauks and Foxes, speak of them as honest in their dealings, and feel safe among them, seldom locking their doors by day or night, and allowing them free ingress to their stores and houses. Their reputation for courage, it appears, does not stand quite so fair. Lieutenant Pike speaks of them as being more dreaded by their savage brethren for "their deceit and inclination for stratagem, than for their open courage." Major Thomas Forsyth, late U.S. agent among the Sacs and Foxes, calls them a dastardly and cowardly set of Indians. The correctness of these charges may be questioned. Mr. Schoolcraft, in speaking of the Foxes says:

> The history of their migrations and wars, shows them to have been a restless and spirited people, erratic in their dispositions, having a great contempt for agriculture, and a predominant passion for war.
>
> They still retain their ancient character, and are constantly embroiled in wars and disputes with their neighbours, the results of which show, that they have more courage in battle, than wisdom in council.

In a report of the war department to the president, made by the secretary Mr. Cass, in 1832, the Sacs and Foxes are spoken of as being distinguished for their "daring spirit of adventure and for their natural courage."

The truth appears to be, that the Sacs and Foxes fought their way from the waters of the St. Lawrence to Green Bay, and after reaching that place, not only sustained themselves against hostile tribes, but were among the most active and courageous in the subjugation or rather extermination of the numerous and powerful Illini confederacy. They have had many wars, offensive and defensive, with the Sioux, the Pawnees, the Osages and other tribes, some of whom are ranked among the most fierce and ferocious warriors on the continent; and, it does not appear, that in these conflicts, running through a long period of years, they were found wanting in this greatest of savage virtues.

In the late war with Great Britain, a party from the Sacs and Foxes, fought under the British standard as a matter of choice: and in the recent contest between a fragment of these tribes and the United States, although defeated and literally cut to pieces by an overwhelming force, it is very questionable whether their reputation as braves, would suffer by a comparison with that of their victors. It is believed that a careful review of their history, from the period when they first established themselves on the waters of the Mississippi, down to the present time, will lead the inquirer to the conclusion, that the Sacs and Foxes are truly a courageous people, shrewd, politic, and enterprising, with not more of ferocity and treachery of character, than is common among the tribes by whom they are surrounded.

CHAPTER 2

Treaty with the Sac and Fox Indians in 1789

The first treaty between the United States and the Sacs, was made at Fort Harmar, on the Muskingum River, on the 9th of January 1789. It was concluded by Arthur St. Clair, governor of the Territory north west of the Ohio, on the part of the United States, and the *sachems* and warriors of the Chippeway, Ottawa, Pottawatamie, Delaware, Wyandotte and Sac tribes of Indians. The object of this treaty seems to have been the confirmation of former treaties and the adjustment of boundary lines of previous cessions of land. By the fourteenth article of this treaty, it is provided, that the United States, "do also receive into their friendship and protection, the nations of the Pottawatamies, and Sacs; and do hereby establish a league of peace and amity between them respectively; and all the articles of this treaty, so far as they apply to these nations, are to be considered as made and concluded, in all and every part, expressly with them and each of them."

On the 27th of June 1804, the President, Mr. Jefferson, directed Governor William H. Harrison, to make a treaty with the Sacs, and obtain, if possible, cessions of land on both sides of the Illinois River, and to give them, in lieu thereof, an annual compensation. In November following, Governor Harrison concluded a treaty with the Sacs and Foxes, under his instructions. As this treaty has formed the basis of all the subsequent ones made with these tribes, and as its validity, has been disputed by some of the Sac nation, it is deemed expedient, to copy it entire, in this place, more especially as it will be matter of frequent reference in the subsequent pages of this work.

Articles of a treaty, made at Saint Louis, in the district of Louisiana, between William Henry Harrison, governor of the Indiana Territory and of the district of Louisiana, superintendent of Indian affairs for the said territory and district, and commissioner plenipotentiary of the United States, for concluding any treaty, or treaties which may be found necessary with any of the north western tribes of Indians, of the one part; and the chiefs and headmen of the united Sac and Fox tribes of the other part.

Article 1. The United States receive the united Sac and Fox tribes into their friendship and protection; and the said tribes agree to consider themselves under the protection of the United States, and of no other power whatsoever.

Art. 2. The general boundary line between the lands of the United States and of the said Indian tribes shall be as follows, *viz*: Beginning at a point on the Missouri River, opposite to the mouth of the Gasconade River; thence, in a direct course so as to strike the river Jeffreon, at the distance of thirty miles from its mouth, and down the said Jeffreon to the Mississippi; thence, up the Mississippi to the mouth of the Ouisconsin River, and up the same to a point which shall be thirty-six miles, in a direct line from the mouth of said river; thence, by a direct line to a point where the Fox River (a branch of the Illinois) leaves the small lake called Sakaegan; thence down the Fox River to the Illinois River, and down the same to the Mississippi. And the said tribes, for and in consideration of the friendship and protection of the United States, which is now extended to them, of the goods (to the value of two thousand, two hundred and thirty-four dollars and fifty cents) which are now delivered, and of the annuity hereinafter stipulated to be paid, do hereby cede and relinquish forever, to the United States, all the lands included within the above described boundary.

Art. 3. In consideration of the cession and relinquishment of land made in the preceding article, the United States will deliver to the said tribes, at the town of St. Louis, or some other convenient place on the Mississippi, yearly and every year, goods suited to the circumstances of the Indians, of the value of one thousand dollars (six hundred of which are intended for the Sacs, and four hundred for the Foxes,) reckoning that value at the first cost of the goods in the city or place in the United States, where they shall be procured. And if the said tribes shall hereafter, at an annual delivery of the goods aforesaid, desire that a part of their annuity should be furnished in domestic animals, implements of husbandry, and other utensils, convenient for them, the same shall at the subsequent annual delivery, be furnished accordingly.

Art. 4. The United States will never interrupt the said tribes, in the possession of the lands which they rightfully claim; but will on the contrary, protect them in the quiet enjoyment of the same, against their own citizens, and against all other white persons, who may intrude upon them. And the said tribes do hereby engage, that they will never sell their land, or any part thereof, to any sovereign power but the United States; nor to the citizens or subjects of any other sovereign power, nor to the citizens of the United States.

Art. 5. Lest the friendship which is now established between the United States and the said Indian tribes, should be interrupted by the misconduct of individuals, it is hereby agreed, that for injuries done by individuals, no private revenge or retaliation shall take place; but, instead thereof, complaint shall be made by the party injured to the other; by the said tribes, or either of them, to the superintendent of Indian affairs, or one of his deputies; and by the superintendent, or other person appointed by the president, to the chiefs of the said tribes. And it shall be the duty of the said chiefs, upon complaint being made, as aforesaid, to deliver up the person, or persons, against whom the complaint is made, to the end that he, or they, may be punished agreeably to the laws of the state or territory where the offence may have been committed.

And, in like manner, if any robbery, violence or murder shall be committed on any Indian, or Indians, belonging to the said tribes, or either of them, the person or persons so offending, shall be tried, and if found guilty, punished, in like manner as if the injury had been done to a white man. And it is further agreed, that the chiefs of the said tribes shall, to the utmost of their power, exert themselves to recover horses, or other property which may be stolen from any citizen or citizens of the United States by any individual or individuals of their tribes. And the property so recovered, shall be forthwith delivered to the superintendent, or other person authorized to receive it, that it may be restored to the proper owner.

And in cases where the exertions of the chiefs shall be ineffectual in recovering the property stolen, as aforesaid, if sufficient proof can be obtained, that such property was actually stolen by any Indian, or Indians, belonging to the said tribes or either of them, the United States may deduct from the annuity of the said tribes, a sum equal to the value of the property which was stolen. And the United States hereby guaranty to any Indian or Indians, of the said tribes, a full indemnification for any horses, or other property, which may be stolen from them, by any of their citizens: *Provided*, that the property so stolen cannot be recovered, and that sufficient proof is produced that it was actually stolen by a citizen of the United States.

Art. 6. If any citizen of the United States, or any other white person, should form a settlement, upon the lands which are the property of the Sac and Fox tribes, upon complaint being made thereof, to the Superintendent, or other person having charge of the affairs of the Indians, such intruder shall forthwith be removed.

Art. 7. As long as the lands which are now ceded to the United States remain their property, the Indians belonging to the said tribes shall enjoy the privilege of living and hunting upon them.

Art. 8. As the laws of the United States regulating trade and intercourse with the Indian tribes, are already extended to the country inhabited by the Sacs and Foxes, and as it is provided by those laws, that no person shall reside, as a trader, in the Indian country, without a licence under the hand and seal of the Superintendent of Indian affairs, or other person appointed for the purpose by the president, the said tribes do promise and agree, that they will not suffer any trader to reside among them, without such licence, and that they will, from time to time, give notice to the superintendent, or to the agent for their tribes, of all the traders that may be in their country.

Art. 9. In order to put a stop to the abuses and impositions which are practised upon the said tribes, by the private traders, the United States will, at a convenient time, establish a trading house, or factory, where the individuals of the said tribes can be supplied with goods at a more reasonable rate, than they have been accustomed to procure them.

Art. 10. In order to evince the sincerity of their friendship and affection for the United States, and a respectful deference for their advice, by an act which will not only be acceptable to them, but to the common father of all the nations of the earth, the said tribes do, hereby, promise and agree that they will put an end to the bloody war which has heretofore raged between their tribe and the Great and Little Osages. And for the purpose of burying the tomahawk, and renewing the friendly intercourse between themselves and the Osages, a meeting of their respective chiefs shall take place, at which, under the direction of the above named commissioner, or the agent of Indian affairs residing at St. Louis, an adjustment of all their differences shall be made, and peace established upon a firm and lasting basis.

Art. 11. As it is probable that the government of the United States will establish a military post at, or near the mouth of the Ouisconsin River, and as the land on the lower side of the river may not be suitable for that purpose, the said tribes hereby agree, that a fort may be built, either on the upper side of the Ouisconsin, or on the right bank of the Mississippi, as the one or the other may be found most convenient; and a tract of land not exceeding two miles square, shall be given for that purpose; and the said tribes do further agree, that they will at all times, allow to traders and other persons travelling through their country, under the authority of the United States, a free and safe passage for themselves and their property of every description; and that for such passage, they shall at no time, and on no account whatever, be subject to any toll or exaction.

Art. 12. This treaty shall take effect and be obligatory on the contracting parties, as soon as the same shall be ratified by the president, by and with the advice and consent of the Senate of the United States.

In testimony whereof, the said William Henry Harrison, and the chiefs and head men of said Sac and Fox tribes, have hereunto set their hands and affixed their seals. Done at St. Louis, in the district of Louisiana, on the third day of November, one thousand, eight hundred and four, and of the independence of the United States the twenty-ninth.
Additional article.

It is agreed that nothing in this treaty contained shall affect the claim of any individual or individuals, who may have obtained grants of land from the Spanish government, and which are not included within the general boundary line, laid down in this treaty: *Provided*, that such grant have at any time been made known to the said tribes and recognised by them.

William Henry Harrison. L. S.
Layowvois, or Laiyuva, his X mark L.S.
Pashepaho, or the Stabber, his X mark. L.S.
Quashquame, or jumping fish, his X mark. L.S.
Outchequaha, or sun fish, his X mark. L.S.
Hashequarhiqua, or the bear, his X mark.L.S.

In presence of

William Prince, Secretary to the Commissioner.
Griffin, one of the Judges of the Indiana Territory
J. Bruff, Maj. Art'y. U.S
Amos Stoddard, Capt. corps of Artillerists
P. Choteau, *Agent de la haute Louisiana,*
                pour le department sauvage
Ch. Gratiot
Aug. Choteau.Vigo
S. Warrel, Lieut. U. States Artillery.
D. Delaunay

Sworn interpreters:

Joseph Barren.
H'polite Bolen, his X mark

On the 31st of December 1804, the President of the United States, submitted this treaty to the Senate for their advice and consent, and it was by that body duly ratified.

In a *Life of Black Hawk,* dictated by himself and written by J.B. Patterson, to which there is a certificate of authenticity appended from Antoine Le Clair. U.S. interpreter, for the Sacs and Foxes, under date of 16th October 1833, there is the following statement concerning the manner in which this treaty was made.

Some moons after this young chief (Lieutenant Pike) descended the Mississippi, one of our people killed an American, and was confined, in the prison at St. Louis for the offence. We held a council at our village to see what could be done for

87

him—which determined that Quash-qua-me, Pa-she-pa-ho, Ou-che-qua-ha, and Ha-she-quar-hi-qua, should go down to St. Louis, and see our American father, and do all they could to have our friend released; by paying for the person killed, thus covering the blood and satisfying the relations of the man murdered! This being the only means with us of saving a person who had killed another, and we *then* thought it was the same way with the whites.

The party started with the good wishes of the whole nation, hoping they would accomplish the object of their mission. The relations of the prisoner blacked their faces and fasted, hoping the Great Spirit would take pity on them, and return the husband and the father to his wife and children.

Quash-qua-me and party remained a long time absent. They at length returned and encamped a short distance below the village, but did not come up that day, nor did any person approach their camp. They appeared to be dressed in fine coats and had medals. From these circumstances, we were in hopes they had brought us good news. Early the next morning, the council lodge was crowded—Quash-qua-me and party came up, and gave us the following account of their mission.

On their arrival at St. Louis, they met their American father, and explained to him their business, and urged the release of their friend. The American chief told them he wanted land, and they agreed to give him some on the west side of the Mississippi, and some on the Illinois side opposite the Jeffreon. When the business was all arranged, they expected to have their friend released to come home with them.—But about the time they were ready to start, their friend was led out of prison, who ran a short distance and was *shot dead*. This is all they could recollect of what was said and done. They had been drunk the greater part of the time they were in St. Louis.

This is all myself or nation knew of the treaty of 1804. It has been explained to me since. I find by that treaty, all our country east of the Mississippi, and south of the Jeffreon was ceded to the United States for one thousand dollars a year! I will leave it to the people of the United States to say, whether our nation was properly represented in this treaty? or whether we received a fair compensation for the extent of country ceded by those four individuals. I could say much more about this treaty but I will not at this time. It has been the origin of all our difficulties.

The power among the Indian tribes of this country to sell their lands, has always been considered as vested in the chiefs. They, however, are accustomed to consult the whole nation, and, possibly, it may be necessary, in all cases, that its assent should be obtained. It has not been the practice of our government, it is believed, in its negotiations with the Indians, to institute particular enquiries for the purpose of ascertaining, how far the chiefs were authorized to act by their people. A number of treaties have been formed, at different times, in which the chiefs must have acted under the general authority with which they are clothed on this point; the circumstances of the case being such, as to have precluded all opportunity of their ascertaining the sense of the tribes, after the negotiations had been commenced.

In the case under consideration, notwithstanding the statement of Black Hawk, there was every reason, especially on the part of the commissioner, for believing, that the chiefs who signed the treaty, were fully authorized to act. In the first place, government, in its instructions to the commissioner, to make a purchase of lands, of the Sacs and Foxes, had given as a reason for it, that it was a matter of complaint, on the part of these two tribes, that they were not, like their neighbours, receiving an annuity from the United States. They owned a very large extent of territory, and had, comparatively, but a limited population. It was natural that they should wish to dispose of some portion of it, for the purpose of receiving an annual supply of goods and money. In the second place, five chiefs of the Sacs and Foxes, united in the treaty, one of them, Pah-she-pa-ho, being at the time the great head-chief of the Sac nation.

It is admitted by Black Hawk that a council had been held by these two tribes, and that Pah-she-pa-ho and his associates had been authorized to visit St. Louis to purchase the release of a prisoner. It is probable that the sale of a part of their territory may have been agreed upon by this council. In the third place, there must have been a prevailing opinion in St. Louis, that these chiefs were authorized to act in the case. The treaty was publicly made, and a number of high-minded and honourable men, are parties to it, in the character of commissioner, secretary, and witnesses. Among them are several officers of the army; the first governor of the territory of Louisiana; and Pierre Chouteau, at that time Agent for the Sac and Fox Indians, and well acquainted with them. These circumstances forbid the idea of the treaty having been formed under circumstances in which there were not satisfactory reasons for believing, that the Indians, parties to it were fully authorized to act.

Black Hawk is mistaken in some things about this treaty, and it may be that he has been misinformed in regard to the authority of his chiefs to make this sale of their lands. He says, for instance, that the treaty was made some moons after the return of Lieutenant Pike from the sources of the Mississippi; when in fact Pike did not leave St. Louis upon his expedition, until the 9th of August 1805, nearly a year after the date of the treaty. Again, he says, it was made by four of the chiefs. The treaty is signed by five. But admitting that the deputation of chiefs transcended their authority in the sale of the lands, made at that time, it would seem that the Sacs and Foxes acquiesced in it. They never disavowed the treaty, but have regularly received their annuity, and, on more than one occasion, have recognised it, as binding. Even Black Hawk and his band, made this recognition, in the treaty of peace which they signed with the United States, at Portage des Sioux, in 1816.

It may be questioned, however, whether good faith towards the Indians and a due regard to national honour, do not make it expedient that our government should invariably hold its treaties with them, in their own country, and in the midst of the tribe owning the lands proposed to be purchased. In such case, the assent of all the Indians might be obtained, and the charge of having formed a fraudulent treaty, with unauthorized individuals, could never be raised. The peculiar relation subsisting between the government of the United States and the Indian tribes, within its territory, demands on the part of the former, great delicacy of action, liberality and perfect good faith. By such a course, alone, can our national honour be preserved untarnished.

Subsequently to the treaty of 1804, the erection by the government of the United States, of Fort Madison on the Mississippi, above the Des Moines rapids, gave some dissatisfaction to the Sacs and Foxes. This was increased by the British agents and traders, who instigated them to resist the encroachments of the Americans, now beginning to press upon their hunting grounds. Of this interference on the part of the British, with the Indians, there can be no doubt. Governor Harrison in a letter to the secretary of war, dated Vincennes, July 15th, 1810, says, "a considerable number of the Sacs went some time since to see the British superintendent, and on the first instant, more passed Chicago, for the same destination." General Clark, under date of St.

Louis, July 20th, 1810, says, in writing to the same department:

> One hundred and fifty Sacs are on a visit to the British agent by invitation, and a smaller party on a visit to the island of St. Joseph, in lake Huron.

John Johnson, Esq. the Indian agent, at Fort Wayne, under date of August 7th, 1810, says, to the secretary at war,:

> About one hundred Saukees have returned from the British agent, who supplied them liberally with everything they stood in need of. The party received forty-seven rifles, and a number of fusils with plenty of powder and lead.

McKee, Dixon, and Girty were open and active agents in exciting the Indians to attack the American frontiers. They held frequent talks with them and supplied them liberally with goods and munitions of war. In 1811, there being a strong probability of a war with Great Britain, a deputation of the Sauks and Foxes, visited Washington city, to see the president, by whom they were told that in the event of a war taking place with England, their great father did not wish them to interfere on either side, but to remain neutral: He did not want their assistance but desired them to hunt and support their families and live in peace. Immediately after the war of 1812, the Sacs and Foxes, with whom, as with Indians generally, war is the great business of life, felt that they ought, as a matter of course, to take sides with one party or the other, and went to St. Louis, to offer their services to the United States agent, to fight against the British; but the offer was declined, on the ground that the government of the United States had resolved not to employ the Indians in that capacity.

The machinations of the British, were successfully continued. The Sacs and Foxes divided upon the question of taking up arms against the United States. A part of them claimed the protection of the American government and received it; a part joined the British standard, Black Hawk among the number, and fought against the Americans until the peace of 1815. The number of warriors who joined the British is supposed to have been about two hundred, and they have ever since been known as the "British Band," at the head of which has been "General Black Hawk."

On the 14th September, 1815, William Clark, Ninian Edwards and Auguste Choteau, commissioners on behalf of the United States, concluded a treaty with the chiefs and warriors of the Fox tribe, by which all injuries and acts of hostility, committed by either party during the late war, were to be forgiven, and peace and friendship established between the two nations. The fourth article of the treaty contains a recognition of the former treaty in these words.

> The said Fox tribe or nation do hereby, assent to, recognise, re-establish and confirm the treaty of St. Louis, which was concluded on the 3rd of November, 1804, to the full extent of their interest in the same, as well as all other contracts and agreements between the parties.

This treaty was made at Portage des Sioux.

On the 13th of September, 1815, the same commissioners, at the same place, concluded a treaty of peace and friendship with the chiefs and warriors of that part of Sac nation of Indians residing on the Mississippi River. The first article recognises the treaty of 1804 in the following words.

> The undersigned chiefs and warriors for themselves and that portion of the Sacs which they represent, do hereby assent to the treaty between the United States of America and the united tribes of Sacs and Foxes, which was concluded at St. Louis on the third of November 1804; and they moreover promise to do all in their power to re-establish and enforce the same.

There is a further provision that they will remain distinct and separate from the Sacs of Rock River, giving them no assistance whatever, until peace shall be established between them and the United States. The Sacs on Rock River were that part of the tribe which had been engaged in the late war, and who now declined making a treaty with the United States, and continued, although officially notified of the peace, to commit occasional depredations on the frontiers; and, it was not until the following spring that hostilities on their part actually ceased.

On the 13th of May, 1816, the same commissioners effected a treaty with the chiefs and warriors of the Sacs of Rock River, and the adjacent country. The first article of this treaty provides, that:

> The Sacs of Rock River and the adjacent country, do hereby unconditionally assent to, recognise, re-establish and confirm the treaty between the United States of America and the united tribes of Sacs and Foxes, which was concluded at St. Louis on the 3rd November 1804, as well as all other contracts and

agreements, heretofore made between the Sac tribe and the United States.

Under the 9th article of the Treaty of Ghent, concluded 24th December 1814, between the United States and Great Britain, it was stipulated, that each party should put an end to Indian hostilities within their respective territory, and place the tribes on the same footing upon which they stood before the war. Under this provision, the second article of the treaty with the Sacs of Rock River, stipulated that they are placed upon the same footing which they occupied before the late war, upon the single condition of their restoring the property stolen by them, from the whites, subsequent to their notification that peace had been made between the United States and Great Britain.

Under the 9th article of the treaty of 1804, the United States agreed to establish a trading-house to supply the Sacs and Foxes with goods at a more reasonable rate than they had been accustomed to procure them. On the third of September 1822, Major Thomas Forsyth, the U.S. Indian agent, made a treaty at Fort Armstrong, with the chiefs, warriors and head men of the Sacs and Foxes, by which, in consideration of the sum of one thousand dollars, they forever released the United States from all obligation contained in said ninth article of the treaty of 1804.

On the fourth of August 1824, at Washington city, William Clark, Indian agent and sole commissioner of the United States, effected a treaty with the Sacs and Foxes through their chiefs and head men, by which, for the sum of one thousand dollars *per annum* for ten years, they ceded all their interest and title to any lands claimed by them in the state of Missouri, which are situated, lying and being between the Mississippi and Missouri Rivers, and a line running from the Missouri at the entrance of Kansas River, north one hundred miles, to the north west corner of the state of Missouri, and from thence east to the Mississippi. By this treaty, these tribes acknowledged the land east and south of the lines above described, so far as the Indians claim the same, to belong to the United States, and that none of their tribes shall be permitted to settle or hunt upon any part of it, after the first day of January 1826, without permission from the Superintendent of Indian affairs.

Upon the 19th of August 1825, William Clark and Lewis Cass, commissioners on behalf of the United States, concluded a treaty at Prairie du Chien, in the territory of Michigan, with the chiefs

93

and warriors of the Sioux, Winnebagoes, Menominees, Chippewas, Ottawas, Pottawatamies, Sacs, Foxes and Ioways. The objects of this treaty were the restoration of peace among the Indian tribes, several of whom had been for some time waging war against each other; the settlement of boundary lines between these tribes respectively, and between them and the United States. The commissioners succeeded in effecting a peace between the Sioux and Chippeways, and between the Sacs, Foxes and Ioways on the one part, and the Sioux on the other; and also in adjusting the boundary lines of the territory of each tribe to the satisfaction of all parties. Under this treaty nothing was asked by the United States nor was anything granted to them: the character in which the government presented itself, being simply that of a pacificator.

The concourse of Indians assembled at this council was very great. About 3000 came to the council ground, clothed in their war dresses, and armed with bows, war-clubs and tomahawks. The Sacs and Foxes were the last to arrive, but were very imposing and warlike in their appearance when they reached the ground. They ascended the Mississippi, to Prairie du Chien, in a fleet of canoes, lashed together. They passed and repassed the town in a connected squadron, standing erect, in their canoes, in full dress, singing their war songs. Upon landing, they drew up in martial order, as if in warlike defiance of their bitter enemies, the Sioux, who were encamped near the shore, and who in turn shot back the fierce look of hostility upon their ancient foe. An eyewitness describes this scene as one unique and singularly magnificent. The council was held under a spacious booth of green boughs, and lasted for several days. Keokuk was present on this occasion, as the head chief of the Sacs, and took an active part in the council; his course being marked by that moderation and sound policy, for which he is eminently distinguished.

In the early part of the year 1828, the President of the United States, appointed Governor Cass and Colonel Pierre Menard, to treat with certain tribes of Indians for the cession of what is called the "mineral region" lying on the Mississippi, south of the Wisconsin. The commissioners arrived at Green Bay late in the summer of that year, and on the 25th of August, made a temporary agreement with the Indians, by which the whites were allowed to occupy the country where the lead mines were worked; and in the ensuing year a treaty was to be held with the Indians for the purchase of the mineral country: in the mean time, no white was to cross a certain line, described in said

94

COUNCIL GROUND AT PRAIRIE DU CHIENS

agreement, to dig for ore; and finally the Indians were paid twenty thousand dollars in goods, for the trespasses already committed on their lands by the miners. This agreement was ratified by the president and senate of the United States on the 7th January, 1829.

Soon after President Jackson came into office in 1829, he appointed General McNeil of the army, to fill the place of Governor Cass in the said commission, which was to meet at St. Louis and under the agreement above described, proceed to the mineral region, to effect by treaty, its purchase. In consequence of some disagreement in opinion between these two commissioners, the president subsequently united with them, Caleb Atwater, Esq. of Ohio. They reached Prairie du Chien about the middle of July, where they met deputies on the part of the Winnebagoes, Chippeways, Ottowas, Pottawatimies, Sioux, Sauks, Foxes and Menominees; and on the first of August, a treaty was concluded for about eight millions of acres, extending from the upper end of Rock island to the mouth of the Wisconsin, from latitude 41° 15' to latitude 43° 15' on the Mississippi.

Following the meanderings of the river the tract is about two hundred and forty miles from south to north. It extends along the Wisconsin and Fox Rivers from west to east so as to give a passage across the country from the Mississippi to lake Michigan. At this treaty Keokuk and Morgan, with two hundred warriors of the Sac and Fox tribes were present, and according to the statement of one of the commissioners, rendered essential service to them, by intimidating the Winebagoes, who from some dissatisfaction, threatened to assassinate the commissioners and those associated with them.

On the 21st Sept. 1832, after the conclusion of the Black Hawk war, General Scott and Governor Reynolds concluded a treaty with the Sacs and Foxes, by which about six million acres of land were acquired, for which the United States were to pay them the sum of twenty thousand dollars *per annum* for thirty years, to pay off the debts of the tribes and to support, at the discretion of the President, a black and gunsmith among them. A reservation was made of forty miles square, on the Ioway River in favour of Keokuk, (since purchased,) including his village, as a reward for his fidelity to the United Slates. Black Hawk, his son and the Prophet were to be held as hostages during the pleasure of the president. This is known as the "Black Hawk purchase."

The whole of the six millions lie upon the west side of the Mississippi and are included within the following boundaries: Beginning on the Mississippi River at the point where the Sac and Fox northern boundary line is established, by the second article of the treaty of Prairie des Chiens of 15th July, 1830, strikes said river; thence up said boundary line to a point fifty miles from the Mississippi, measured on said line to the nearest point on the Red Cedar of Iowa, forty miles from the Mississippi River; thence in a right line to a point in the northern boundary of the state of Missouri fifty miles measured on said boundary from the Mississippi River; thence by the last mentioned boundary to the Mississippi River, and by the western shore of said river to the place of beginning.

The Sac and Fox tribes are now residing, (as at time of first publication), on the west side of the Mississippi, and are living upon friendly terms with the United States. As a general remark, it may be said, that their intercourse with the United States has been of a pacific character. They took no part in the war of the Revolution: they were not parties to the Indian disturbances which terminated in the treaty of Greenville in 1795. Tecumseh and the Prophet failed to enlist them in their grand confederacy against the Americans, which was nearly broken up by the premature battle of Tippecanoe. The machinations of the British agents and traders, backed by the most liberal distribution of goods and fire arms, induced but a small party of them, not exceeding two hundred, to join the British standard in the late war with England. In the still more recent disturbance, on the frontiers of Illinois, called the "Black Hawk war," but a portion of these tribes, took up arms against the United States, the great mass of them refusing to take any part in it; while Keokuk, their principal chief, exerted all his influence to dissuade the "British Band" from engaging in so hopeless a contest.

Chapter 3

Birth of Black Hawk

Black Hawk is a remarkable instance of an individual, in no wise gifted with any uncommon physical, moral or intellectual endowments, obtaining, by the force of circumstances, the most extraordinary celebrity. Since the year 1831, his name has been familiarly known to the people of the United States; and the terror, which for a brief period, it excited upon the frontiers of Illinois, Missouri and Indiana, was only surpassed by the curiosity which pervaded every part of the union, to behold this notable chief of the woods, after he had been conquered, and was carried a prisoner of state, from the wilds of the West to the Atlantic sea-board. His tour through the United States, partook largely of the triumphal march of a successful hero. In the number of persons who flocked around him, the honours which he received were scarcely less flattering than those awarded to the illustrious Lafayette, while the "nation's guest." In the one case there was curiosity alone, in the other, curiosity and gratitude blended. To the casual observer, the distinction between the two cases is not very apparent.

The causes which created a desire so universal, to behold this aboriginal chief, have awakened a corresponding interest in the public mind, to learn more of his history, than was revealed in the events of the campaign of 1832. To gratify this curiosity, is the object of the present volume. The author has carefully consulted all the sources of information, touching the life and character of Black Hawk, that were within his reach; and has studiously avoided the presentation of any fact which did not seem to be well authenticated. Should the incidents here narrated, in the life of this celebrated Indian, not prove as rich and amusing as might be anticipated, from the wide spread notoriety which he has obtained, the work will still be found of some value.

It presents in a connected form, and as the author trusts, with historic accuracy, one link in the great chain of political relations between the United States and the Indian tribes of North America. Every day is increasing the interest and magnitude of these relations, and any effort to preserve the facts with which they are associated, would seem to be worthy of public consideration. Black Hawk may die, his name be forgotten, and the smoke of his wigwam be seen no more, but the "Black Hawk war" will long form a page of deep interest, in the history of this country.

The subject of this memoir is by birth a Sac, having been born at the principal Sac village, on Rock River, in the year, as he himself states, 1767. His father's name was Py-e-sa, his grandfather's Na-na-ma-kee or Thunder. Black Hawk was not by birth a chief, but at the early age of fifteen, having distinguished himself by wounding an enemy, he was permitted to paint and wear feathers; and was placed in the rank of the Braves. About the year 1783, he united in an expedition against the Osages, and had the good fortune to kill and scalp one of the enemy: for this act of youthful valour, he was, for the first time, permitted to mingle in the scalp-dance.

This triumph was followed shortly afterwards by two more excursions against the same tribe. In the first, Black Hawk was the leader of seven men, who suddenly attacked a party of one hundred Osages, killed one of them, and as suddenly retreated without loss. This exploit, so far increased the number of his followers, that he soon afterwards started with a party of one hundred and eighty braves, and marched to an Osage village, on the Missouri; but found it deserted. Most of the party being disappointed, left their leader and returned home. Black Hawk, however, with but five followers, pursued the trail of the enemy, and after some days succeeded in killing one man and a boy; and, securing their scalps, returned home.

In the year 1786, having recovered from the effect of his late unsuccessful excursion, Black Hawk found himself once more at the head of two hundred braves, and again set off to avenge the repeated outrages of the Osages upon the Sac nation. Soon after he reached the enemy's country, he met a party about equal in number to his own. A battle ensued. The Osages lost near one hundred men, and Black Hawk nineteen. He claims, in the attack, to have killed five of the enemy, with his own hand. This severe engagement had the effect, for some time, of keeping the Osages upon their own lands and arresting their depredations upon the Sacs.

This cessation of hostilities gave the latter an opportunity of redressing the wrongs which the Cherokees had committed upon them, by murdering some of their women and children. A party was raised for this purpose, and met the Cherokees upon the Merrimack River, below St. Louis, the latter being most numerous. In this battle Py-e-sa, the father of Black Hawk was killed. The Cherokees were compelled to retreat with the loss of twenty-eight men, the Sacs having but seven killed. Upon the fall of Py-e-sa, Black Hawk assumed the command and also took possession of the "medicine bag," then in the keeping of his father.

Owing to the disasters of this expedition, and especially the death of his father, Black Hawk, for the ensuing five years, refrained from all warlike operations, and spent his time in fishing and hunting. At the end of this period, being about the year 1800, he made another excursion, against the Osages, at the head of about five hundred Sacs and Foxes and a hundred Ioways, who had joined him as allies. After a long march they reached and destroyed about forty lodges of the enemy, killing many of their bravest warriors, five of whom were slain by the leader of the invading army. In the year 1802, he terminated a severe and protracted campaign against the Chippewas, Kaskaskias and Osages, during which six or seven battles were fought and more than one hundred of the enemy killed. The following summer Black Hawk made one of his periodical visits to St. Louis to see his Spanish father, by whom he was well received.

Upon his next visit to this Spanish dignitary, he found many sad and gloomy faces, because the United States were about to take possession of the town and country around it. Black Hawk says:

Soon after the Americans arrived I took my band and went to take leave, for the last time, of our father. The Americans came to see him also. Seeing them approach, we passed out at one door, as they entered at another—and immediately started, in our canoes, for our village on Rock River—not liking the change any more than our friends appeared to at St. Louis. On arriving at our village, we gave the news that strange people had taken St. Louis, and that we should never see our Spanish father again. This information made all our people sorry. Sometime afterwards (1805) a boat came up the river with a young American chief (Lieutenant, afterwards General Pike,) and a small party of soldiers. We heard of them, soon after he had passed Salt river.

Some of our young braves watched him every day, to see what sort of people he had on board. The boat at length arrived at Rock River, and the young chief came on shore with his interpreter—made a speech, and gave us some presents. We, in return, presented him with meat and such provisions as we could spare. We were well pleased with the speech of the young chief. He gave us good advice; said our American father would treat us well. He presented us an American flag, which was hoisted. He then requested us to pull down our British flags, and give him our British medals—promising to send us others on his return to St. Louis. This we declined as we wished to have *two fathers*.

Subsequently to this period, the building of Fort Edwards, near the head of the Des Moyens rapids, gave much uneasiness to the Sacs. Some of the chiefs and a party of their followers went down to this point, and had an interview with the war chief who had command of the troops engaged in constructing the fort. The Indians became satisfied and returned home. Not long afterwards a party, of which Black Hawk was one, determined to attack and take Fort Madison, standing upon the west side of the Mississippi, above the mouth of the Des Moyens, which was then garrisoned with about fifty men. Their spies having ascertained that the troops marched out of the fort every morning to exercise, they concealed themselves near it, with an agreement to fire upon them when they came out.

About sunrise, on the morning of the proposed attack, the gate opened, and a young man made his appearance, but was suffered to return without being molested. The gate was again opened and four soldiers came out. They were followed by a fifth, who was instantly killed. The others then ran for the fort, but two of them were shot down before they reached it. The Indians continued for two days, shooting into the fort, and endeavouring to set fire to it. Finding their efforts unavailing, they gave up the attack and returned home.

The period had now arrived when the difficulties between this country and Great Britain, were to be settled by an appeal to arms. Some discontent had prevailed among the Sacs, in regard to the encroachments of the Americans upon their hunting grounds. They, however, offered their services to the United States, to fight against the British, but their offer was declined. They had not been as liberally supplied with presents and goods at Fort Madison, as they had anticipated, and in the meantime, the British agents had artfully fomented their discontent, and laboured to win their confidence by the most liberal distribution among them of goods and ardent spirits.

Shortly after the declaration of war, Girty, a British trader, arrived at Rock island with two boats loaded with goods, and the British flag was hoisted. He informed the Indians that he had been sent to them by Colonel Dixon, with presents, a large silk flag and a keg of rum. The day after his arrival, the goods were divided among the Indians, they promising to pay for them, in furs, in the following spring. Girty informed Black Hawk that Colonel Dixon was then at Green Bay, with a large quantity of goods, arms and ammunition, and was desirous that he should raise a party of warriors and join him. Black Hawk succeeded in collecting about two hundred braves, and soon reached Green Bay, where he found Dixon encamped, with a large body of Indians, assembled from other tribes, who had been already furnished with clothing and with arms. Black Hawk had an interview with Dixon, two other war chiefs and the interpreter.

> He received me with a hearty shake of the hand, and presented me to the other chiefs, who shook my hand cordially, and seemed much pleased to see me. After I was seated, Colonel Dixon said, "General Black Hawk, I sent for you, to explain to you, what we are going to do, and the reasons that have brought us here. Our friend Girty, informs us in the letter you brought from him, what has taken place. You will now have to hold us fast by the hand. Your English father has found out that the Americans want to take your country from you, and has sent me and his braves to drive them back to their own country. He has likewise sent a large quantity of arms and ammunition, and we want all your warriors to join us." He then placed a medal round my neck, and gave me a paper, (which I lost in the late war,) and a silk flag, saying, "You are to command all the braves that will leave here the day after tomorrow, to join our braves near Detroit.

On the following day, arms, clothing, knives and tomahawks, were distributed to Black Hawk's band, and upon the succeeding morning, they started, in all near five hundred braves, to join the British Army. This was in August, 1812, shortly after the surrender and massacre of the American troops at Chicago, which place they passed a few days after it had been evacuated. Of the movements of Black Hawk during his connection with the British upon our north west, no satisfactory information has been obtained. It appears that he was in two engagements, but seems not to have distinguished himself. The last of these was the attack, in August 1813, upon Fort Stephenson, then under the command of Major Croghan. The gallant defence of this post, and the fatal repulse given to the combined British and Indian forces, seem to have disheartened Black Hawk; for soon afterwards, tired of successive defeats, and disappointed in not obtaining the "spoils of victory," he left the army, with about twenty of his followers, and returned to his village on Rock River.

It is probable that he would have remained neutral during the remainder of the war, had it not been for one of those border outrages, which lawless and unprincipled white men but too often commit upon the Indians, under pretence of self defence or retaliation, often a mere pretext for wanton bloodshed and murder. Previous to joining Colonel Dixon, Black Hawk had visited the lodge of an old friend, whose son he had adopted and taught to hunt. He was anxious that this youth should go with him and his band and join the British standard, but the father objected on the ground that he was dependent upon his son for game; and, moreover, that he did not wish him to fight against the Americans who had always treated him kindly. He had agreed to spend the following winter near a white settler, upon Salt River, one of the tributaries of the Mississippi which enters that stream below the Des Moyens, and intended to take his son with him.

As Black Hawk was approaching his village on Rock River, after his campaign on the lakes with Dixon, he observed a smoke rising from a hollow in the bluff of the stream. He went to see who was there. Upon drawing near to the fire, he discovered a mat stretched, and an old man of sorrowful aspect sitting under it, alone, and evidently humbling himself before the Great Spirit, by fasting and prayer. It proved to be his old friend, the father of his adopted son. Black Hawk seated himself beside him and inquired what had happened, but received no answer, for indeed he seemed scarcely alive. Being revived by some water, he looked up, recognised the friend of his youth, and in reply to Black Hawk's second inquiry, said, in a feeble voice,

Soon after your departure to join the British, I descended the river with a small party, to winter at the place I told you the white man had requested me to come to. When we arrived, I found a fort built, and the white family that had invited me to come and hunt near them, had removed to it. I then paid a visit to the fort, to tell the white people that myself and little band were friendly, and that we wished to hunt in the vicinity of their fort. The war chief, who commanded it, told me that we might hunt on the Illinois side of the Mississippi, and no person would trouble us. That the horsemen only ranged on the Missouri side, and he had directed them not to cross the river. I was pleased with this assurance of safety, and immediately crossed over and made my winter's camp. Game was plenty: We lived happy and often talked of you. My boy regretted your absence, and the hardships you would have to undergo. We had been here about two moons, when my boy went out as usual to hunt. Night came on and he did not return. I was alarmed for his safety and passed a sleepless night. In the morning my old woman went to the other lodges and gave the alarm, and all turned out in pursuit.

There being snow on the ground, they soon came upon his track, and after pursuing it some distance, found that he was on the trail of a deer, that led to the river. They soon came to the place where he had stood and fired, and found a deer hanging upon the branch of a tree, which had been skinned. But here also were found the tracks of white men. They had taken my boy prisoner. Their tracks led across the river, and then down towards the fort. My friends followed them, and soon found my boy lying dead. He had been most cruelly murdered. His face was shot to pieces, his body stabbed in several places, and his head scalped. His arms were tied behind him.

The old man ceased his narrative, relapsed into the stupor from which he had been aroused and in a few minutes, expired. Black Hawk remained by his body during the night, and next day buried upon the peak of the bluff. Shocked at the cruel fate of his adopted son, and deeply touched by the mournful death of his old comrade, he was roused to vengeance against the Americans, and after remaining a few days at the village, and raising a band of braves, prepared for offensive operations upon the frontiers.

Having narrated to his band the murder of his adopted son, they began to thirst for blood, and agreed to follow Black Hawk wheresoever he might lead. The party consisted of about thirty. They descended the Mississippi in canoes to the place where Fort Madison had stood, but found it abandoned by the American troops and burnt. They continued their course down the river and landed near Cap au Gris, on the 10th of May, where they killed one of the United States Rangers, named Bernard, but were driven off by Lieutenant Massey, with a detachment from Fort Howard. The Indians, however, rallied in the woods, and on the 24th of May, a severe battle and of a character somewhat novel, was fought between the troops at Fort Howard, under Lieutenant Drakeford of the U. S. Rangers, and Black Hawk and his party. The former, in his official report of this engagement, says,

Yesterday, about twelve o'clock, five of our men went out to some cabins on the bluff, about one quarter of a mile below the fort, to bring a grind-stone. The backwater of the Mississippi, rendered it so they went in a canoe. On their return they were attacked by a party of Indians, supposed to be about fifty in number; they killed and tomahawked three and wounded one mortally. While about this mischief, we gave them as good a fire from a little below the fort, as the breadth of the backwater would permit. Captain Craig and myself with about forty men, waded across the water and pursued them: in going about half a mile, we came on them and commenced a fire which continued about one hour, part of which time at a distance of forty steps, and no part of the time further than a hundred and fifty steps.

Shortly after the commencement of the battle, we were reinforced by Captain Musick and twenty of his men; the enemy now ran; some made their escape, and others made to a sink-hole that is in the battle ground, and from there they returned a most rapid fire; it being very dangerous, to approach nearer than fifty steps of the sink, we at length erected a breastwork, on the two wheels of a wagon, and resolved upon moving it up to the edge of the sink, to fire from behind, down into the sink and preserve us from theirs. We got the moving battery finished about sunset, and moved it up with a sufficient number of men behind it, whilst all other posts round were sufficiently guarded, in case they should be put to the route.

We had not moved to within less than ten steps of the sink, before they commenced a fire, which we returned at every

Battle of Sink Hole.

opportunity. Night came on and we were obliged to leave the ground, and decline the expectation of taking them out without risking man for man, which we thought not a good exchange on our side.

During the time of the battle another party of Indians commenced a brisk fire on the fort. Captain Craig was killed in the commencement of the battle, Lieut. Edward Spears at the moving of the breast work to the sink. The morning of the 25th we returned to the ground and found five Indians killed and the sign of a great many wounded, that had been taken off in the night. The aggregate number of killed on our part is one captain, one third lieutenant, and five privates; three wounded, one missing, one citizen killed and two wounded mortally.

Black Hawk states that but eighteen of his men were in the sink with him, and that they dug holes in the sides of the bank, with their knives, to protect them from the fire of the Americans: Some of his warriors commenced singing their death songs; but he, several times called out to the enemy, if brave men, to come down and fight them. He describes the wagon-battery, and its inefficiency in dislodging them from their depressed but safe situation. His retreat to the sink-hole under the circumstances, was a sound military movement. Lieutenant Drakeford having withdrawn his forces, Black Hawk and his party left their entrenchment and returned by land, to their village.

The tribes of Indians on the Mississippi, were notified in the early part of this year, 1815, that peace had been concluded between the United States and England. Most of those who had been engaged in the war, ceased hostilities. Black Hawk, however, and his band, and some of the Pottawatamies, were not inclined to bury the tomahawk. Even as late as the spring of 1816, they committed depredations. Some palliation for these outrages may be found in the fact, that the British, on the north-west frontier, long after they were officially notified of the peace, continued to excite the Indians to acts of violence against the United States; and, indeed, participated in them likewise.

It was in the spring of this year that they captured the garrison at Prairie du Chien, and instigated Black Hawk and his party to attack some boats, which were ascending the Mississippi to that point, with troops and provisions. In this attack, Black Hawk was the leader. One of the boats was captured and several of the crew killed. They were compelled to return, and dropped down to the fort at the mouth of the Des Moyens river. As a reward for their attack upon these boats, the British agents distributed rum among the Indians engaged in the affair, and joined with them in dancing and feasting.

In May, Black Hawk and his party, having been again summoned by the Americans, to make peace, concluded to descend the Mississippi to Portage des Sioux, to meet the American commissioners who were there for that purpose. On the 13th of May, 1816, a treaty of peace was signed by Clark, Edwards, and Choteau on behalf of the United States, and the chiefs and warriors of the Sacs of Rock River and the adjacent country. To this treaty Black Hawk was a party. It recognises the validity of the treaty of St. Louis, of November 1804.

CHAPTER 4

Black Hawk's Visit to Malden

From the treaty of peace, between the United States and the Sac Indians of Rock River, in 1816, to the commencement of hostilities between these parties in 1832, the life of Black Hawk seems to have been quiet and monotonous, occasionally relieved by a warlike excursion, but generally spent in hunting, throughout the winter, and in loitering about his village, during the summer. Such, indeed, is the life of most Indians. Having no intellectual pursuits and little desire for the acquisition of property, beyond the supply of their immediate wants, they have in reality but two sources of excitement—war and the chase. They take no interest in the domestic affairs of their families, have little taste for the pursuits of agriculture, and, if not engaged in hostile excursions, in following the deer, or in trapping the beaver, they sink into listless inactivity.

It is highly probable that many of their wars are undertaken, more for the gratification of that love of excitement, which is an indestructible element of the human mind, than from any constitutional proneness to cruelty and bloodshed. They need both physical and intellectual excitation, and having none of the resources which mental and moral culture throws open to civilized man, they seek it in making war upon each other or upon the wild animals which share with them the woods and the prairies.

Subsequently to the treaty of 1816, and perhaps in that year, the government of the United States built Fort Armstrong, upon Rock Island, in the Mississippi River, and but a few miles from the village where Black Hawk and his band resided. This measure, though not actually opposed, was by no means acceptable to them. They probably did not relish the gradual advances upon them, of the white population; but they entertained, moreover, a special regard for this beautiful island, which is justly considered one of the finest in the whole extent of the Mississippi. It is fertile, and produces many varieties of nuts and fruits, and being in the rapids of the stream, the waters which lave its shores, yield an abundance of excellent fish. In addition to all this, they have a traditionary belief, that the island was the favourite residence of a good spirit which dwelt in a cave in the rocks on which Fort Armstrong now stands. This spirit had often been seen by the Indians, but after the erection of the Fort, alarmed by the noise and intrusion of the white man, it spread its beautiful, swan-like wings, and disappeared.

During the year 1817, the Sacs sent out some warriors against the Sioux, and succeeded in killing several of them, but Black Hawk was not of the party. About this time, his eldest son sickened and died, and within a short period afterwards, he lost his youngest daughter. This affliction seems to have made a deep impression upon him; and according to a custom common among the Indians, he blacked his face, and for the ensuing two years lived at home, in seclusion, drinking water at mid-day, and eating boiled corn but sparingly, in the evening. In the winter of 1819-20, there was a disturbance between the Sacs and Ioways, one of the latter having killed a young man belonging to the former. Under the agreement of a late council between these two tribes, the old custom of appeasing the friends of one who had been killed, by presents, had been abolished, and each party had promised, that in future, the murderer should be surrendered up, that he might be punished with death.

A party of Sacs, of which Black Hawk was one, agreed to visit the Ioway village on this occasion, and when about to depart, called at the lodge of the young man who had committed the outrage, to take him along. He was sick, but still ready to accompany them. His brother interfered, and insisted that he was too unwell to travel; that he would himself go and die in his place, and finally set off with the party.

On the seventh day, they reached the Ioway village. They dismounted a short distance from it, and bid farewell to their young brave, who went calmly forwards, alone, singing his death-song, and seated himself in the middle of the lodges. One of the Ioway chiefs went out to Black Hawk, who told him the brother had come in the place of the young man that had committed the murder, he being sick. Black Hawk and his party, now mounted their horses and set off on their return; and casting their eyes towards the village, saw the Ioways, armed with spears and clubs, gathering around the young prisoner.

At night the returning party, having stopped and kindled a fire, were suddenly alarmed by the tramping of horses. They immediately stood to their arms, but were soon relieved, by finding, instead of a foe, their young brave, unhurt and in the possession of two horses.

They ascertained that the Ioways, at first threatened him with instant death, but finally, changing their purpose, had given him something to eat, smoked the pipe with him, and presenting him with two horses, bid him return home in safety. The generous conduct of the Ioways is deserving of praise, but the genuine affection of this young brave, in nobly volunteering to die in place of his sick brother, presents one of those rare cases of self-devotion, which should be held in remembrance.

In the following autumn, Black Hawk and some of his band went on a visit to their British father at Malden and received presents from him. A medal was given to Black Hawk for his fidelity to the British in the late war, and he was requested to come up annually, to that place, with his band, and receive such presents, as had been promised them by Colonel Dixon, when they joined the English forces. These visits were regularly made, it is believed, from that time down to the year 1832. It is owing to this circumstance that Black Hawk's party has long been known by the appellation of the "British Band."

In the winter of 1822, Black Hawk and his party, encamped on the Two-Rivers, for the purpose of hunting, and while there was so badly treated by some white men, that his prejudices against the Americans were greatly strengthened. He was accused of having killed the hogs of some settlers, who, meeting him one day in the woods, wrested his gun from his hands, and discharging it in the air, beat him so severely with sticks that for several nights he was unable to sleep. They then returned him his gun and ordered him to leave the neighbourhood.

Of the perpetration of this outrage, there is little doubt, while the fact of Black Hawk's having committed the offence charged upon him, rests, at best, upon suspicion. Supposing him to have been guilty, and the supposition is at variance with the whole tenor of his intercourse with the whites, it was on their part, one of those brutal appeals to *club* law, which are but too often practised towards the Indians; and which, when avenged by them, not infrequently brings upon their nation, the power and the arms of the United States.

The ensuing summer, the expediency of a removal of the whole of the Sacs and Foxes, to the west side of the Mississippi, was urged upon them by the agent at Fort Armstrong. The principal Fox chief, as well as Keokuk, assented to the removal. The latter sent a messenger through the village informing the Indians that it was the wish of their Great Father, the president, that they should remove, and he pointed out the Ioway River as presenting a fine situation for their new village. There was a party, however, among the Sacs, made up principally of the "British Band," who were decidedly opposed to a removal; and they called upon their old leader, Black Hawk, for his opinion on the question. He took the ground that the land on which their village stood had never been sold; that the Americans had, therefore, no right to insist upon the measure, and that as a matter of policy he was opposed to it.

The old man was probably swayed in his decision by another cause. He felt that his power in the tribe was waning before the rising popularity of Keokuk. Here was a question on which their people differed in opinion. By placing himself at the head of one of the parties, he might recover his influence, or at least sustain himself against the overshadowing ascendancy of his rival. He had an interview with Keokuk to see if the matter could not be adjusted with the President, by giving him other lands in exchange for those on which their village stood; and the latter promised to see the great chief at St. Louis, on the subject.

During the following winter, while Black Hawk and his party were absent on a hunting expedition, several white families arrived at their village, destroyed some of their lodges and commenced making fences over their cornfields. Black Hawk upon hearing of this movement, promptly returned to Rock River, and found his own lodge occupied by the whites. He went to Fort Armstrong and complained to the interpreter, the agent being absent. He crossed the Mississippi and travelled several days to converse with the Winnebago sub-agent, who concurred with the interpreter in advising the Sacs to remove to Keokuk's settlement on the Ioway. He then visited the prophet, Wabokieshiek, or White Cloud, whose opinions were held in much respect by the Sacs and Winnebagoes.

He urged Black Hawk not to remove, but to persuade Keokuk and his party to return to Rock River, assuring them that if they remained quietly at their village, the whites would not venture to disturb them. He then rejoined his hunting party, and in the spring when they returned to their village, they found the white settlers still there, and that the greater part of their cornfields had been enclosed by fences. About that time Keokuk visited Rock River and endeavoured to persuade the remainder of the Sacs to follow him to the Ioway. He had ac-complished nothing with the great chief at St. Louis, in regard to their remaining at their village, and as a matter of policy, that peace might be preserved, he was warmly in favour of the proposed removal. Black Hawk considered it an act of cowardice to yield up their village and the graves of their fathers, to strangers, who had no right to the soil, and the breach between Keokuk and himself was widened.

The white immigrants continued to increase, and the Sac village was the great point of attraction to them. It was situated on the neck of land formed by the junction of Rock River with the Mississippi, and had been the chief village of the tribe for sixty or seventy years.

Their women had broken the surface of the surrounding prai-rie with their hoes, and enclosed with a kind of flimsy pole fence, many fields, which were annually cultivated by them, in the raising of corn, beans, potatoes and squashes. They had also erected several hundred houses of various dimensions, some probably an hundred feet in length by forty or fifty broad; which were constructed of poles and forks, arranged so as to form a kind of frame, which was then enclosed with the bark of trees, which, being peeled off and dried under a weight for the purpose of keeping it expanded, was afterwards confined to the walls and roof by means of cords, composed of the bark of other trees.

This indeed is a delightful spot:—on the north-west rolls the majestic Mississippi, while the dark forests which clothe the numerous islands of Rock River, with its several rippling streams on the south-east, form a delightful contrast, which is rendered still more pleasing from the general declivity of the surrounding country, as it sinks gradually away to the shores of these rivers.

This ancient village had literally become the graveyard of the nation. Scarcely an individual could be found in the whole na-tion, who had not deposited the remains of some relative, in or near to this place. Thither the mother, with mournful and melancholy step, annually repaired to pay a tribute of respect to her departed offspring; while the weeping sisters and loud lamenting widows, joined the procession of grief; sometimes, in accordance with their own feelings, no doubt, but always in pursuance of an established custom of their nation, from time immemorial. On these occasions they carefully clear away every spear of grass or other vegetable, which they find growing near the grave, and make such repairs as may be thought necessary.

They also carry to the grave some kind of food, which they leave there for the spirit of the deceased: and before they conclude these ceremonies, they often, in a very melancholy and lamenting mood, address the dead, enquiring how they fare, and who, or whether any one performs for them the kind offices of mother, sister or wife; together with many other enquiries which a frantic imagination may happen to suggest. This being one of the most important religious duties, is scrupulously observed by all the better class of this people. (*Chronicles of the North American Savages*, No. 4.)

The whites who established themselves at this place, in violation of the laws of congress, and the provisions of the treaty of 1804, committed various aggressions upon the Indians, such as destroying their corn, killing their domestic animals, and whipping the women and children. They carried with them, as articles of traffic, whiskey and other intoxicating liquors, and by distributing them in the tribe, made drunkenness and scenes of debauchery common. Black Hawk and the other chiefs of the band, remonstrated against these encroachments, and especially in regard to the introduction of spirituous liquors among their people: and, upon one occasion, when a white man continued, openly, to sell whiskey to them, the old chief, taking with him one or two companions, went to his house, rolled out the barrel of whiskey, broke in the head, and emptied its contents upon the ground, in presence of the owner.

This was done, as he alleges, from the fear that some of the white persons would be killed by his people when in a state of intoxication. Thus things wore on until 1827. During that winter, while the Indians were making their periodical hunt, some of the whites, in the hope of expediting their removal to the west side of the Mississippi, set on fire, in one day, about forty of their lodges, a number of which were entirely consumed. When the Indians returned in the spring and demanded satisfaction for the destruction of their property, they were met by new insults and outrages.

In the summer of 1829, Black Hawk happened to meet, at Rock island, with the late Governor Coles, of whom he had heard as a great chief of Illinois, in company with "another chief" as he calls him—Judge Hall. Having failed in his appeals to the Indian agents, for redress of the grievances of his people, he determined to apply to these two chiefs, on the subject, and accordingly waited upon them for that purpose.

> He spoke of the indignity perpetrated upon himself, (his hav-
> ing been beaten with sticks by the whites,) with the feeling
> that a respectable person among us would have shown under
> such circumstances; and pointing to a black mark on his face,
> said that he wore it as a symbol of disgrace. The customs of his
> nation required, that he should avenge the wrong that he had
> received, but he chose rather to submit to it for the present than
> involve them in a war. And this was the only alternative, for if
> an Indian should kill, or even strike a white man, the aggres-
> sion would be eagerly seized upon and exaggerated; the whole
> frontier population would rush to war, and the Indians would
> be hunted from their houses like wild beasts. He spoke of the
> intrusion upon their fields, the destruction of their growing
> corn, the ploughing up of the graves of their fathers, and the
> beating of their women; and added:
> "We dare not resent any of these things. If we did, it would
> be said that the Indians were disturbing the white people, and
> troops would be sent out to destroy us. We enquired, "why do
> you not represent these things to our government?"
> "The president is a wise and a good ruler, who would protect
> you."
> "Our great father is too far off, he cannot hear our voice."
> "But you could have letters written and sent to him."
> "So we could but the white men would write letters, and say
> that we told lies. Our great father would not believe an Indian,
> in preference to his own children."
> (*History of the North American Indians,* by James Hall, Esq.)

Black Hawk in reference to this interview, says:

> Neither of them could do anything for us; but both evidently
> appeared very sorry. It would give me great pleasure at all times,
> to take these two chiefs by the hand.

Under the seventh article of the treaty made at St. Louis in 1804, it is provided that:

As long as the lands which are now ceded to the United States remain their property, the Indians, belonging to the said tribes, shall enjoy the privilege of living and hunting upon them.

It was not until the year, 1829, that any part of the lands upon Rock River, were brought into market by the United States. It follows as a matter of course, that all the white settlers upon them prior to this period, were trespassers, being there in violation of the laws of Congress, and the provisions of the treaty. Although the frontier settlements of Illinois, had not approached within fifty or sixty miles of Rock River, and the lands for a still greater distance around it, had not been offered for sale, yet in this year, government was induced to make sale of a few quarter sections, at the mouth of Rock River, including the Sac village. The reason for this uncalled for measure, is obvious—to evade the provisions of the foregoing treaty of cession, and create a pretext for the immediate removal of the Indians to the west side of the Mississippi.

In the spring of 1830, when Black Hawk and his band returned from their annual hunt, to occupy their lodges, and prepare as usual for raising their crop of vegetables, they found, that the land in and around their village, had been brought into market, and that their old friend, the trader at Rock Island had purchased a considerable part of it. Black Hawk, greatly disturbed at this new condition of things, appealed to the agent at that place, who informed him, that the lands having been sold by government to individuals, he and his party had no longer any *right* to remain upon them. Black Hawk was still unwilling to assent to a removal, and in the course of the summer, he visited Malden to consult his British father on the subject, and returned by Detroit to see the great American chief, Governor Cass, residing there. Both of these persons told him that if the Indians had not sold their lands and would remain quietly upon them, they would not be disturbed.

Black Hawk, acting upon the assumption that the land on which their village stood, never had been legally sold to the United States, returned home determined to keep possession of it. It was late in the fall when he arrived: his people had gone to their hunting grounds for the winter and he followed them. They made an unsuccessful hunt and the season passed off in gloom. Keokuk again exerted his influence to induce them to desert Black Hawk and remove to the Ioway. Such, however, was their attachment to their favourite village, that the

116

whole band returned to it in the spring of 1831. The agent at Rock island forthwith notified them that if they did not remove from the land, troops would be sent by the United States to drive them off. Black Hawk says, he had a conference, about this time, with the trader at Rock Island, who enquired of him, if some terms could not be made, upon which he and his party would agree to remove to the west side of the Mississippi.

To this he replied, that if his great father would do justice to them and make the proposition, they would remove. He was asked by the trader, "if the great chief at St. Louis would give six thousand dollars, to purchase provisions and other articles," if he would give up peaceably and remove. To this he agreed. The trader accordingly sent a message to the agent at St. Louis, that Black Hawk, and his whole band, could be removed for the sum of six thousand dollars, but the answer was, that nothing would be given, and that if they did not remove immediately, an armed force would be sent to compel them.

The squaws had now planted their corn, and it was beginning to grow, when the whites again commenced ploughing it up. Black Hawk at last determined to put a stop to these aggressions upon his people, and accordingly gave notice to those who were perpetrating them, that they must remove, forthwith, from his village. In the meantime, after the return of the Indians, which took place in April, eight of the white settlers united in a memorial to the Executive of the state of Illinois, in which they set forth that the Sac Indians of Rock River had:

> Threatened to kill them; that they had acted in a most outrageous manner; threw down their fences, turned horses into their cornfields, stole their potatoes, saying *the land was theirs and that they had not sold it,*—although said deponents had purchased the land of the United States' government: levelled deadly weapons at the citizens, and on some occasions hurt said citizens for attempting to prevent the destruction of their property, &c. &c.

The memorial concludes with the still more startling outrage, that the said Indians went "to a house, rolled out a barrel of whiskey and destroyed it." One of these eight afflicted memorialists, swore the other seven to the truth of their statements, and with an earnest prayer for immediate relief, it was placed before His Excellency, on the 19th of May.

This long catalogue of outrages, backed by other memorials, and divers rumours of border depredations, committed by "General Black Hawk" and his "British Band," called into immediate action the patriotism and official power of the governor. Under date of Bellville, May 26, 1831, he writes to the superintendent of Indian affairs, General William Clark, at St. Louis, that in order to protect the citizens of Illinois, which he considered in a state of "actual invasion," he had called out seven hundred militia to remove a band of Sac Indians, then residing at Rock River, and he pledges himself to the superintendent, that in fifteen days he will have a force in the field, sufficient to "remove them *dead* or *alive*, over to the west side of the Mississippi."

But to save all this disagreeable business, His Excellency suggests to General Clark that perhaps a request from him to these Indians, to remove to the west side of the river, would effect the object of procuring peace to the citizens of the state. The letter concludes with the magnanimous declaration that there is no disposition on the part of the people of the state of Illinois to injure these unfortunate, deluded savages, "if they will let us alone."

General Clark, under date of St. Louis, 28 May, 1831, acknowledges the receipt of the above letter, and says, that he had already made every effort in his power, to get all the Indians who had ceded their lands to remove.

On the same day, 28th May, 1831, Governor Reynolds writes to General Gaines, then at St. Louis, that he had received information that Black Hawk and his band had invaded the state of Illinois; and that he had called out seven hundred troops to meet them. General Gaines, on the 29th of May, replies to His Excellency that he had ordered six companies of United States troops from Jefferson Barracks to Rock Island, and that they would be joined by four other companies from Prairie des Chiens, making in all ten companies; a force which he deemed sufficient to repel the invasion and give security to the frontier: That if the residue of the Sacs and Foxes, or other tribes should unite with the band of Black Hawk, he would call on His Excellency for some militia, but did not then deem it necessary.

On the 30th of May, the troops, accompanied by General Gaines, left Jefferson barracks, in a steamboat, for Fort Armstrong; and upon the 7th of June, the commanding general held a council on Rock Island, at which Black Hawk and some of his braves were present. Keokuk, Wa-pel-lo and other chiefs from the west side of the Mississippi were also in attendance. When the council was opened, General Gaines rose and stated that the president was displeased with the refusal of the Sacs of Rock River, to go to the right bank of the Mississippi, that their great father wanted only that which was reasonable and right, and insisted that they should remove. Black Hawk replied, in substance, that the Sacs had never sold their lands and were determined to hold on to their village. General Gaines inquired, "who is Black Hawk? Is he a chief? By what right does he appear in council?"

No reply was made; Black Hawk arose, gathered his blanket around him, and stalked out of the council room. On the following morning he was again in his seat, and when the council was opened, he arose and said, "My father, you inquired yesterday, "who is Black Hawk? why does he sit among the chiefs?" I will tell you who I am. I am a Sac, my father was a Sac—I am a warrior and so was my father. Ask those young men, who have followed me to battle, and they will tell you who Black Hawk is—provoke our people to war, and you will learn who Black Hawk is." He then sat down, and nothing more was said on the subject. The result of this conference was, that Black Hawk refused to leave his village, and that General Gaines informed him and his party, if they were not on the West side of the Mississippi within a few days, he should be compelled to remove them by force.

The general anxious, if possible, to effect the object without bloodshed, deemed it expedient to increase his forces, that the Indians might be intimidated, and thus induced to submit; or, in case of a resort to hostile measures, that he might be fully prepared to act with efficiency. He accordingly called upon the Governor of Illinois for some militia, to co-operate with the United States' troops under his command. On the 25th of June, Governor Reynolds, and General Joseph Duncan with 1600 mounted militiamen, principally volunteers, reached Rock River. On the morning of the 26th, General Gaines with his combined forces, took possession of the Sac village without firing a gun or finding an Indian; the whole party, with their wives and children, having crossed over the Mississippi the previous night. On the following day they were found on the west bank of that stream, encamped under the protection of a white flag.

On the 30th of June, General Gaines and Governor Reynolds signed a treaty of capitulation and peace, with Black Hawk, Pa-she-pa-how, Wee-sheat, Kah-ke-ka-mah, and other chiefs and head men of the British band of Sac Indians, and their old allies of the Winnebago, Pottawatamie and Kickapoo nations. The preamble to this treaty is worthy of preservation. It is in these words.

Whereas, the British Band of Sac Indians, have in violation of the several treaties, entered into between the United States and the Sac and Fox nations, in the year 1804, 1816 and 1825, continued to remain upon and to cultivate the lands on Rock river, ceded to the United States by said treaties, after the said lands had been sold by the United States, to individual citizens of Illinois and other states: and whereas the said British Band of Sac Indians, in order to sustain their pretensions to continue upon said Rock River lands, have assumed the attitude of actual hostility towards the United States, and have had the audacity to drive citizens of the state of Illinois from their homes, destroy their corn, and invite many of their old friends of the Pottawatamies, Winnebagoes, and Kickapoos, to unite with them the said British band of Sacs, in war, to prevent their removal from said lands: and whereas many of the most disorderly of these several tribes of Indians, did actually join the said British band of Sac Indians prepared for war against the United States, and more particularly against the state of Illinois; from which purpose they confess nothing could have restrained them, but the apprehension of force far exceeding the combined strength of the said British Band of Sac Indians, with such of their aforesaid allies, as had actually joined them; but, being now convinced that such a war would tend speedily to annihilate them, they have voluntarily abandoned their hostile attitude and sued for peace. Therefore, &c.

The first article stipulates that peace is granted by the United States to the British Band of Sac Indians—the second that they are required to submit to the chiefs of the Sac and Fox nations, who reside on the west side of the Mississippi—the third that the United States guarantee to them the integrity of their lands west of that river under the treaties of 1825 and 1830—the fourth that the said British Band shall not trade with any nation but the United States—that the United States have a right to establish military posts and roads within their country—the sixth that the chiefs and head men of the Sac and Fox nations shall enforce the provisions of this treaty—and finally that permanent peace and friendship be established between the United States and the said British Band of Sac Indians, and that the latter are not to return to the east side of the Mississippi without the permission of the former.

The commanding general, under date of sixth of July, 1831, informs the war department, that:

The mounted volunteers, the regulars, two pieces of artillery, and some musquetry and riflemen, induced the Indians to abandon the village before our arrival, without firing a gun. Deserted by their allies, this disorderly band was left alone to seek security in a speedy flight to the right bank of the Mississippi, where they were found the next day, under the protection of a white flag.

Governor Reynolds in his official despatch to the same department, under date of Belleville. Ill. 7th July 1831, says:

The Indians with some exceptions, from Canada to Mexico, along the northern frontier of the United States, are more hostile to the whites, than at any other period since the last war; particularly the band of Sac Indians, usually and truly called the "British Band," became extremely unfriendly to the citizens of Illinois and others. This band had determined for some years past to remain at all hazards, on certain lands which had been purchased by the United States, and afterwards some of them sold to private individuals by the general government. They also determined to drive off the citizens from this disputed territory. In order to effect this object, they committed various outrages on the persons and property of the citizens of this state. That this band might the more effectually resist all force that would be employed against them, they treated with many other tribes to combine together for the purpose of aiding this British Band to continue in possession of the country in question.

General William Clark, the Indian agent at St. Louis, in his official communication to the department, says:

The disaffected Sacs were depending for an increase to their number from the discontented parts of the Kickapoos, Pottawatamies and Winnebagoes, (and that they exhibited a daring opposition, &c. &c.)

From the tone and pomposity of these documents, commencing with Governor Reynold's annunciation to General Clark, that Illinois was in a state of "actual invasion," and ending with the letters to the war department, just cited, it might appear, to one not familiar with

121

the facts in the case, that a powerful confederacy of warlike Indians, after years of secret preparation, had made a sudden and bold descent upon the state of Illinois, and were about to carry war and desolation throughout the frontiers—to make the heavens lurid with the conflagration of dwelling houses, and the air resonant with the wails of women and children sinking beneath the murderous tomahawk: and, that this banded horde of northern savages, had been successfully met, captured or dispersed, by the patriotism, valour and overwhelming power of the combined army of the United States and the militia of Illinois! And yet, will it be credited by posterity, that this "actual invasion" of the state, fierce and appalling as it has been represented, consisted simply in this: a part of the Sac tribe of Indians, residing within the boundaries of Illinois, at their village on Rock River, where they were born and had lived all their lives, refused to give up their cornfields to some white men, who had purchased the same, under a sale made by the government of the United States for the purpose of a technical evasion of one of its own treaties.

In short, thus far, it was little more than a neighbourhood quarrel between the squaws of the "British Band" of Indians, and a few white settlers,—most of whom were there in violation of the laws of the country—about the occupancy of some cornfields, which, from time immemorial, had been annually cultivated by the Indian women. Black Hawk became excited by these outrages, as he deemed them, upon the rights of his people; but instead of killing every white man in his vicinity, which he could have done in one night, he simply commanded them to leave his village: and threatened in case they did not, to remove them by force. Such is the substance of the "actual invasion" of the state of Illinois, by the British Band of Sac Indians.

It is alleged, however, by the defenders of this memorable campaign, that this band of Sacs had, in violation of the treaties of 1804, 1816 and 1825, continued to remain upon and cultivate the land on Rock river, ceded to the United States, after it had been sold by the United States to individual citizens of Illinois and other states—that they had refused positively to remove to the west side of the Mississippi—that they had endeavoured to persuade some of the neighbouring tribes to unite with them in defending this land against the rightful occupancy of the white purchasers—that they had "threatened to kill" them—"thrown down their fences"—on some occasions "hurt" said settlers—"stole their potatoes" saying they had not sold these lands—otherwise "acted in a most outrageous manner," and finally, in the words of the capitulation on the 30th June, 1831, "assumed the attitude of actual hostility towards the United States, and had the audacity to drive citizens of the state of Illinois, from their homes."

Admitting these allegations to be true, what may be said in behalf of the party against which they are made? It may be replied, that under the treaty of 1804, the Indians had an undoubted right to "live and hunt" upon the land ceded by that treaty, so long as it remained the property of the United States: that as early as 1823-4 the whites had intruded upon the land on Rock River around the principal village of the Sacs and Foxes—the United States neglecting to have these intruders removed, as by the treaty they were solemnly bound to do: that these whites frequently beat the Indian men, women, and children with sticks, destroyed their cornfields, distributed whiskey among them, cheated them out of their furs and peltries and on one occasion, when the Indians were absent on a hunting excursion, set fire to some thirty or forty of their lodges, by which many of them were totally destroyed.

These outrages were perpetrated before a single acre of the land upon Rock River, had been sold by the United States, and when in fact, the regular frontier settlements of Illinois, had not approached within fifty miles of the Sac village. Consequently they were committed in express violation of the most solemn treaties and of the laws of the United States, for the protection of the Indians. In 1829, clearly with a view, on the part of those who brought about the measure, of evading the force of that article of the treaty of 1804, which permitted the Indians to live and hunt upon these lands, so long as they remained the property of the United States, a few quarter sections were sold, on Rock River, including the Sac village.

New insults and outrages were now offered to the Indians, and they were again ordered to remove, not from the quarter sections which had actually been sold, but to the west side of the Mississippi. Against this, they remonstrated and finally refused, positively, to be driven away. The results of this refusal have already been shown in the narration which has been made of the events following upon the "actual invasion" of the state of Illinois, in the spring of 1831. But it has been said that these Indians endeavoured to form an alliance with some of the neighbouring tribes to defend their lands. There is no doubt that Black Hawk laboured to persuade Keokuk and the Sac Indians residing with him, to return to the east side of the Mississippi and assist in defending their village.

His effort to unite with him, in alliance against the United States, the Winnebagoes, Pottawatamies and Kickapoos, was probably for the same object, though the case is not so clearly made out. Mr. Schoolcraft in his "Narrative" speaks of a war message having been transmitted to the Torch lake Indians, by Black Hawk, or his counsellors, in 1830, and repeated in the two succeeding years; and adds that similar communications were made to other tribes. The message, continues Mr. Schoolcraft, was very equivocal. It invited these tribes to aid the Sacs in fighting their enemies. Whatever may have been the object, no success attended the effort. Other motives than that of retaining possession of these lands, may have prompted Black Hawk to seek this alliance. Being an ambitious, restless man, he may have thought it expedient to do something to keep himself in power with his people.

A military campaign is occasionally a fortunate circumstance for a politician, whether his skin be red or white. Gunpowder-popularity is of equal importance to the chiefs of the Sacs and the chiefs of the Illini. An "actual invasion" of a state—which, in these modern times, is supposed to consist in "levelling deadly weapons" at the inhabitants thereof, and "stealing their potatoes," is quite a wind-fall to political aspirants.

That the British Band of Sac Indians cherished the feeling of active hostility towards the whites, that has been attributed to them, may well be questioned. That they were provoked to a feeble assertion of their rights by the injustice of our government and the lawless conduct of the white settlers among them, is unquestionably true. But it should be recollected, that from the period of their treaty with the United States, in 1816, to their capitulation in 1831, they had not killed one of our people. For a number of years prior to 1831, the Americans had constantly passed through their country, unarmed, carrying with them large amounts of money and of goods, for the trade at the lead mines: and yet not one of these travellers, sleeping in the woods and the Indian lodges, had been molested in person or property.

For several years, the whites residing at and around the Sac village on Rock River were trespassing upon these Indians, for the purpose of driving them to the west side of the Mississippi, but still the tomahawk was not raised for retaliation. If Black Hawk and his party, had really intended to resort to arms, who that understands the Indian character, can doubt for a moment, that they would have struck a decisive blow, and murdered every white settler upon Rock River, before General Gaines ascended the Mississippi? After our army reached Fort Armstrong and General Gaines had been informed by Black Hawk that he would not remove, he gave orders to his braves, that if the American war chief came to the village to force them away, not a gun should be fired, nor any resistance offered; but that they must remain quietly in their lodges and let the war chief kill them if he chose.

Under these circumstances, it is as difficult to believe that Black Hawk and his band seriously intended to make war upon the whites at that time, as it is to admit that the United States had a right to force the Indians to remove to the west side of the Mississippi, because a few quarter sections of the land at the mouth of Rock River, had been prematurely sold; while millions of acres around, were still the property of the United States, and as such, under the treaty of 1804, the Indians were expressly permitted to live and hunt upon them.

In the course of this narrative, frequent mention has been made of the leading chief of the Sac nation, who is highly distinguished by his influence, pacific character and fine talents. The relation he sustains to Black Hawk and his band, connects him directly with our narrative. On this account, as well as to gratify the interest which is felt in his history, the succeeding chapter will be occupied with a brief sketch of the life and adventures of Keokuk, the Watchful Fox.

KEOKUK, THE WATCHFUL FOX

CHAPTER 5

Keokuk's Birth

It is no easy task to present in a satisfactory manner, a biographical sketch of an Indian. However eventful his life may have been, it is only a few of the more prominent of his deeds which become known to the world; while the minor incidents, those small matters, which make up the sum of human character, pass unobserved by his companions, or if noticed, are soon forgotten. The subject of the present chapter, is yet in the meridian of life, high in power, and in the enjoyment of a distinguished reputation. Yet the materials for estimating his character, and for tracing his progress, step by step, from the obscurity of a private station, to the most honourable post in the nation over which he now presides, are neither full nor satisfactory. Barely enough is known of him, throughout the United States, to create the desire to know more; and it is to be regretted that the means of gratifying this laudable curiosity, are not more abundant.

Keokuk is a native of the Sac nation of Indians, and was born near or upon Rock river in the north western part of what now constitutes the state of Illinois, about the year 1780. He is not a hereditary chief, and consequently has risen to his present elevation by the force of talent and of enterprise. He began to manifest these qualities at a very early period of his life. While but a youth he performed an act, which placed him, as it were by *brevet*, in the ranks of manhood. In the first battle in which he engaged, he encountered and killed a Sioux warrior, with his spear, while on horseback; and as the Sioux are distinguished for their horsemanship, this was looked upon as so great an achievement, that a public feast was made in commemoration of it, by his tribe; and the youthful Keokuk, was forthwith admitted to all the rights and privileges of a brave. It was further allowed, that ever afterwards, on all public occasions, he might appear on horseback, even if the rest of the chiefs and braves were not mounted.

During the late war between the United States and Great Britain, and before Keokuk was entitled to take his seat in the councils of his nation, an expedition was sent by our government, to destroy the Indian village at Peoria, on the Illinois River. A rumour reached the Sac village, in which he resided, that this expedition was also to attack the Sacs, and the whole tribe was thrown into consternation. The Indians were panic stricken, and the council hastily determined to abandon their village. Keokuk happened to be standing near the council-lodge when this decision was made. It was no sooner announced than he boldly advanced to the door and requested admission. It was granted. He asked leave to speak, and permission was given him. He commenced by saying he had heard with deep regret, the decision of the council—that he himself was wholly opposed to flight, before an enemy still distant, and whose strength was entirely unknown. He called the attention of the council to the importance of meeting the enemy in their approach—of harassing their progress—cutting them off in detail—of driving them back, or of nobly dying in defence of their country and their homes.

He boldly exclaimed:

Make me your leader, let our young men follow me, and the pale-faces shall be driven back to their towns. Let the old men and the women, and all who are afraid to meet the white man, stay here, but let your braves go to battle.

Such intrepid conduct, could not fail to produce its effect upon a race so excitable as the Indians. The warriors with one voice, declared they were ready to follow Keokuk; and he was at once chosen to lead them against the enemy. It turned out, however, that the alarm was false, but the eloquence of Keokuk in the council, and his energy in preparing for the expedition, placed him at once in the first rank of the braves.

His military reputation, was, on another occasion, much increased, by the skill and promptness with which he met a sudden emergency on the battlefield. With a party of his braves, Keokuk was hunting in the country which lies between the residence of the Sacs and that of the Sioux, betwixt whom, for many years, a deadly hatred had existed. Very unexpectedly, a party of the latter well mounted, came upon them. The Sacs were also on horseback, but their enemies being superior horsemen and fully equipped for war, had a decided advantage. There was no covert from behind which the Sacs could fight, and flight was impossible. Keokuk's mode of defence was as novel as ingenious. He instantly formed his men into a compact circle, ordered them to dismount, and take shelter behind their horses, by which movement they were protected from the missiles of the Sioux, and at the same time placed under circumstances in which they could avail themselves of their superiority as marksmen.

The Sioux, raising the war-whoop, charged upon their entrenched foe with great fury, but were received with a fire so destructive that they were compelled to fall back. The attack was repeated but with the same result. The hordes could not be forced upon those whose guns were pouring forth volleys of fire and smoke, and after several unsuccessful attempts to break the line, the Sioux retreated with considerable loss.

At a subsequent period, during a cessation of hostilities between these tribes, the Sacs had gone to the prairies to hunt buffalo, leaving their village but slightly protected by braves. During the hunt Keokuk and his band, unexpectedly approached an encampment of a large number of Sioux, painted for war, and evidently on their way to attack his village. His own braves were widely scattered over the extensive plains, and could not be speedily gathered together. Possessing the spirit of a fearless and generous mind, he instantly resolved upon the bold expedient of throwing himself between the impending danger and his people. Unattended, he deliberately rode into the camp of his enemy. In the midst of their lodges rose the war-pole, and around it the Sioux were dancing, and partaking of those fierce excitements, by means of which the Indians usually prepare themselves for battle.

It happened that revenge upon the Sacs constituted the burden of their songs, at the moment of Keokuk's approach. He dashed into the midst of them and boldly demanded to see their chief.

I have come to let you know that there are traitors in your camp: they have told me that you are preparing to attack my village: I know they told me lies, for you could not, after smoking the pipe of peace, be so base as to murder my women and children in my absence. None but cowards would be guilty of such conduct.

When the first feeling of amazement began to subside, the Sioux crowded around him in a manner evincing a determination to seize his person, and they had already laid hold of his legs, when he added, in a loud voice, "I supposed they told me lies, but if what I have heard is true, then the Sacs are ready for you." With a sudden effort, he dashed aside those who had seized him, plunged his spurs into his gallant horse, and rode off at full speed. Several guns were discharged at him, but fortunately without effect: a number of the Sioux warriors instantly sprung upon their horses and pursued him, but in vain. Keokuk, on horseback, was in his element; he made the woods resound with the war-whoop, and brandishing his tomahawk in defiance of his foes, soon left them far behind, and joined his little party of braves. His pursuers, fearful of some stratagem, gave up the pursuit, after having followed him for some distance, and retired to their camp. Keokuk took immediate steps to call in his braves and speedily returned to protect his village. His enemies, however, finding themselves discovered, abandoned the contemplated attack and retraced their steps to their own country.

The eloquence of Keokuk and his sagacity in the civil affairs of his nation, are, like his military talents, of a high order. One or two cases in which these have been exhibited, are worthy of being recorded. A few years since, some of his warriors fell in with a party of unarmed Menominies, at Prairie des Chiens, in sight of Fort Crawford, and murdered the whole of them. Justly incensed at this outrage, the Menominies prepared to take up arms against the Sacs, and prevailed upon the Winnebagoes to join them. For the purpose of allaying the rising storm, the United States' agent, at Prairie des Chiens, General Street, invited the several parties to a council at that place for the purpose of adjusting the difficulty, without a resort to arms. They accordingly, out of respect to the agent, assembled at Fort Crawford, but the Menominies refused, sternly, to hold any conference with the Sacs on the subject.

Keokuk told the agent not to be discouraged, for he would adjust the difficulty with them, before they separated, in despite of their prejudices and their positive refusal to treat: He only asked an opportunity of meeting them face to face in the council-lodge. The tribes were brought together, but the Menominies persevered in their determination to hold no conference with the Sacs. The negotiation proceeded, and a friendly feeling was re-established between the Winnebagoes and the Sacs. Keokuk then rose and with much deliberation, began his address to the Menominies. At first they averted their faces or listened with looks of defiance. He had commenced his speech without smok-

KEOKUK LEAVING THE SIOUX ENCAMPMENT

ing the pipe or shaking hands, which was a breach of etiquette; and, above all, he was the chief of a tribe that had inflicted upon them an injury, for which blood alone could atone. Under these discouraging circumstances, Keokuk proceeded, in his forcible, persuasive and impressive manner. Such was the touching character of his appeal, such the power of his eloquence, that the features of his enemies gradually relaxed; they listened; they assented; and when he concluded by remarking, proudly, but in a conciliating tone, "I came here to say that I am sorry for the imprudence of my young men; I came to make peace; I now offer you the hand of Keokuk; who will refuse it?" they rose one by one and accepted the proffered grasp.

In the late contest between the United States and Black Hawk's band, Keokuk and a majority of the Sacs and Foxes, took no part. Black Hawk made several efforts to induce them to unite against the whites, which they were strongly inclined to do, not only from their love of war and of plunder but on account of the injustice with which very many of them believed they had been treated by the people of the United States. It required all of Keokuk's influence and moderation to prevent the whole nation from enlisting under the Black Hawk banner. He requested the agent of the American Government to send to his village, on the west side of the Mississippi, a white man who understood the Sac language, and who might bear witness to his, Keokuk's sincerity and faithfulness to the whites. Such a person was sent. The excitement raised by Black Hawk and the war in which he was engaged, continued to increase among Keokuk's people.

He stood on a mine, liable to be exploded by a single spark. He was in peril of being slain as the friend of the whites. He remained calm and unawed, ruling his turbulent little state with mildness and firmness, but at the constant risk of his life. One day, a new emissary arrived from Black Hawk's party. Whiskey was introduced into the camp, and Keokuk saw that the crisis was at hand. He warned the white man who was his guest, of the impending danger, and advised him to conceal himself. A scene of tumult ensued. The emissary spoke of blood that had been shed—of their relations being driven from their hunting grounds—of recent insults—of injuries long inflicted by the whites—hinted at the ready vengeance that might be taken on an exposed frontier—of defenceless cabins—and of rich booty. The desired effect was produced.

The braves began to dance around the war pole, to paint and to give other evidences of a warlike character. Keokuk watched the rising storm and appeared to mingle in it. He drank and listened and apparently assented to all that was said. At length his warriors called out to be led to battle, and he was asked to lead them. He arose and spoke with that power which had never failed him. He sympathized in their wrongs—their thirst for vengeance—he won their confidence by giving utterance to the passions by which they were moved, and echoing back their own thoughts with a master spirit. He then considered the proposition to go to war, alluded to the power of the whites—the hopelessness of the contest: He told them he was their chief—that it was his duty to rule them as a father at home: to lead them to war if they determined to go.

But in the proposed war, there was no middle course: The power of the United States was such, that unless they conquered that great nation, they must perish; that he would lead them instantly against the whites on one condition, and that was, that they should first put all their women and children to death, and then resolve, that having crossed the Mississippi, they would never return, but perish among the graves of their fathers rather than yield them to the white-men. This proposal, desperate as it was, presented the true issue: it calmed the disturbed passions of his people, the turmoil subsided, order was restored, and the authority of Keokuk, became for the time being firmly re-established. (James Hall, Esq.)

Black Hawk and his band have always been opposed to Keokuk, and since the late war, which proved so disastrous to them, and into which they were plunged, in opposition to his counsel, they have looked upon him with increased aversion.

They have made repeated efforts to destroy his influence with the remainder of the tribe, and owing to the monotony of his pacific rule, were, on one occasion, nearly successful. A spirit of discontent pervaded his people—they complained of the extent of the power which he wielded—they needed excitement, and as his measures were all of a peaceful character, they sought it in a change of rulers. The matter was at length openly and formally discussed. The voice of the nation was taken, Keokuk was removed from his post of headman and a young chief placed in his stead. He made not the smallest opposition to this measure of his people, but calmly awaited the result. When his young successor was chosen, Keokuk was the first to salute him with the title of Father. But the matter did not rest here.

With great courtesy, he begged to accompany the new chief to the agent of the United States, then at Rock island; and with profound respect, introduced him as his chief and his father—urged the agent to receive him as such, and solicited, as a personal favour, that the same regard that had ever been paid to him, by the whites, might be transferred to his worthy successor. The sequel may be readily inferred. The nation could not remain blind to the error they had committed. Keokuk as a private individual was still the first man among his people. His ready and noble acquiescence in their wishes, won both their sympathy and admiration. He rose rapidly but silently to his former elevated station, while the young chief sunk as rapidly to his former obscurity.

Some time in 1832, five of the friendly Sacs belonging to Keokuk's party, murdered a man by the name of Martin, in Warren County, Illinois. One of these, proved to be a nephew of Keokuk, but by the orders of his uncle, he was seized and delivered over to the civil authority of that state to be tried for the murder. The other four made their escape. Some time afterwards, Keokuk was called upon to deliver up the other four Sacs, who had been concerned in the outrage, that they also might be brought to justice. He replied that they were beyond his reach, but that he would call a council of his headmen and take measures to give satisfaction to the whites. The council was held, and Keokuk stated the demand of their Great Father, the president; and that if satisfaction were not made to him, he feared an army would be sent into their country, and that many troubles would overtake them.

Immediately four young warriors arose and offered to be surrendered up to the whites, and suffer death in place of the real offenders, to prevent their nation from incurring the displeasure of the president. Keokuk, supposing that this would satisfy the demands of justice, delivered them up as the murderers and they were imprisoned. Upon their trial, Keokuk was present, as a witness. In giving his testimony, he stated with honest simplicity, that the young men then arraigned in court, for the murder of Martin, were not the guilty ones, but they had agreed to die in place of the real murderers who could not be found. The prisoners were, as a matter of course, set at liberty.

Some months after the close of the "Black Hawk war," Keokuk was informed that reports were in circulation, in the state of Illinois, that the Indians were dissatisfied and preparing for fresh hostilities. He dictated a letter to the governor upon the subject, which was forwarded to him. It is in these words.

Raccoon Fork of Des Moines River, Nov. 30, 1832.
To the Great Chief of Illinois.
My Father:

I have been told by a trader, that several of your village criers (editors) have been circulating bad news, informing the whites that the Indians are preparing for war, and that we are dissatisfied. My Father, you were present when the tomahawk was buried, and assisted me to place it so deep, that it will never again be raised against your white children of Illinois.

My Father, very few of that misguided band that entered Rock River last summer, remain. You have humbled them by war, and have made them friendly by your generous conduct to them after they were defeated.

Myself and the greater part of the Sacs and Foxes, have firmly held you by the hand: We followed your advice and did as you told us. My Father, take pity on those of my nation that you forgave, and never mention the disasters of last summer. I wish them to be forgotten.

I do not permit the criers of our village or camps to proclaim any bad news against the whites, not even the truth. Last fall an old man, a Fox, was hunting on an island, a short distance below Rock River for turkeys to carry to Fort Armstrong: he was killed by a white man. My Father, we passed it over: we have only spoken of it in whispers; our agent has not heard of it. We wish to live in friendship with the whites; if a white man comes to our camp or village, we give him a share of what we have to eat, a lodging if he wants it, and put him on the trail if he has lost it.

My Father, advise the criers of your villages to tell the truth respecting us, and assist in strengthening the chain of friendship, that your children may treat us friendly when they meet us: and be assured that we are friends, and have feelings as well as they have.

My Father, this is all I have to say at present.
Keokuk, Chief of the Sac nation.

In the autumn of the year 1837, Keokuk and a party of his warriors made a visit to Washington city. Black Hawk was of the party, having been taken along, it is supposed by the politic Keokuk, lest in his absence, the restless spirit of the old man should create some new difficulties at home. We are indebted to a gentleman, (Judge Hall), who happened to be at the capital at the time of this visit, for the following sketch of a council, held under the direction of the Secretary at War, Mr. Poinsett, for the laudable purpose of reconciling the long cherished feeling of hostility between the Sacs and Foxes, and the Sioux,—a deputation of chiefs from this latter nation being also at the seat of government. The council was held in a church. The Indians were seated on a platform erected for the purpose, the spectators occupying the pews. The secretary, representing the president, was seated on the centre of the platform, facing the audience—the Sioux on his right hand and the Sauks and Foxes on his left, forming a semi-circle.

These hostile tribes, presented in their appearance a remarkable contrast. The Sioux tricked out in blue coats, epaulettes, fur hats and various articles of finery, which had been presented to them, and which were now incongruously worn in conjunction with portions of their own proper costume; while the Saukies and Foxes, with a commendable pride and good taste, wore their national dress, without any admixture, and were studiously painted according to their own notions of propriety. But the most striking object was Keokuk, who sat at the head of his delegation, on the extreme left, facing his mortal enemies the Sioux, who occupied the opposite side of the stage; having the audience upon his left side, and his own people on his right, and beyond them the Secretary at War.

He sat grasping in his right hand the war banner, the symbol of his station as ruling chief. His person was erect and his eye fixed calmly but steadily upon the enemies of his people. On the floor, and leaning upon the knee of the chief, sat his son, a boy of nine or ten years old, whose fragile figure and innocent countenance, afforded a beautiful contrast with the athletic and warlike form and the intellectual though weather-beaten features of his father. The effect was in the highest degree picturesque and imposing. The council was opened by smoking the pipe, which was passed from mouth to mouth.

The secretary then briefly addressed both parties, in a conciliating strain, urging them, in the name of their great father,

135

the president, to abandon those sanguinary wars, by means of which their race was becoming extinct, and to cultivate the arts, the thrift and industry of the white men. The Sioux spoke next. The orator, on rising first stepped forward, and shook hands with the secretary, and then delivered his harangue in his own tongue, stopping at the end of each sentence, until it was rendered into English by the interpreter, who stood by his side, and into the Saukie language by the interpreter of that tribe. Another and another followed, all speaking vehemently and with much acrimony.

The burthen of their harangue was, the folly of addressing pacific language to the Sauks and Foxes, who were faithless and in whom no confidence could be placed. 'My father,' said one of them, 'you cannot make these people hear any good words unless you bore their ears with sticks.' 'We have often made peace with them,' said another speaker, an old man, who endeavoured to be witty, 'but they would never observe any treaty. I would as soon think of making a treaty with that child,' pointing to Keokuk's little boy, 'as with a Saukie or Musquakee.'

The Sioux were evidently gratified and excited by the sarcasms of their orators, while their opponents sat motionless, their dark eyes flashing, but their features as composed and stolid, as if they did not understand that disparaging language that was used. We remarked a decided want of gracefulness in all these speakers. Each of them having shaken hands with the secretary, who sat facing the audience, stood immediately before and near to him, with the interpreter at his elbow, both having their backs to the spectators; and in this awkward position, speaking low and rapidly—but little of what they said could be heard except by the persons near them.

Not so Keokuk. When it came to his turn to speak, he rose deliberately, advanced to the secretary, and having saluted him, returned to his place, which being at the foot of the stage, and on one side of it, his face was not concealed from any of the several parties present. His interpreter stood beside him. The whole arrangement was judicious, and though apparently unstudied, shewed the tact of an orator. He stood erect, in an easy, but martial posture, with his robe thrown over his left shoulder and arm, leaving the right arm bare, to be used in action. His voice was firm, his enunciation remarkably clear, distinct, and rapid. Those who have had the gratification of hearing a distinguished senator from South Carolina, now in Congress, whose rapidity of utterance, concentration of thought and conciseness of language are alike peculiar to himself, may form some idea of the style of Keokuk, the latter adding, however, an attention to the graces of attitude and action, to which the former makes no pretension.

He spoke with dignity but great animation, and some of his retorts were excellent. 'They tell you,' said he, 'that our ears must be bored with sticks, but, my father, you could not penetrate their thick skulls in that way—it would require hot iron.'

'They say they would as soon make peace with a child, as with us,—they know better, for when they made war upon us they found us men.'

'They tell you that peace has often been made, and that we have broken it. How happens it then that so many of their braves have been slain in our country? I will tell you—they invaded us; we never invaded them: none of my braves have been killed in their land. We have their scalps and can tell where we took them.

As we have given the palm to Keokuk, at this meeting, we must in justice to the Sioux, mention an eloquent reply, made by one of the same party, on a different day. The Secretary at War, met the Sioux delegation in council to treat for the purchase of some of their territory. A certain sum of money being offered them for the land, they demanded a greater price. They were then told that the Americans were a great people, who would not traffic with them like a trader—that the president had satisfied himself as to the value of the territory, and offered them the full price.

Big Thunder, a son of the Little Crow, replied that the Sioux were a great nation, and could not, like a trader, ask a price and then take less: and, then to illustrate the equality of dignity, between the high contracting parties, he used a figure, which struck us as eminently beautiful—'the children of our white parent are very many, they possess all the country from the rising of the sun to noon-day:—the Sioux are very many, the land is all theirs from the noon-day to the setting sun.'

After leaving Washington City, Keokuk, attended by his wife and son, four chiefs of the united Sac and Fox tribes, and several warriors among whom were Black Hawk and his son, proceeded as far north as Boston, and attracted in all the cities through which they passed great attention. They were met in Boston, with distinguished honours, being received by governor Everett on behalf of the state, and the mayor, on behalf of the city.

The ceremony of receiving the Indians occurred on the 30th of October, and no public spectacle in the history of Boston, ever assembled so great a number of its citizens. Between the hours of ten and twelve, the chiefs held a levee in Faneuil Hall, for the visits of the ladies, exclusively, an immense concourse of whom, thronged the old "cradle of liberty" to look upon the stranger guests. At 2 o'clock, p.m. the chiefs were escorted by the lancers to the State House, which was filled with ladies, the members of the legislature, the civil authorities, &c. Governor Everett, first addressed the audience, by giving them a brief account of the different tribes represented by the Indian chiefs then present. Then turning to the Indians, he said,

Chiefs and warriors of the united Sac and Fox tribes, you are welcome to our hall of council. You have come a far way from your homes in the west to visit your white brethren. We are glad to take you by the hand. We have heard before of the Sacs and Foxes—our travellers have told us the names of their great men and chiefs. We are glad to see them with our own eyes.

We are called the Massachusetts. It is the name of the red men who once lived here. In former times the red man's *wigwam*, stood on these fields, and his council fires were kindled on this spot.

When our fathers came over the great waters, they were a small band. The red man stood on the rock by the sea side, and looked at them. He might have pushed them into the water and drowned them; but he took hold of their hands and said, welcome, white man. Our fathers were hungry, and the red man gave them corn and venison. Our fathers were cold, and the red man spread his blanket over them and made them warm.

We are now grown great and powerful, but we remember the kindness of the red man to our fathers.

Brothers, our faces are pale and yours are red, but our hearts are alike. The Great Spirit has made his children of different complexions, but he loves them all.

Brothers, you dwell between the Mississippi and the Missouri—they are mighty streams. They have great arms—one stretches out to the east and the other away west to the Rocky Mountains. But they make one river and they run together into the sea.

Brothers, we dwell in the east and you in the far west, but we are one family, of many branches but one head.

Brothers, as you passed through the hall below, you stopped to look at the great image of our father Washington. It is a cold stone and cannot speak to you. But our great father Washington loved his red children, and bade us love them also. He is dead but his words have made a great print in our hearts, like the step of a strong buffalo on the clay in the prairies.

My brother, (addressing Keokuk) I perceive by your side your young child sitting in the council hall with you. May the Great Spirit preserve the life of your son. May he grow up by your side like the tender sapling by the side of the mighty oak. May you long flourish both together, and when the mighty oak is fallen in the forest, may the young tree take its place, and spread out its branches over the tribe.

Brothers, I make you a short talk, and bid you welcome once more to our council hall.

Keokuk rose first in reply, and shaking hands with the governor and others near to him, spoke with fine emphasis and much earnest and graceful gesticulation, holding his staff, which he frequently shifted from hand to hand.

Keokuk and his chiefs are very much gratified that they have had the pleasure of shaking hands with the head man or governor of this great state, and also with all the men that surround him.

You well say, brother, that the Great Spirit has made both of us, though your colour is white and mine is red; but he made your heart and mine the same. The only difference I find is, he made you speak one language, and I another. He made the same sky above our heads for both. He gave us hands to take each other by, and eyes to see each other. I wish to take all present by the hand,—to shake hands with all my white brethren.

I am very happy to say, before I die, that I have been in the great house where my fathers and your fathers used to speak together as we do now. And I hope the Great Spirit is pleased with this sight; and will long continue to keep friendship between the white and red men. I hope that now, in this presence, he sees us; and hears our hearts proffer friendship to each other; and that he will aid us in what we are now engaged in.

My remarks are short and this is what I say to you. I take my friends all by the hand, and wish the Great Spirit to give them all a blessing.

Several other chiefs spoke, and after them Black Hawk made a short address. To these several speeches the governor replied collectively. Presents were then distributed among them by the governor. Keokuk received a splendid sword and brace of pistols; his son, Musanwont, a handsome little rifle: The head chiefs received long swords and the others short ones. Black Hawk was also presented with a brace of pistols and a sword. When this ceremony had ended, the Indians repaired to the common in front of the capitol, and there, in the presence of some thirty thousand spectators, exhibited themselves in a war dance, for about half an hour; and from thence returned to their lodging.

Throughout the whole of his visit in Boston, Keokuk preserved his grave and dignified manners, winning the respect and admiration of all who had an opportunity of coming in contact with him. Upon his return to the west, he spent a few hours in Cincinnati, and was visited by a great number of persons. We had the pleasure of taking him by the hand, and of making some inquiries in regard to his character, of those who were personally acquainted with him.

In person, Keokuk, is stout, graceful and commanding, with fine features and an intelligent countenance. His broad expanded chest and muscular limbs, denote activity and physical power; and he is known to excel in dancing, horsemanship, and all athletic exercises. He has acquired considerable property, and lives in princely style. He is fond of travelling, and makes frequent visits of state to the Osages, the Ottaways, the Omahas and the Winnebagoes. On these occasions he is uniformly mounted on a fine horse, clad in a showy robe wrought by his six wives, equipped with his rifle, pipe, tomahawk and war-club. He is usually attended in these excursions by forty or fifty of his young men, well mounted and handsomely dressed.

A man precedes the party to announce his approach to the tribe he is about to honor with a visit; and such is his popularity, that his reception is generally in a style corresponding with the state in which he moves. These visits are most frequently made in autumn, and are enlivened by hunting, feasting, dancing, horse-racing and various athletic games, in all of which Keokuk takes an active part. He moves, it is supposed, in more savage magnificence, than any other Indian chief upon the continent.

In point of intellect, integrity of character, and the capacity for governing others, he is supposed to have no superior among the Indians: Bold, courageous, and skilful in war—mild, firm and politic in peace: He has great enterprise and active impulses, with a freshness and enthusiasm of feeling, which might readily lead him astray, but for his quick perception of human character, his uncommon prudence and his calm, sound judgment. At an early period of his life he became the chief warrior of his tribe, and by his superior talents, eloquence, and intelligence, really directed the civil affairs of his nation for many years, while they were nominally conducted in the name of the hereditary peace chief. Such is Keokuk, the Watchful Fox, who prides himself upon being the friend of the white man.

CHAPTER 6

Black Hawk Recrosses the Mississippi

Black Hawk and his band were not long upon the west side of the Mississippi, before new difficulties arose, calculated to disturb the harmony which it was hoped the treaty of the 30th of June, had established between them and the United States. The period of their removal to the west side of the Mississippi, was too late in the season to enable them to plant corn and beans a second time; and before autumn was over they were without provisions. Some of them, one night, recrossed the river to *steal roasting-ears from their own fields,*—to quote the language of Black Hawk,—and were shot at by the whites, who made loud complaints of this depredation. They, in turn, were highly exasperated at having been fired upon for attempting to carry off the corn which they had raised, and which they insisted, belonged to them.

Shortly after this, a party of Foxes, belonging, it is believed, to Black Hawk's band, went up the Mississippi, to Prairie des Chiens, to avenge the murder of some of their tribe, which had been committed in the summer of 1830, by a party of the Menominies and Sioux. The Foxes attacked the camp of the Menominies and killed twenty-eight of them. The authorities at Prairie des Chiens, made a demand of the murderers, that they might be tried and punished under the laws of the United States, according to the treaty of 1825. Black Hawk, with other chiefs, took the ground that the United States had no right to make this demand, and refused to give them up. Here then was another source of difficulty.

Neapope, a chief of the British band, and second in command to Black Hawk, prior to the removal of the Indians to the west side of the Mississippi, had started on a visit to Malden, to consult their British Father in regard to the right to retain their lands on Rock River. He returned late in the fall, bringing word that in his opinion, the Americans could not take their lands, unless by purchase; and this purchase, it was contended by Black Hawk had never been made. Neapope on his way from Malden, called to see the Prophet, who assured him that early the ensuing spring, not only the British, but the Ottawas, Chippewas, Pottawatomies and Winnebagoes, would assist them to regain their village and the lands around it.

Black Hawk believed, or affected to believe, this information, and began to make preparations to increase the number of his braves by recruiting from different villages. He sent a messenger to Keokuk, and to the Fox tribe, to inform them of the good news he had heard, and to ask their co-operation. Keokuk had too much sagacity to be imposed upon by tales of either British or Indian assistance, and sent word to Black Hawk that he was deceived and had better remain quiet. With a view of preventing further difficulty, he is said to have made application to the agent at St. Louis, that the chiefs of the Sacs and Foxes might be permitted to visit Washington City, to see the president, and if possible make a final adjustment of the matter in dispute. Black Hawk alleges he was anxious to make this visit to his Great Father, and had determined, to submit peaceably to his counsel, whatever it might be.

But the arrangement for the visit, from some cause, was not perfected, and Black Hawk proceeded with his own plans. He established his head quarters at the point where Fort Madison formerly stood, on the west side of the Mississippi, and made another unsuccessful effort to draw into his support some of the braves under Keokuk. Having assembled his own party he began to ascend the Mississippi—the women and children in canoes with their provisions, camp equipage and property—his warriors armed and mounted on their horses. Below Rock island, they were met by the Prophet, who informed them that there was a great war chief then at Fort Armstrong, with a large body of soldiers. The Prophet stated that the agent and trader at Rock island, had attempted to dissuade him from joining Black Hawk, but he had refused to take their advice, because so long as they remained at peace, the Americans dare not molest them.

Having reached the mouth of Rock River, in the early part of April 1832, the whole party rashly and in violation of the treaty of the previous year, crossed to the east side of the Mississippi, for the avowed purpose of ascending Rock River, to the territory of their friends, the Winnebagoes, and raising a crop of corn and beans with them. General Atkinson with a body of troops was then at Fort Armstrong, having been ordered by government to that point, for the purpose of preventing a war between the Menomenies and the Foxes, and demanding the surrender of those Indians who had committed the murders at Fort Crawford. After Black Hawk and his party had proceeded some distance up Rock River, he was overtaken by an express from General Atkinson, with an order for him to return and recross the Mississippi, which he refused to obey, on the ground that the general had no right to make such an order; the Indians being at peace and on their way to the prophet's village, at his request, to make corn.

Before they had reached this point, they were overtaken by a second express from General Atkinson, with a threat, that if they did not return, peaceably, he would pursue and force them back. The Indians replied that they were determined not to be driven back, and equally so not to make the first attack on the whites. Black Hawk now ascertained that the Winnebagoes, although willing that he should raise a crop of corn with them, would not join in any hostile action against the United States. The Pottowatomies manifested the same determination, and both denied having given the prophet any assurances of co-operation. Black Hawk immediately came to the conclusion, that if pursued by General Atkinson, he would peaceably return with his party, and recross the Mississippi. He was encamped at Kish-wa-cokee, and was preparing to compliment some Pottowatomie chiefs, then on a visit to him, by a dog-feast.

In the mean time the Illinois militia, ordered out by Governor Reynolds, upon his hearing of this second "invasion," of the state, had formed a junction with the regular troops under General Atkinson at Rock Island, the latter assuming the command of the whole. From this point, the militia, being generally mounted, proceeded by land to Dixon's Ferry on Rock River, about halfway between the mouth of that stream and the encampment of Black Hawk. General Atkinson with three hundred regulars and three hundred militia ascended Rock river in boats to the same point. Major Stillman, having under his command a body of two hundred and seventy-five mounted volunteers, obtained leave of General Whitesides, then in command of the Illinois militia, at Dixon's Ferry, to go out on a scouting expedition. He proceeded up Rock River about thirty miles, to Sycamore Creek, which empties into that river on the east side. This movement brought

144

Battle of Sycamore Creek.

him within a few miles of the camp of Black Hawk and a part of his braves, at the time when the old chief was engaged in getting up a dog-feast in honour of his Pottowatomie visitors.

It was on the 14th of May, that Black Hawk, while engaged in this ceremony, was informed that a large number of mounted volunteers, had been seen about eight miles from his camp.

I immediately started three young men, with a white flag, to meet them and conduct them to our camp, that we might hold a council with them, and descend Rock River again: and directed them in case the whites had encamped, to return, and I would go and see them. After this party had started, I sent five young men to see what might take place. The first party went to the encampment of the whites, and were taken prisoners. The last party had not proceeded far, before they saw about twenty men coming towards them in full gallop. They stopped and finding that the whites were coming so fast, in a warlike attitude, they turned and retreated, but were pursued and overtaken and two of them killed.

The others made their escape. When they came in with the news, I was preparing my flags to meet the war chief. The alarm was given. Nearly all my young men were absent about ten miles off. I started with what I had left, (about *forty*,) and had proceeded but a short distance, before we saw a part of the army approaching. I raised a yell, and said to my braves; "some of our people have been killed, wantonly and cruelly murdered! we must avenge their death." In a little while we discovered the whole army coming towards us in full gallop! We were now confident that our first party had been killed. I immediately placed my men in front of some bushes, that we might have the first fire, when they approached close enough.

They made a halt some distance from us. I gave another yell, and ordered my brave warriors to charge upon them, expecting that we would all be killed! they did charge—every man rushed and fired, and the enemy retreated in the utmost confusion, and consternation; before my little but brave band of warriors. After pursuing the enemy for some distance, I found it useless to follow them, as they rode so fast, and returned to my encampment with a few of my braves, (about twenty-five having gone in pursuit of the enemy.) I lighted my pipe, and sat down to thank the Great Spirit for what he had done. I had not been long meditating, when two of the three young men I had sent out with the flag, to meet the American war chief, entered. My astonishment was not greater than my joy to see them living and well. I eagerly listened to their story, which was as follows:

When we arrived near to the encampment of the whites, a number of them rushed out to meet us, bringing their guns with them. They took us into the camp, when an American who spoke the Sac language a little, told us that his chief wanted to know how we were, where we were going, where our camp was, and where Black Hawk was. We told him that we had come to see his chief: that our chief had directed us to conduct him to our camp, in case he had not encamped; and in that event to tell him, that he (Black Hawk) would come to see him; he wished to hold a council with him, as he had given up all intention of going to war.

At the conclusion of this talk, a party of white men came in on horseback. We saw by their countenances that something had happened. A general tumult arose. They looked at us with indignation—talked among themselves for a moment, when several cocked their guns; in a second they fired at us in the crowd; our companion fell dead. We rushed through the crowd and made our escape. We remained in ambush but a short time, before we heard yelling, like Indians running an enemy. In a little while we saw some of the whites in full speed.

One of them came near us. I threw my tomahawk and struck him on the head, which brought him to the ground. I ran to him and with his own knife took off his scalp. I took his gun, mounted his horse, and took my friend here behind me. We turned to follow our braves, who were running the enemy, and had not gone far before we overtook a white man, whose horse had mired in a swamp. My friend alighted and tomahawked the man, who was apparently fast under his horse. He took his scalp, horse and gun. By this time our party was some distance ahead. We followed on and saw several white men lying dead on the way.

After riding about six miles, we met our party returning.

We asked them how many of our men had been killed. They said none after the Americans had retreated. We inquired then how many whites had been killed? They replied they did not know; but said we will soon ascertain, as we must scalp them as we go back. On our return we found ten men, besides the two we had killed before we joined our friends. Seeing that they did not yet recognise us, it being dark, we again asked, how many of our braves had been killed? They said five.

We asked who they were. They replied that the first party of three, who went out to meet the American war chief, had all been taken prisoners, and killed in the encampment; and that out of a party of five who followed to see the meeting of the first party and the whites, two had been killed. We were now certain that they did not recognise us, nor did we tell them who we were, until we arrived at our camp. The news of our death had reached it some time before, and all were surprised to see us again. (Patterson's *Life of Black Hawk*, dictated by himself.)

Such is the narrative of this defeat, as given by Black Hawk, and two of his men who were the bearers of his white flag and a proposition to surrender. The accounts given by Major Stillman's troops—for it is not ascertained that the commander published any official statement of the battle—is in substance about the following. The force under Major Stillman, two hundred and seventy-five in number, on the afternoon of the fourteenth of May, met three Indians bearing a white flag, one of whom, after having been taken prisoner, was shot down. The army encamped just before sunset, in a piece of woods, surrounded by an open prairie, about three miles from Sycamore Creek. Soon after they had halted, five more Indians, with apparent pacific intentions, were seen approaching the camp. Captain Eades, with a party of armed troops, dashed at full speed towards them, when they became alarmed and commenced a retreat.

The captain, after following them for some distance, and killing two of the party, gave up the pursuit, and was on his return to the camp, when he was met by the whole detachment. The pursuit of the retreating Indians was immediately renewed, and continued until both parties had crossed Sycamore Creek. This brought them upon the camp of Black Hawk, who having been apprized of the approach of the whites, had mounted his men and prepared for action. The Indians were concealed behind some bushes, and after having fired their guns, raised the war-whoop and resorted to the tomahawk. Their fire was returned, with but little effect, and then Major Stillman, instantly ordered a retreat across the creek, and the route became general. His troops fled through their camp, and did not stop until they reached Dixon's Ferry, distant thirty miles.

Some of them deemed it prudent to seek a place of still greater safety, than the flag of General Atkinson, and continued their flight for more than fifty miles, and until they reached their own fire-sides. The roll was called at Dixon's ferry next morning, and fifty-two were found missing. It was, however, subsequently ascertained that more than half of this number were among those who rode express to the "settlements" to carry the news of their gallant attack upon General Black Hawk and his British band. Such was the panic among the troops engaged in this skirmish, that they reported the Indian force at 1500 and even 2000 men! Black Hawk's statement has already been given, in which he places his number at forty; and one of the volunteers whose horse was lame, and who hid himself, and watched the Indians as they passed him in the pursuit and on their return, did not estimate them at more than a hundred.

It is probable the real number of the Indians did not exceed fifty. It is painful to contemplate this whole affair, for it is alike discreditable to the national faith and the national arms. The violation of a flag of truce, and the wanton destruction of the lives of some of those who bore it, not only placed an indelible stigma upon the character of the country, but led to a war, in the prosecution of which, much blood and much treasure were expended. Had a conference with Black Hawk been held, scarcely a doubt remains, considering his failure to secure the co-operation of other tribes, and his utter destitution of provisions, that he and his band would have returned, peaceably, to the west side of the Mississippi. The precipitate flight of the troops under Major Stillman, has no justification.

Supposing the panic to have been such as to render a retreat across Sycamore Creek necessary, it should have terminated when the troops reached their encampment; which, being in a copse of woods, surrounded by a prairie, they would have been protected by trees, while the Indians, if they continued the attack, must have fought in the open plain. But no effort was made to rally at the encampment, and all the baggage of our troops—blankets, saddle-bags, camp equipage and provisions,—fell into the hands of the Indians. Black Hawk finding that there was now no alternative, determined to fight. Indignant at the attack upon his flag of peace—encouraged by his signal success in putting to flight, a force vastly superior in numbers to his own—and strengthened by the booty—especially the provisions—he had taken, he assembled his braves and prepared for an active border war.

He immediately sent out spies to watch the movements of General Atkinson, and prepared to remove his women and children, from the seat of war to the head waters of Rock River, where he supposed they would be safe from the attacks of the whites. In passing to this point, by the sources of the Kish-wa-co-kee, he was met by some Winnebagoes, who had heard of his victory, and were now disposed to join him. Some additional war parties were sent out, the new recruits from the Winnebagoes, constituting one of them. This arrangement completed, Black Hawk proceeded with the women and children to the Four Lakes, in which Catfish, one of the tributaries to Rock River, has its origin.

Stillman's defeat spread consternation throughout the state of Illinois. The Indian forces were greatly magnified in number, and Black Hawk's name carried with it associations of uncommon military talent, and of savage cunning and cruelty. General Atkinson proceeded to fortify his camp, at Dixon's Ferry, and the Executive of the State made a call for more mounted volunteers. The Secretary at War sent about 1000 United States' troops from the sea-board to the scene of action; and General Winfield Scott was ordered to proceed to the northwest, and direct the future operations of the campaign. A bloody border contest ensued. Many frontier families were massacred with savage ferocity, and some were carried into captivity.

A party of Pottowattomies, thirty in number, fell upon a little settlement on Indian creek, one of the tributaries of Fox River, and murdered fifteen men, women and children, taking two prisoners, the Misses Hall; who were subsequently placed in charge of some Winnebagoes, and by them returned in safety, a few weeks afterwards, to their friends. At Kellog's Grove, not far from Galena, in the early part of June, a party of Indians stole some horses. Captain J.W. Stephenson pursued them with twelve men. A skirmish ensued, which resulted in the death of three of our troops and five or six of the enemy.

On the evening of the 14th of June, a party of eleven Sacs, killed five white men at Spafford's farm. General Dodge with twenty-nine men, followed and overtook them in a swamp, where the whole were shot down and scalped, they having first killed three of Dodge's men. The barbarous practice of scalping the dead, was in this case adopted by our troops and sanctioned by their officers. (See Adjutant W. W. Woodbridge's statement.)

On the 24th of June, the Indians made an attack upon the fort at Buffalo grove, twelve miles north of Dixon's ferry. It was defended by a hundred and fifty men, under the command of Captain Dement, some of whom, with about forty horses, were killed. The commander did not deem it prudent to march out and encounter the Indians, who finding that they could not take the fort, secured a quantity of provisions, some horses and cattle, and commenced a retreat. They had not proceeded far, before they were overtaken by a detachment of volunteers under Colonel Posey, who had come to relieve the fort. Black Hawk, who commanded the Indians in this affair, says:

> We concealed ourselves until they came near enough, and then commenced yelling and firing and made a rush upon them.
> About this time their chief, with a party of men, rushed up to the rescue of those we had fired upon. In a little while they commenced retreating, and left their chief and a few braves, who seemed willing and anxious to fight. They acted like braves, but were forced to give way when I rushed upon them with my braves. In a short time, the chief returned with a larger party. He seemed determined to fight and anxious for battle. When he came near enough, I raised the yell, and firing commenced from both sides.
> The chief, who is a small man, addressed his warriors in a loud voice; but they soon retreated, leaving him and a few braves on the battlefield. A great number of my warriors pursued the retreating party, and killed a number of their horses as they ran. The chief and his braves were unwilling to leave the field. I ordered my braves to rush upon them, and had the mortification of seeing two of my chiefs killed, before the enemy retreated. This young chief deserves great praise for his courage, but fortunately for us, his army was not all composed of such brave men.

The Indians had about two hundred men in this engagement. The troops in the fort united with those under Colonel Posey, exceeded, in number Black Hawk's party. The loss of life was inconsiderable on either side.

On the 4th of July, the main army under General Atkinson, arrived at the foot of lake Coshconong, formed by an expansion of Rock River, in the vicinity of which the Indians had been embodied. On the 9th of July, General Atkinson says, in a letter to General Scott, that he had not yet been enabled to find the Indians, who he supposes to be seven or eight hundred strong, his own force amounting to four hundred regulars and 2100 mounted volunteers.

Two brigades of the mounted volunteers, under General Dodge, pursued the Indians from this place towards Fort Winnebago. They were overtaken on the 21st of July, about sun down, on the banks of the Wisconsin. An attack was immediately made, and about forty of the Indians are supposed to have been killed. General Dodge lost one man and had eight wounded. The exact loss of the Indians in this engagement cannot be ascertained. One account places the number at sixteen. (*The Book of the Indians of North America.*) Black Hawk says he had but fifty warriors with him in the engagement, the rest being engaged in assisting the women and children in crossing the Wisconsin to an island, to protect them from the fury of the whites: That he was compelled to fall back into a deep ravine where he continued to maintain his ground until dark, and until his people had had time to reach the island, and that he lost but six of his men.

This is undoubtedly a mistake, owing in all probability to the interpreter in taking down his statement; for some of his men, subsequently, placed the number at sixty. The condition of the Indians at this time was most deplorable. Before breaking up their encampment, upon the Four Lakes, they were almost destitute of provisions. In pursuing their trail from this point to the Wisconsin, many were found literally starved to death. They were compelled to live upon roots, the bark of trees and horse flesh. A party of Black Hawk's band, including many women and children, now attempted to descend the Wisconsin upon rafts and in canoes, that they might escape, by recrossing the Mississippi. They were attacked however, in their descent, by troops stationed on the bank of the river, and some were killed, others drowned, a few taken prisoners, and the remainder, escaping to the woods, perished from hunger.

Black Hawk, and such of his party as had not the means of descending the Wisconsin, having abandoned all idea of any farther resistance, and unwilling to trust themselves to a capitulation, now determined to strike across the country, and reach the Mississippi, some

BATTLE OF BAD-AXE.

distance above the mouth of the former stream, and thus effect their escape. They struck it at a point opposite the Ioway, and about forty miles above the Wisconsin, losing on their route, many of their people from starvation. So soon as they reached the Mississippi, a part of the women and children, in such canoes as they could procure, undertook to descend it, to Prairie des Chiens, but many of them were drowned before they reached that place, and those who did arrive at it, were found to be in a starving condition. On the first of August, while in the act of crossing the Mississippi, an attack was made upon Black Hawk and his party by the steamboat *Warrior*, with an armed force on board. The commander of the boat, under date of Prairie des Chiens, 3rd August 1832, gives the following account of it.

I arrived at this place on monday last, (July 30th) and was despatched with the *Warrior* alone, to Wapeshaws village, one hundred and twenty miles above, to inform them of the approach of the Sacs, and to order down all the friendly Indians to this place. On our way down we met one of the Sioux band, who informed us that the Indians, our enemies, were on Bad-axe River, to the number of four hundred. We stopped and cut some wood and prepared for action. About four o'clock on Wednesday afternoon (August 1st) we found the *gentlemen* (Indians) where he stated he left them.

As we neared them, they raised a white flag, and endeavored to decoy us; but we were a little too old for them; for instead of landing, we ordered them to send a boat on board, which they declined. After about fifteen minutes delay, giving them time to remove a few of their women and children, we let slip a six-pounder, loaded with canister, followed by a severe fire of musketry; and if ever you saw straight blankets, you would have seen them there. I fought them at anchor most of the time and we were all very much exposed. I have a ball which came in close by where I was standing, and passed through the bulkhead of the wheel room.

We fought them for about an hour or more until our wood began to fail, and night coming on, we left and went on to the prairie. This little fight cost them twenty-three killed, and of course a great many wounded. We never lost a man, and had but one man wounded, (shot through the leg.) The next morning before we could get back again, on account of a heavy fog,

154

they had the whole of General Atkinson's army upon them. We found them at it, walked in, and took a hand ourselves. The first shot from the *Warrior* laid out three.

I can hardly tell you anything about it, for I am in great haste, as I am now on my way to the field again. The army lost eight or nine killed, and seventeen wounded, whom we brought down. One died on deck last night. We brought down thirty-six prisoners, women and children. I tell you what, *Sam*, there is no fun in fighting Indians, particularly at this season, when the grass is so very bright. Every man, and even my cabin-boy, fought well. We had sixteen regulars, five rifle men, and twenty of ourselves. Mr. How, of Platt, Mr. James G. Soulard, and one of the Rolettes, were with us and fought well.

The flippant and vaunting style of this letter is in good keeping with the spirit which prompted the firing upon a flag of truce. By what circumstance the commander of the *Warrior* ascertained that this white flag was intended as a decoy, is left wholly unexplained. As he and his men, were beyond the reach of the Indians, humanity and the rules of war, required that he should have allowed himself more than *fifteen minutes*, to ascertain the true object of the Indians, in raising the symbol of a capitulation. Black Hawk himself, asserts that he directed his braves not to fire upon the *Warrior*, as he intended going on board in order to save the women and children; that he raised a white flag and called to the captain of the boat, desiring him to send his canoe on shore, that he might go on board, as he wanted to give himself up.

The deplorable condition to which Black Hawk was at this time reduced, flying for safety to the west side of the Mississippi, encumbered by his women and children, and his whole party exhausted by fatigue and hunger, renders it extremely difficult to believe that any decoy was intended by him. Indeed, nothing can be more certain, than that he was most heartily desirous of ending the disastrous and fatal contest in which he had become involved, without the slaughter of any more of his people. If the thirst for blood had been less rapacious on the part of the Americans, or their respect for a flag of truce something greater, the further destruction of life would have been spared; and the nation preserved from the charge of having fired upon a flag, held sacred throughout the world.

CHAPTER 7

Capture of Black Hawk and the Prophet

After the battle upon the Wisconsin, the whole army, under the command of General Atkinson, crossed to the north side of that river, at Helena, and on the twenty-ninth of July, commenced the pursuit of the Indians, by forced marches, over a rugged and mountainous country. On the morning of the second of August, while ten miles from the Mississippi, it was ascertained that the enemy were upon the bank of that stream, near the Bad-Axe, and in the act of crossing to the west side. Arrangements were immediately made for an attack. General Dodge's squadron was placed in front, followed by the infantry, and these by the brigades of Henry, Alexander, and Posey. The army had proceeded in this order about five miles, when some Indians were discovered and fired upon. They immediately retreated to the main body, on the bank of the river.

To prevent the possibility of the escape of the enemy, Generals Alexander and Posey, were directed to form the right wing of the army, and march to the river, above the Indian encampment, and then to move down along the bank. General Henry formed the left wing, and the United States' infantry and General Dodge's squadron, occupied the centre. In this order, the army descended a bluff bank into a river bottom, heavily timbered, and covered with weeds and brushwood. General Henry first came upon a portion of the enemy, and commenced a heavy fire upon them, which was returned. General Dodge's squadron and the United States' troops, soon came into the action, and with General Henry's men, rushed upon the Indians, killing all in the way, except a few who succeeded in swimming a slough of the Mississippi, about a hundred and fifty yards wide.

During this time the brigades of Alexander and Posey, in marching

156

down the bank of the river, fell in with another party of Indians, and killed or routed the whole of them. When the Indians were driven to the brink of the river, a large number of men, women and children, plunged into the water to save themselves by swimming; but only a few escaped "our sharpshooters." The battle lasted about three hours. In the afternoon, of the same day, Generals Atkinson, Dodge and Posey, descended the Mississippi, to Prairie des Chiens, in the *Warrior*, and there awaited the arrival of the mounted volunteers, who reached that place on the fourth. Among the Indians who escaped the slaughter was Black Hawk. Twelve of those who effected their escape, were captured on the fourth, by a party of whites, from Cassville, under the command of Captain Price, and most of those who succeeded in reaching the west side of the Mississippi, were subsequently attacked by a party of hostile Sioux, and either killed or taken prisoners. The brief, but official account of this battle is given by the commanding general, in these words.

Headquarters, First Artillery Corps, North-western Army
Prairie des Chiens, Augt. 25, 1832.

Sir: I have the honour to report to you that I crossed the Ouisconsin on the 27th and 28th *ultimo*, with a select body of troops, consisting of the regulars under Colonel Taylor, four hundred in number, part of Henry's, Posey's and Alexander's brigades, amounting in all to 1300 men, and immediately fell upon the trail of the enemy, and pursued it by a forced march, through a mountainous and difficult country, till the morning of the 2nd inst., when we came up with his main body on the left bank of the Mississippi, nearly opposite the mouth of the Ioway, which we attacked, defeated and dispersed, with a loss on his part of about a hundred and fifty men killed, thirty-nine women and children taken prisoners—the precise number could not be ascertained, as the greater portion was slain after being forced into the river.

Our loss in killed and wounded, which is stated below, is very small in comparison with the enemy, which may be attributed to the enemy's being forced from his positions by a rapid charge at the commencement, and throughout the engagement—the remnant of the enemy, cut up and disheartened, crossed to the opposite side of the river, and has fled into the interior, with a view, it is supposed, of joining Keokuk and Wapello's bands of

Sacs and Foxes.

The horses of the volunteer troops being exhausted by long marches, and the regular troops without shoes, it was not thought advisable to continue the pursuit; indeed a stop to the further effusion of blood seemed to be called for, till it might be ascertained if the enemy would surrender.

It is ascertained from our prisoners, that the enemy lost in the Battle of the Ouisconsin sixty-eight killed and a very large number wounded; his whole loss does not fall short of three hundred;—after the battle on the Ouisconsin, those of the enemy's women and children, and some who were dismounted, attempted to make their escape by descending that river, but judicious measures being taken by Captain Loomis and Lieutenant Street, Indian agent, thirty-two women and children and four men have been captured, and some fifteen men killed by the detachment under Lieutenant Ritner.

The day after the battle on this river, I fell down with the regular troops to this place by water, and the mounted men will join us today. It is now my purpose to direct Keokuk, to demand a surrender of the remaining principal men of the hostile party, which, from the large number of women and children we hold prisoners, I have every reason to believe will be complied with. Should it not, they should be pursued and subdued, a step Maj. General Scott will take upon his arrival.

I cannot speak too highly of the brave conduct of the regular and volunteer forces engaged in the last battle and the fatiguing march that preceded it, as soon as the reports of officers of the brigades and corps are handed in, they shall be submitted with further remarks.

5 killed, 2 wounded, 6th inf.
2 do. 5th inf.
1 captain, 5 privates Dodge's Bat. mounted
1 Lieutenant 6 privates Henry's
1 private wounded, Alexander's
1 private,   Posey's

    I have the honour to be with great respect,
        Your obedient servant, H. Atkinson,
            Brevet Brig. General U.S.A.

Maj. General Macomb, Com. in Chief, Washington.

The destruction of life in the Battle of the Bad-Axe, was not confined to the Indian warriors. Little discrimination seems to have been made between the slaughter of those in arms and the rest of the tribe. After they had sought refuge in the waters of the Mississippi, and the women, with their children on their backs, were buffeting the waves, in an attempt to swim to the opposite shore, numbers of them were shot by our troops. Many painful pictures might be recorded of the adventures and horrors of that day. One or two cases may be cited. A Sac woman, named Na-ni-sa, the sister of a warrior of some note among the Indians, found herself in the hottest of the fight. She succeeded at length in reaching the river, and keeping her infant child, close in its blanket, by force of her teeth, plunged into the water, seized hold upon the tail of a horse, whose rider was swimming him to the opposite shore, and was carried safely across the Mississippi.

When our troops charged upon the Indians, in their defiles near the river, men, women and children were so huddled together, that the slaughter fell alike upon all of them. A young squaw was standing in the grass, a short distance from the American line, holding her child, a little girl of four years old, in her arms. In this position, a ball struck the right arm of the child, just above the elbow, and shattering the bone, passed into the breast of its young mother, and instantly killed her. She fell upon the child and confined it to the ground.

When the battle was nearly over, and the Indians had been driven from this point, Lieutenant Anderson of the United States Army, hearing the cries of the child, went to the spot, and taking it from under the dead mother, carried it to the place for surgical aid. The arm was amputated, and during the operation, the half starved child did not cry, but sat quietly eating a piece of hard biscuit. It was sent to Prairie des Chiens, and entirely recovered from its wound.

When the fortunes of Black Hawk became desperate, his few straggling allies, from other tribes, not only deserted him, but joined his enemies. It is to two Winnebagoes, Decorie, and Chaetar, that the fallen chief is indebted for being taken captive. On the 27th of August, they delivered Black Hawk and the Prophet to the Indian agent, General Street, at Prairie des Chiens. Upon their delivery, Decorie, the One-eyed, rose and said:

My father, I now stand before you. When we parted, I told you I would return soon; but I could not come any sooner. We have had to go a great distance (to the Dalle, on the Wisconsin, above the portage.) You see we have done what you sent us to do. These, (pointing to the prisoners) are the two you told us to get. We have done what you told us to do. We always do what you tell us, because we know it is for our good. Father, you told us to get these men, and it would be the cause of much good to the Winnebagoes. We have brought them, but it has been very hard for us to do so. That one, Black Hawk was a great way off. You told us to bring them to you alive: we have done so. If you had told us to bring their heads alone, we would have done so, and it would have been less difficult than what we have done. Father, we deliver these men into your hands.

We would not deliver them even to our brother, the chief of the warriors, but to you; because we know you, and we believe you are our friend. We want you to keep them safe; if they are to be hurt we do not wish to see it. Wait until we are gone before it is done. Father, many little birds have been flying about our ears of late, and we thought they whispered to us that there was evil intended for us; but now we hope these evil birds will let our ears alone. We know you are our friend, because you take our part, and that is the reason we do what you tell us to do.

You say you love your red children: we think we love you as much if not more than you love us. We have confidence in you and you may rely on us. We have been promised a great deal if we would take these men—that it would do much good to our people. We now hope to see what will be done for us. We have come in haste; we are tired and hungry. We now put these men into your hands. We have done all that you told us to do.

The agent, General Street, replied:

My children, you have done well. I told you to bring these men to me, and you have done so. I am pleased at what you have done. It is for your good, and for this reason I am pleased. I assured the great chief of the warriors, (General Atkinson) that if these men were in your country, you would find them and bring them to me, and now I can say much for your good. I will go down to Rock island with the prisoners, and I wish you who have brought these men, especially, to go with me, with such other chiefs and warriors as you may select. My children, the great chief of the warriors, when he left this place, directed me to deliver these and all other prisoners, to the chief of the warriors at this place, Colonel Taylor, who is here by me.

Some of the Winnebagoes, south of the Wisconsin, have be-
friended the Saukies, and some of the Indians of my agency
have also given them aid. This displeases the great chief of the
warriors, and your great father the president, and was calculated
to do much harm. Your great father, the president at Washington, has sent a great war chief from the far east, General Scott,
with a fresh army of soldiers. He is now at Rock Island. Your
great father the president has sent him and the governor and
chief of Illinois to hold a council with the Indians. He has sent
a speech to you, and wishes the chiefs and warriors of the Winnebagoes to go to Rock Island, to the council on the tenth of
next month.

I wish you to be ready in three days, when I will go with you.
I am well pleased that you have taken the Black Hawk, the
Prophet and other prisoners. This will enable me to say much
for you to the great chief of the warriors, and to the president
your great father. My children, I shall now deliver the two men,
Black Hawk and the prophet, to the chief of the warriors here.
He will take care of them till we start to Rock Island.

Colonel Taylor upon taking charge of the prisoners made a few
remarks to their captors, after which Chaetar, the associate of Decorie,
rose and said,

My father, I am young, and do not know how to make speeches. This is the second time I ever spoke to you before people. I
am no chief; I am no orator; but I have been allowed to speak to
you. If I should not speak as well as others, still you must listen
to me. Father, when you made the speech to the chiefs, Waugh-
Kon-Decorie-Carramani, the one-eyed Decorie, and others, I
was there. I heard you. I thought what you said to them, you
also said to me. You said if these two, (pointing to Black Hawk
and the prophet) were taken by us and brought to you, there
would never more a black cloud hang over your Winnebagoes.
Your words entered into my ear, my brains and my heart. I left
here that same night, and you know that you have not seen me
since until now.

I have been a great way; I had much trouble; but when I remembered what you said, I knew what you said was right. This
made me continue and do what you told me to do. Near the

161

Dalle on the Wisconsin, I took Black Hawk. No one did it but me. I say this in the ears of all present, and they know it—and I now appeal to the Great Spirit, our grandfather, and the Earth, our grandmother, for the truth of what I say. Father, I am no chief, but what I have done is for the benefit of my nation, and I hope to see the good that has been promised us. That one, Wabokieshiek, the prophet, is my relation—if he is to be hurt, I do not wish to see it. Father, soldiers sometimes stick the ends of their guns into the backs of Indian prisoners, when they are going about in the hands of the guard. I hope this will not be done to this man.

Naopope the second in command, with a few other Indians who escaped from the battle of the Bad-Axe, were also brought in by the Sioux, who being the ancient enemy of the Sacs and Foxes, seized upon this opportunity of waging war upon the remnant of Black Hawk's band. They were placed by General Street, in the custody of Colonel Taylor.

On the seventh of September, the prisoners were placed on board the steamboat *Winnebago*, and sent down to Jefferson Barracks, a few miles below St. Louis. The arrival of General Scott at the scene of action, was unfortunately delayed until after the campaign was closed, in consequence of the Asiatic cholera having broken out, among the troops under his command, while ascending the lakes. The disease continued to rage among them, with dreadful mortality, for some time after their arrival at Rock Island. Of course, this campaign added no new laurels to the military reputation of General Scott; but, by his humane and tireless exertions for the alleviation of the sufferings of his soldiers, he won for himself more true glory, than the most brilliant victory, over an Indian enemy, could confer.

While at Rock Island, General Scott instituted some inquiries among the Indians, in regard to the difficulties between them and the whites. Among others interrogated was Naopope, the friend and counsellor of Black Hawk, who participated in the campaign, and on account of his courage and skill as a warrior, directed to a great extent, the movements of the band, from the period of their recrossing the Mississippi, until the Battle of the Bad-Axe. His statement confirms the declaration of Black Hawk, that in coming over to the east side of the river, there was no intention of making war upon the frontier settlers; and that they really intended to surrender to Major Stillman,

162

upon Sycamore Creek, on the 14th of May, and actually sent a white flag, in evidence of their submission, which was fired upon by the American troops.

I always belonged to Black Hawk's band. Last summer I went to Malden; when I came back, I found that by the treaty with General Gaines, the Sacs had moved across the Mississippi. I remained during the winter with the Prophet, on Rock River, thirty-five miles above the mouth. During the winter the Prophet sent me across the Mississippi, to Black Hawk, with a message, to tell him and his band to cross back to his village and make corn: that if the Americans came and told them to remove again, they would shake hands with them. If the Americans had come and told us to move, we should have shaken hands, and immediately have moved peaceably.
We encamped on Sycamore Creek. We met some Pottowatomies and made a feast for them. At that time I heard there were some Americans (under Major Stillman) near us. I prepared a white flag to go and see them, and sent two or three young men on a hill to see what they were doing. Before the feast was finished, I heard my young men were killed. This was at sunset. Some of my young men ran out; two killed, and the Americans were seen rushing on to our camp. My young men fired a few guns, and the Americans ran off, and my young men chased them about six miles.

Naopope further stated that the Pottowatomies immediately left them, and that none of the Kickapoos ever joined them. A few of the Winnebagoes did, and brought in scalps at different times; but so soon as they discovered that the whites were too powerful for the Sacks, they turned round and fought against them. Some of the other witnesses examined on this occasion, testify, that when Black Hawk saw the steam boat *Warrior* approaching them, on the first of August, he said he pitied the women and children; and, having determined to surrender to the commander of the boat, raised a white flag which was immediately fired upon. This fact is stated in the letter of the captain of the *Warrior*, and is corroborated by Lieutenant Kingsbury, who had charge of the troops on board.
Among the prisoners delivered to General Street, was the Prophet Wabokieshiek, or the White Cloud, a stout, shrewd looking Indian about forty years of age. This individual exercised considerable influ-

ence over Black Hawk and his band. He had a village, called after him, upon Rock River, where he usually resided, and was recognised among the village chiefs. He claimed to be part Winnebago and part Sac, his father belonging to one and his mother to the other of these tribes. He wore a full suit of hair, with a white head-dress rising several inches above the top of his hair—a style of dress suited, it is supposed, to his profession. He seems to have had sagacity and cunning—two qualities essential to the character of a prophet, and without which they could not long retain their influence and sacred character. Wabokieshiek has been represented as the priest of assassination, but the evidence on which this charge is made, seems to be wanting.

He was instrumental in persuading Black Hawk and his party to return to the east side of the Mississippi in 1832, and went down to the mouth of Rock River to meet them, and encourage the belief that the Americans would not interfere with them, so long as they refrained from any offensive operations. He made a speech to the braves and warriors of Black Hawk, in which he told them they had nothing to fear and much to gain: That the American war chief, would not molest them so long as they acted peaceably: That the time would come when they would be ready to pursue a different course; but that they must await such reinforcements as would enable them to resist the army of the whites.

The Prophet was either duped himself, or playing upon the credulity of Black Hawk and Naopope. He was constantly giving them assurances of assistance from the other tribes and from their British Father at Malden. There may have been reason for expecting it from the former, but none from the latter. He entertained strong prejudices against the whites, and being naturally prone to mischief making, was willing to stir up the Indians to resistance, without caring for the results that would be likely to follow a border war. The likeness of him, which is here given, is said to convey a good idea of his style of dress and the expression of his face.

On the 21st of September, General Scott and Governor Reynolds concluded a treaty with the Winnebagoes, and the Sacs and Foxes; the provisions of which have been stated. For the faithful performance of it, on the part of the Indians, it was stipulated that Black Hawk and his two sons, Wabokieshiek the Prophet, Naopope and five other chiefs of the hostile band, should be retained as hostages during the pleasure of the president. The remainder of the prisoners, captured during the campaign, were set at liberty.

WABOKIESHIEK, THE PROPHET.

In recurring to the causes which led to this war and the spirit and military skill with which it was conducted, there is nothing on which a citizen of the United States can dwell with satisfaction. Looking alone to the official documents, that have been published on the subject, it would appear that the Indians were the aggressors—that they invaded the territory of the United States, marking their path with outrages upon the unoffending citizens; and that they were met, encountered, and defeated, under circumstances which shed renown upon the arms and humane policy of the government. But it is necessary, in doing justice to both parties in this contest, to destroy this flattering picture.

Some of the causes which operated to render Black Hawk and his band, discontented with the conduct of the United States, and with their condition upon the west side of the Mississippi, have been enumerated. Whatever may have been their ulterior views, in returning within the limits of the state of Illinois, in the spring of 1832, it cannot be supposed that they came with any immediate hostile intentions. Had they been determined upon war, they would neither have encumbered themselves with their wives and children, nor have openly recrossed the Mississippi, near to Fort Armstrong, when they knew there was an officer of the United States army, with a body of troops, stationed at that point, for the express purpose of preserving peace upon the frontier. Such movements would have been at variance with the well known military policy of the Indians.

Judging from the success of General Gaines, in removing this same band, in 1831, without bloodshed, to the west side of the Mississippi, it has been supposed, that a pacific conference between the commandant of Fort Armstrong and Black Hawk, in 1832, before he had commenced his ascent up Rock river, would have resulted in the peaceable return of the Indians to their own hunting grounds. The condition of things at that time, warrants such a belief, and the subsequent declarations of the Indians, strengthen the opinion, that had the experiment been made, it would have been successful. It is true, that the commanding officer at Fort Armstrong, sent two messages to Black Hawk upon this subject; but the first is represented by the Indians to have been an *order* for them to return; and the second, that if they did not, they would be pursued and *forced* to recross the Mississippi. These efforts failed, but it does not follow that a friendly council upon the subject, would not have resulted differently.

Many causes operate in bringing about an Indian war, and in plunging the government of the United States, prematurely and unnecessarily, into it. There is generally upon the frontiers a class of persons who have nothing to lose, and much to gain by such a contest. It gives them employment and circulates money among them. With such pioneer loafers, an Indian war is always popular. Then there is the "Indian Hater," (this class is admirably described by the author of Legends of the West), a numerous and respectable body of men, to be found upon the frontier settlements, who, from having suffered in their persons and property by the barbarities and plunder of the Indians, have come at length to look upon them as no better than the wild beasts of the forest, and whose many atrocities make it a moral duty, on the part of the whites, to exterminate by fire and the sword. Again there is the regular *squatter*and land speculator, whose interest is always promoted by a war, because it usually results in driving the Indians further back from the frontier.

Intermixed with these classes, are many quiet and worthy citizens, who with their families, have been carried to the frontiers, in the ordinary course of events, by the tide of emigration. These may have neither a desire for war nor a feeling of hostility towards the Indians, but when the tomahawk is raised, they contribute to swell the alarum, and oftentimes, by their very fears of a war, do much to bring it about. Finally, it is not to be disguised, that there are many individuals, in the states, who are prone to look to an Indian war, as a means of gratifying their love for adventure and excitement; or who, having political aspirations, are disposed to make the military renown, which may be gained in a campaign, the means of attaining civic honours. It is obvious, if there be any foundation for these positions, that an Indian war may oftentimes be undertaken without any just cause, prosecuted without system and terminated in dishonour to our government.

When Black Hawk and his party rashly determined, in the spring of 1832, to recross the Mississippi, a fine opportunity was presented, for getting up a border war, and the necessary machinery was speedily put in motion. The old chief, with a few hundred braves and their women and children, carrying with them their cooking utensils and personal property, had no sooner reached the east bank of the Mississippi, than the alarm note was sounded upon the frontier, and echoed from cabin to cabin, until it was spread throughout the state of Illinois. The most dreadful anticipations of savage cruelty were indulged—the force of Black Hawk was greatly magnified—his thirst for vengeance upon the whites was only to be appeased by blood—the state was actually invaded by a powerful and remorseless enemy—and memorials and petitions, for an armed force to repulse the invaders and protect the frontiers, flowed in upon the governor, from all quarters. Such was the excited state of public feeling, such the force of public sentiment, that little time was left for Executive deliberation.

Governor Reynolds issued his proclamation, reiterating the dangers of the frontier, and calling for a body of the militia to march and protect it. A call under such circumstances was promptly responded to, and in a short time, a large body of mounted volunteers, embracing many of the most respectable and influential citizens of Illinois, were in the vicinity of the invading foe, and ready for co-operation with the regular troops under General Atkinson. A concentration of these two forces was made at Dixon's Ferry, on Rock River, about thirty miles below the encampment of Black Hawk and his party. Had a conference now been sought with the Indians, their prompt submission cannot be doubted. Black Hawk, whatever might have been his previous expectations, had received no addition of strength from other tribes—he was almost destitute of provisions—had committed no act of hostility against the whites, and with all his women, children and baggage, was in the vicinity of an army, principally of mounted volunteers, many times greater than his own band of braves. He would probably have been glad of any reasonable pretext for retracing his precipitate steps. Unfortunately no effort for a council was made.

A body of impetuous volunteers dashed on, without caution or order, to Sycamore Creek, within three miles of the camp of a part of Black Hawk's party. He instantly sent a white flag to meet them for the purpose of holding a council, and agreeing to return to the west side of the Mississippi. Unfortunately, for the cause of humanity, as well as the good faith of the United States, this flag was held to be but a decoy, and without waiting to ascertain its true character, the bearers of it were fired upon and one of them killed. An onset was immediately made by Major Stillman upon Black Hawk, who finding there was no alternative but war, met our troops, and put them to flight in the manner already described.

Emboldened by his brilliant success in this engagement, and finding that he would not be permitted to capitulate, he sent out his war parties, removed his women and children up Rock River, and a regular border war was commenced. The murders which his men committed upon the frontier settlers, naturally increased the alarm throughout the state, additional volunteers rushed to the seat of war, and the commanding general commenced his military operations for a regular campaign.

In about two months, Black Hawk, having lost many of his men, in the different skirmishes with the American troops, and not a few of his women and children by actual starvation, found himself upon the bank of the Mississippi, endeavouring to escape the pursuing enemy, by crossing to the west side of that stream. While engaged in this act, the steamboat *Warrior*, having an armed force on board, ascended the river for the purpose of cutting off his retreat. Once more Black Hawk raised the white flag, and sought to surrender himself and his whole band, to the whites. Again his flag was looked upon as a decoy, and in fifteen minutes, a round of canister shot, from the boat, was fired, with deadly fatality into the midst of his men, women and children.

The following morning, the main army, under General Atkinson, reached the scene of action. His force must have been six or eight times greater than that of the Indians, and by a judicious movement, the latter was promptly surrounded on three sides by the pursuing army, while on the other, the steam boat *Warrior*, the waters of the Mississippi, and a band of hostile Sioux on its west bank, precluded all chance of escape in that quarter. A demand upon the Indians, at this time, to surrender, unconditionally, would undoubtedly have been most cheerfully acceded to.

But it appears not to have been made. It is probable that General Atkinson whose character for humanity, has always stood high, could not restrain the impetuosity of his troops long enough to propose a capitulation. They had been deeply excited by the murders perpetrated by the Black Hawk band—had been harassed by a long and fatiguing march—and perhaps felt, that the results of the campaign, thus far, had been rather inglorious to their arms. These causes may have conspired to precipitate them into a battle, which had been better spared than fought, inasmuch as it resulted, necessarily, in the death of a great many miserable women and children, who were already on the brink of the grave, from hunger and exhaustion.

A brief recapitulation of a few of the events of this disastrous campaign, has thus been made, for the purpose of showing, that however hostile Black Hawk and his band may have been, originally, towards the whites, he did not make the first attack upon them; and that the war might in all probability have been prevented, or arrested in any stage of its progress, by the exercise of that forbearance, good faith and sound policy, which should ever be cherished by the United States.

The official report of General Atkinson to General Macomb, after the Battle of the Bad-Axe has been quoted in full. On the 25th of November 1832, the Secretary at War, Mr. Cass, in his annual report to the president, says, in speaking of this campaign,

> General Atkinson, with the regular troops and militia under his command, pursued the Indians through a country very difficult to be penetrated, of which little was known, and where much exertion was required to procure regular supplies. These circumstances necessarily delayed the operations, and were productive of great responsibility to the commanding officer, and of great sufferings and privations to all employed in this harassing warfare. The Indians, however, were driven from their fastnesses, and fled towards the Mississippi, with the intention of seeking refuge in the country west of that river. They were immediately followed by General Atkinson, with a mounted force, overtaken, and completely vanquished. The arrangements of the commanding general, as well in the pursuit as in the action, were prompt and judicious, and the conduct of the officers and men was exemplary. The campaign terminated in the unqualified submission of the hostile party, and in the adoption of measures for the permanent security of the frontiers, and the result has produced upon the Indians of that region, a salutary impression, which it is to be hoped will prevent the recurrence of similar scenes.

On the 25th of October 1832, General Macomb transmitted to General Atkinson, the following letter, from the Secretary at War.

> Department at War, Oct. 24th. 1832.
> Sir: The return of the president to the seat of government, enables me to communicate to you his sentiments in relation to the operations and result of the campaign, recently conducted under your orders, against the hostile Indians; and it is with great pleasure, I have received his instructions to inform you, that he appreciates the difficulties you had to encounter; and that he has been highly gratified at the termination of your arduous and responsible duties. Great privations and embarrassments, necessarily attend such a warfare, and particularly in the difficult country occupied by the enemy. The arrangements which led to the defeat of the Indians, were adopted with judgment and pursued with decision, and the result was honourable to yourself, and to the officers and men acting under your orders.

I will thank you to communicate to the forces that served with you, both regulars and militia, the feelings of the president upon this occasion. I have the honour to be very respectfully, your obedient servant.

Lewis Cass.

General H. Atkinson, Jefferson Barracks, Missouri.

In the report of the Secretary at War which has just been referred to, there is the following statement of the causes which led to this contest.

The recent hostilities, commenced by the Sac and Fox Indians, may be traced to causes, which have been for some time in operation, and which left little doubt upon the minds of those acquainted with the savage character, that they were determined to commit some aggression upon the frontier. The confederated tribes of the Sacs and Foxes have been long distinguished for their daring spirit of adventure and for their restless and reckless disposition. At the commencement of the eighteenth century, one of these tribes made a desperate attempt to seize the post of Detroit; and during a period of forty years, subsequent to that effort, they caused great trouble and embarrassment to the French colonial government, which was only terminated by a most formidable military expedition, sent by that enterprising people into their remote regions west of Green Bay. During the last war with Great Britain, this confederacy entered zealously into the contest, and was among the most active and determined of our enemies.

After the peace their communication with the Canadian authorities was preserved; and, in every year, large parties of the most influential chiefs and warriors visited Upper Canada, and returned laden with presents. That this continued intercourse kept alive feelings of attachment to a foreign power and weakened the proper and necessary influence of the United States, is known to every one who has marked the progress of events and conduct of the Indians upon the north western frontier. The tribes upon the upper Mississippi, particularly the Sacs and Foxes and Winnebagoes, confident in their position and in their natural courage, and totally ignorant of the vast disproportion between their power, and that of the United States, have always been discontented, keeping the frontier in alarm, and continually committing some outrage upon the persons or property of the inhabitants.

All this is the result of impulse, and is the necessary and almost inevitable consequence of institutions, which make war the great object of life. It is not probable, that any Indian seriously bent up on hostilities, ever stops to calculate the force of the white man, and to estimate the disastrous consequences which we know must be the result. He is impelled onward in his desperate career, by passions which are fostered and encouraged by the whole frame of society; and he is, very probably, stimulated by the predictions of some fanatical leader, who promises him glory, victory and scalps.

In this state of feeling, and with these incitements to war, the Sacs and Foxes claimed the right of occupying a part of the country on Rock river, even after it had been sold to citizens of the United States, and settled by them. In 1829 and in 1830, serious difficulties resulted from their efforts to establish themselves in that section, and frequent collisions were the consequence. Representations were made to them, and every effort, short of actual hostilities, used by the proper officers, to induce them to abandon their unfounded pretensions, and to confine themselves to their own country on the west side of the Mississippi River. These efforts were successful, with the well disposed portion of the tribes, but were wholly unavailing with the band known by the name of the "British party."

In 1831, their aggressions were so serious, and the attitude they assumed, so formidable, that a considerable detachment of the army, and of the militia of Illinois, was called into the field; and the disaffected Indians, alarmed by the preparation for their chastisement, agreed to reside and hunt, "upon their own lands west of the Mississippi River," and that they would not recross this river to the usual place of their residence, nor to any part of their old hunting grounds east of the Mississippi, without the express permission of the President of the United States, or the Governor of the state of Illinois.

This arrangement had scarcely been concluded, before a flagrant outrage was committed, by a party of these Indians, upon a band of friendly Menomomies, almost under the guns of Fort Crawford. Twenty-five persons were wantonly murdered, and many wounded, while encamped in the Prairie du Chien, and resting in fancied security upon our soil, and under our flag. If an act like this, had been suffered to pass unnoticed and unpunished, a war between these tribes would have been the consequence, in which our frontiers would have been involved, and the character and influence of the government, would have been lost in the opinion of the Indians.

Apprehensive, from the course of events already stated, and from other circumstances, that the disaffected band of Sacs and Foxes, would again harass and disturb the settlements upon our borders, and determined that the murderers of the Menomenies should be surrendered or taken, the department ordered General Atkinson, on the 7th of March last, to ascend the Mississippi with the disposable regular troops at Jefferson barracks, and to carry into effect the instructions issued by your direction. Still further to strengthen the frontiers, orders were given for the re-occupation of Chicago.

The demand for the surrender of the Menomenie murderers was entirely disregarded: and the British party of the Sacs and Foxes recrossed the Mississippi, and assuming a hostile attitude, established themselves upon Rock river. The subsequent events are well known, and the result has already been stated in this report.

In the annual report of Major-General Macomb to Congress, of November 1832, very much the same positions are taken in regard to the causes which led to this contest with the Indians, that are contained in the report from the War Department. Its leading object seems to be to place the United States in the right—the Indians in the wrong.

It is to be regretted that the Honourable Secretary, whose opinions and statements on all subjects connected with the Indians, carry with them great weight, had not been more explicit, in assigning the causes which led to the late war, with a portion of the Sacs and Foxes. It is not to be supposed that the Secretary would designedly omit any thing, which in his opinion, was necessary, to a fair presentation of this matter; but as the case stands, his statement does not, it is believed, do justice to the Indians. The Secretary says the Sacs and Foxes "have always been discontented, keeping the frontier in alarm, and continually committing some outrage on the persons or property of the inhabitants." Between the treaty of peace at Portage des Sioux, in 1816, and the attack of Major Stillman, in 1832, it is supposed that the Sacs and Foxes never killed one American; and, their aggressions upon the persons and property of the whites, consisted principally, in an attempt to retain possession of their village and cornfields, when pressed upon by the white settlers, who, in violation of the laws of Congress and express treaty provisions, were committing outrages upon the Indians:

The report of the secretary further states, that the Sacs and Foxes "claimed the right of occupying a part of the country upon Rock River, even after it had been sold to citizens of the United States, and settled by them." But the report does not state that under the treaty of 1804, by which these lands were ceded, it is expressly provided that so long as they remain the property of the United States, the Indians of said tribes shall enjoy the privilege of "living and hunting upon them;" it does not state that for six or eight years before the government had sold an acre of land upon Rock River, the white settlers were there, in violation of the laws, trespassing upon these Indians, and thus creating that very hostility of feeling, which, is subsequently cited as a reason for the chastisement inflicted upon them by the United States: it does not state, that in the year 1829, government, for the purpose of creating a pretext for the removal of the Indians from Rock River, directed a few quarter sections of land, including the Sac village, to be sold, although the frontier settlements of Illinois had not then reached within fifty or sixty miles of that place, and millions of acres of land around it, were unoccupied and unsold

It does not state that instead of requiring the Indians to remove from the quarter sections thus prematurely sold, to other lands on Rock River, owned by the United States, and on which, under the treaty, they had a right to hunt and reside, they were commanded to remove to the west side of the Mississippi: it does not state, that the "serious aggressions" and "formidable attitude" assumed by the "British party," in 1831, consisted in their attempt to raise a crop of corn and beans, in throwing down the fences of the whites who were enclosing their fields, in "pointing deadly weapons" at them and in "stealing their potatoes:" it does not state that the murder of the Menominie Indians, at Fort Crawford, by a party of the "British band," was in retaliation, for a similar "flagrant outrage," committed the summer previous, by the Menominies, upon Peah-mus-ka, a principal chief of the Foxes and nine or ten of his tribe, who were going up to Prairie des Chiens on business and were within one day's travel of that place: it does not state that one reason assigned by the "British party" for refusing to surrender the murderers of the Menominies, was the fact that the government had not made a similar demand of that tribe for the murderers of the Sacs.

It does not state that the "hostile attitude" assumed by the Sacs and Foxes, in 1832, after recrossing the Mississippi, and their establishment on Rock River, simply amounted to this; that they came over with their women and children for the avowed purpose of raising a crop of corn with the Winnebagoes—were temporarily encamped on that stream—had committed no outrage upon person or property—and were actually engaged in entertaining some guests with a dog-feast, when the Illinois militia approached their camp, and killed the bearer of a white flag, which Black Hawk sent to them, in token of his peaceable disposition. These may be unimportant omissions, in the opinion of the secretary, but in looking to the causes which led to this contest, and the spirit in which it was conducted, they have been deemed of sufficient importance, to receive a passing notice, when referring to his report.

The opinion has been expressed more than once in the course of this work, that there was in reality, no necessity for this war. A firm but forbearing course of policy, on the part of the United States, towards this discontented fragment of the Sacs and Foxes, would, it is believed, have prevented any serious aggression upon our people or their property. Certain it is, that a few thousand dollars, superadded to a humane spirit of conciliation, would have effected the permanent removal of Black Hawk and his band, to the west side of the Mississippi: and, as the government was not contending with them, in support of its national faith, nor about to punish them for an insult to its national honour, there could have been no disgrace in purchasing the settlement of the difficulty, on such terms. It has been stated that in the spring of 1831, Black Hawk agreed to remove his band to the west side of the Mississippi, and relinquish all claims to the lands upon Rock River, if the United States would pay him six thousand dollars, with which to purchase provisions and other necessaries for his people; and that the Indian agent at St. Louis, was informed of this fact.

Moreover, it has been publicly alleged that before the campaign against Black Hawk, in the summer of 1832, the President and Secretary at War, were both informed, that the "British Band" of the Sacs and Foxes, could be peaceably removed to the west side of the Mississippi for six or eight thousand dollars. The secretary was assured, in the presence of a member of congress, that the inquiry had been made by a person familiar with the Indians, and the fact of their willingness to remove upon these terms distinctly ascertained. (*St. Louis Times* of 13th April, 1833.)

Under the treaty of 1804, the Sacs and Foxes ceded to the United States, more than twenty millions of acres of first rate land, for less than twenty thousand dollars. Black Hawk not only contended for the invalidity of this treaty, but insisted that the price paid by the United States was wholly below the value of the land. Under such circumstances, the course of the government was obvious—to have quieted the complaints of the Indians and secured their peaceable removal to the west, by a second purchase of their interest to the territory in question. Had it cost twenty, fifty or one hundred thousand dollars, to effect this object, our country would still have been the gainer, both by the preservation of the national faith and the national treasure—for the former was wantonly violated, and the latter uselessly squandered.

The contest with Black Hawk and his party, destroyed the lives of four or five hundred Indian men, women and children—about two hundred citizens of the United States—and cost the government near two millions of dollars! Such are the results of a war commenced and waged by a great nation, upon a remnant of poor ignorant savages;—a war which had its origin in avarice and political ambition, which was prosecuted in bad faith and closed in dishonour.

CHAPTER 8

Black Hawk's Visit to Washington in 1837

Black Hawk, his two sons, Naopope, Wabokiesheik, and the other prisoners, who under the treaty of 21st September, were to be held as hostages, during the pleasure of the president, having been sent down the Mississippi, to Jefferson Barracks, under charge of Lieutenant Davis, were immediately put in irons, a measure of precaution, apparently, as unnecessary as it was cruel.

The old chief says:

We were now confined to the barracks, and forced to wear the *ball and chain*! This was extremely mortifying, and altogether useless. Was the White Beaver (General Atkinson) afraid that I would break out of his barracks and run away? Or was he ordered to inflict this punishment upon me? If I had taken him prisoner upon the field of battle, I would not have wounded his feelings so much, by such treatment, knowing that a brave war chief would prefer death to dishonour. But I do not blame the White Beaver for the course he pursued—it is the custom among white soldiers, and I suppose was a part of his duty.

The time dragged heavily and gloomily along throughout the winter, although the White Beaver did every thing in his power to render us comfortable. Having been accustomed throughout a long life, to roam through the forests—to come and go at liberty—confinement under any such circumstances, could not be less than torture.

We passed away the time making pipes, until spring, when we were visited by the agent, trader, and interpreter, from Rock

Island, Keokuk, and several chiefs and braves of our nation, and my wife and daughter. I was rejoiced to see the two latter, and spent my time very agreeably with them and my people as long as they remained.

During the winter they were visited by a great number of persons, one of whom remarks:

We were immediately struck with admiration at the gigantic and symmetrical figures of most of the warriors, who seemed as they reclined, in native ease and gracefulness, with their half naked bodies exposed to view, rather like statues from some master hand, than beings of a race whom we had heard characterized as degenerate and debased. They were clad in leggins and *moccasins* of buckskin, and wore blankets, which were thrown around them in the manner of the Roman *toga*, so as to leave their right arms bare.

The youngest among them were painted on their necks, with a bright vermilion colour, and had their faces transversely streaked, with alternate red and black stripes. From their faces and eyebrows, they pluck out the hair with the most assiduous care. They also shave or pull it out from their heads, with the exception of a tuft about three fingers width, extending from between the forehead and crown to the back of the head; this they sometimes plait into a queue on the crown, and cut the edges of it down to an inch in length, and plaster it with the vermilion which keeps it erect, and gives it the appearance of a cock's comb.

The same writer adds, that, "but for the want of that peculiar expression which emanates from a cultivated intellect," Nasinewiskuk, the eldest son of Black Hawk, could have "been looked upon as the very personification, of the *beau ideal* of manly beauty." Among their many visitors while at this place, was the distinguished author of the *Sketch Book*, who in a letter, under date of 18th of Dec. 1832, says:

From St. Louis, I went to Fort Jefferson, about nine miles distant, to see Black Hawk, the Indian warrior and his fellow prisoners—a forlorn crew—emaciated and dejected—the redoubtable chieftain himself, a meagre old man upwards of seventy. He has, however, a fine head, a Roman style of face, and a prepossessing countenance.(*The Book of the Indians of North*

America, by Samuel G. Drake of Boston, containing much interesting matter about the aborigines of this country, and from which we have copied several of the speeches made upon the liberation of Black Hawk.)

When Catlin the artist, visited Jefferson Barracks for the purpose of painting the portraits of these chiefs, and was about to commence the likeness of Naopope, he seized the ball and chain that were fastened to his leg, and raising them on high, exclaimed with a look of scorn, "make me so, and show me to the great father." Upon the artist's refusing to paint him as he wished, he kept varying his countenance with grimaces, to prevent him from catching a likeness.

During the visit of Keokuk to Jefferson Barracks, he made exertions to obtain the release of the prisoners, pledging himself to the Indian agent at St. Louis, and to General Atkinson, to be responsible for their good conduct in future. Soon afterwards, however, the General received orders from the secretary at war to have the prisoners sent to Washington city. It was in the latter part of April, 1833, that they reached the capitol, under the escort of an officer of the army. In the first interview between President Jackson and Black Hawk, the latter is represented to have said, "I am a man and you are another." In the course of their interview, the president informed him that he and his companions must proceed on the following day to Fortress Monroe, there to remain, until the conduct of their people at home was such as to justify their being set at liberty. In reply to this, the Prophet said:

We expected to return immediately to our people. The war in which we have been involved was occasioned by our attempting to raise provisions on our own lands, or where we thought we had a right so to do. We have lost many of our people, as well as the whites. Our tribes and families are now exposed to the attacks of our enemies, the Sioux, and the Menominies. We hope, therefore, to be permitted to return home to take care of them.

Black Hawk concluded his address to the president, which embraced a history of the late war, by saying:

We did not expect to conquer the whites, no. They had too many houses, too many men. I took up the hatchet, for my part, to revenge injuries which my people could no longer endure. Had I borne them longer without striking, my people

179

would have said, Black Hawk is a woman. He is too old to be a chief—he is no Sac. These reflections caused me to raise the war-whoop. I say no more of it; it is known to you. Keokuk once was here; you took him by the hand, and when he wished to return to his home, you were willing. Black Hawk expects, that, like Keokuk, we shall be permitted to return too.

The president gave them assurances that their women and children should be protected from the Sioux and the Menominies, and that so soon as he was satisfied that peace was restored on the frontiers, they should be permitted to return home.

On the 26th of April, they set off for Fortress Monroe, at Old Point Comfort, where they remained until the fourth of June, when, an order was received, from the president, by the commanding officer, for the liberation of the Indian captives. The kind treatment of the prisoners by Colonel Eustis, then in command at Fortress Monroe, had won greatly upon their regard. When about to depart, Black Hawk waited upon the colonel, and said;—

Brother, I have come on my own part, and in behalf of my companions, to bid you farewell. Our great father has at length been pleased to permit us to return to our hunting grounds. We have buried the tomahawk, and the sound of the rifle will hereafter only bring death to the deer and the buffalo. Brother, you have treated the red men very kindly. Your squaws have made them presents, and you have given them plenty to eat and drink. The memory of your friendship will remain till the Great Spirit says it is time for Black Hawk to sing his death-song. Brother, your houses are as numerous as the leaves upon the trees, and your young warriors, like the sands upon the shore of the big lake that rolls before us. The red man has but few houses, and few warriors, but the red man has a heart which throbs as warmly as the heart of his white brother. The Great Spirit has given us our hunting grounds, and the skin of the deer which we kill there, is his favourite, for its colour is white, and this is the emblem of peace. This hunting dress and these feathers of the eagle are white. Accept them, my brother; I have given one like this to the White Otter. Accept of it as a memorial of Black Hawk. When he is far away this will serve to remind you of him. May the Great Spirit bless you and your children—farewell.

On the fifth of June, under the charge of Major John Garland of the United States army, Black Hawk and his five companions, took their departure from Fortress Monroe. Before leaving the Chesapeake, they visited Norfolk and the Navy Yard at Gosport. They were taken on board the *Delaware*, 74, and were much delighted with its appearance. Black Hawk expressed a strong desire to see the chief who commanded it, and to take the man who built it, by the hand.

At Norfolk a large concourse of persons visited them. Wabokieshiek, the prophet, addressed them from the balcony of their hotel, as follows:

> The Great Spirit sent us here, and now happily we are about to return, to our own Mississippi, and our own people. It affords us much happiness to rejoin our friends and kindred. We would shake hands with all our white friends assembled here. Should any of them go to our country on the Mississippi, we would take pleasure in returning their kindness to us. We will go home with peaceable dispositions towards our white brethren, and make our conduct hereafter, more satisfactory to them. We bid you all farewell, as it is the last time we shall see each other.

Black Hawk made a few remarks, and at one o'clock, June the fifth, they started for Baltimore, which place they reached at eleven o'clock on the following day, and were greeted by crowds of curious spectators. The renown of Black Hawk had every where preceded him, and all were anxious to behold the old chief whose name and deeds had excited so much commotion on the frontiers of the north west. The president happened to be in Baltimore at the same time, and, the "monumental city" was never, perhaps, honoured by the presence of two more distinguished "lions" upon the same day, than upon this occasion. They both attended the theatre on the evening of the sixth; and, it is said, that the attention of the house was very equally divided between them. On the following day an interview took place between them, when the president said to the old chief;—

> When I saw you in Washington, I told you that you had behaved very badly, in raising the tomahawk against the white people, and killing men, women and children upon the frontier. Your conduct last year, compelled me to send my warriors against you, and your people were defeated, with great loss, and your men surrendered, to be kept until I should be satisfied, that you would not try to do any more injury. I told you, I would en-

quire whether your people wished you to return, and, whether if you did return, there would be any danger to the frontier. General Clark and General Atkinson, whom you know, have informed me that Sheckak, your principal chief, and the rest of your people are anxious you should return, and Keokuk has asked me to send you back. Your chiefs have pledged themselves for your good conduct, and I have given directions that you should be taken to your own country.

Major Garland who is with you will conduct you through some of our towns. You will see the strength of the white people. You will see that our young men are as numerous, as the leaves in the woods. What can you do against us? You may kill a few women and children, but such a force would soon be sent against you, as would destroy your whole tribe. Let the red men hunt and take care of their families, but I hope they will not again raise their hands against their white brethren.

We do not wish to injure you. We desire your prosperity and improvement. But if you again plunge your knives into the breasts of our people, I shall send a force, which will severely punish you for all your cruelties. When you go back, listen to the councils of Keokuk and the other friendly chiefs. Bury the tomahawk and live in peace with the frontiers. And I pray the Great Spirit to give you a smooth path and a fair sky to return.

The reply of Black Hawk to this address, was brief, and the Prophet merely said,

My father,—my ears are open to your words. I am glad to hear them. I am glad to go back to my people. I want to see my family. I did not behave well last summer. I ought not to have taken up the tomahawk. But my people have suffered a great deal. When I get back I will remember your words. I won't go to war again. I will live in peace. I shall hold you by the hand.

The object of the president, in directing the captives to be taken home through some of the principal cities of the union, was to exhibit to them the extent of the population, wealth, and means of defence of the United States; in the hope, that such impressions would be made on their minds, as would induce them to refrain from creating disturbances in future upon the frontiers. They were accordingly directed to be carried as far north as Boston, and thence through Albany, Buffalo and Detroit, to their own country.

The captives reached Philadelphia on the 10th of June, and remained at Congress Hall, until the 14th. During their stay in the city, which was prolonged to four or five days, they visited the United States' Mint, the Fair Mount Water Works and other objects of curiosity. They had also an opportunity of witnessing a grand military display in front of their quarters in Congress Hall. Black Hawk wished to know if these were the same soldiers, who were in his country last summer. In making reference to his late contest with the United States, he said to those around him,

> My heart grew bitter against the whites, and my hands strong. I dug up the tomahawk, and led on my warriors to fight. I fought hard. I was no coward. Much blood was shed. But the white men were mighty. They were many as the leaves of the forest. I and my people failed. I am sorry the tomahawk was raised. I have been a prisoner. I see the strength of the white men. They are many, very many. The Indians are but few. They are not cowards. They are brave, but they are few. While the Great Spirit above, keeps my heart as it now is, I will be the white man's friend. I will remain in peace. I will go to my people and speak good of the white man. I will tell them, they are as the leaves of the forest. Very many—very strong; and that I will fight no more against them.

On the morning of the 14th, they set off for New York, and reached that city at 5 p.m. and had an opportunity, at the moment of their arrival at the battery, of beholding the greatest assemblage of people they had yet seen, drawn together to witness the ascent of a balloon from Castle Garden. This novel spectacle, greatly astonished the Indians, and one of them asked the prophet, if the aeronaut was "going to see the Great Spirit." When the crowd ascertained that Black Hawk and his party were on the steamboat, the air resounded with shouts of welcome. Upon their landing, such was the press of the multitude to get a look at the strangers, that they could not reach their lodgings until placed in carriages, and committed to the charge of the police officers.

They were finally, with much difficulty, taken to the Exchange Hotel, which was immediately surrounded by thousands of people, who would not retire to their houses, until "General Black Hawk," had presented himself several times at the window, and graciously bowed to the eager and admiring multitude. During their whole visit to the city of New York, they were treated with marked attention. Their rooms were crowded, daily, with ladies and gentlemen, and they were conducted with ceremony to the theatres, the public gardens, the arsenal, and other places of interest. Speeches were made to them, and they received many handsome presents. Among other civilities, John A. Graham, Esq., waited upon them, and made the following address.

Brothers, open your ears. You are brave men. You have fought like tigers, but in a bad cause. We have conquered you. We were sorry last year, that you raised the tomahawk against us; but we believe you did not know us then as you do now. We think that in time to come, you will be wise and that we shall be friends forever. You see that we are a great people—numerous as the flowers of the field, as the shells on the sea-shore, or the fish in the sea. We put one hand on the eastern, and, at the same time, the other on the western ocean. We all act together.

If some time our great men talk long and loud at our council fires, but shed one drop of white men's blood, our young warriors, as thick as the stars of the night, will leap on board of our great boats, which fly on the waves, and over the lakes—swift as the eagle in the air—then penetrate the woods, make the big guns thunder, and the whole heavens red with the flames of the dwellings of their enemies. Brothers, the president has made you a great talk. He has but one mouth. That one has sounded the sentiments of all the people. Listen to what he has said to you. Write it on your memories. It is good—very good.

Black Hawk, take these jewels, a pair of topaz earrings, beautifully set in gold, for your wife or daughter, as a token of friendship, keeping always in mind, that women and children are the favourites of the Great Spirit. These jewels are from an old man, whose head is whitened with the snows of seventy winters, an old man who has thrown down his bow, put off his sword, and now stands leaning on his staff, waiting the commands of the Great Spirit. Look around you, see all this mighty people, then go to your homes, open your arms, to receive your families.

Tell them to bury the hatchet, to make bright the chain of friendship, to love the white men, and to live in peace with them, as long as the rivers run into the sea, and the sun rises and sets. If you do so, you will be happy. You will then ensure the prosperity of unborn generations of your tribes, who will go hand in hand with the sons of the white men, and all shall be blessed by the Great Spirit. Peace and happiness by the blessing of the Great Spirit attend you. Farewell.

Black Hawk accepted the present and said in reply.

Brother, we like your talk. We will be friends. We like the white people. They are very kind to us. We shall not forget it. Your counsel is good. We shall attend to it. Your valuable present shall go to my squaw. We shall always be friends.

While at New York, Major Garland came to the determination not to take the captives to Boston, but to ascend the North River, and proceed directly to the west. This created much disappointment, among the citizens of that city, who were generally anxious to behold the "great agitator" of the north western frontier.

In pursuance of this new arrangement, on the 22nd of June, the party left New York, in a steam boat for Albany, where they arrived on the following day. At this city, they were met by a crowd of spectators, drawn together by their anxiety to see Black Hawk, so numerous, that it was found necessary to disguise the Indians, in order to enable them to reach their lodgings. They remained in Albany until the morning of the 25th, when they departed for Buffalo, which place they reached on the twenty-eighth. During their stay in Buffalo which lasted for three days, they had an interesting interview with some of the Seneca Indians, who are residing on their reservation near that place. They were addressed by Karlundawana, a worthy Seneca chief, who after expressing the pleasure of his people to meet the Sacs and Foxes, and referring to the condition of the Indians generally, respectfully counselled Black Hawk and his party, to return home in a peaceable mind; to take up the tomahawk no more against the white people; but to cultivate the earth, and be happy.

Black Hawk replied:

Our aged brother of the Senecas, who has spoken to us, has spoken the words of a good and a wise man. We are strangers to each other, though we have the same colour, and the same Great Spirit made us all, and gave us this country together. Brothers we have seen how great a people the whites are. They are very rich and very strong. It is folly for us to fight with them. We shall go home with much knowledge. For myself I shall advise my people to be quiet, and live like good men. The advice which you gave us, brother, is very good, and we tell you now we mean to walk the straight path in future, and to content ourselves with what we have, and with cultivating our lands.

From Buffalo the captives were taken by water to Detroit, where their reception is said to have been much less enthusiastic than in the other cities through which they had passed. It was stated in the newspapers of the day, that they were burnt in effigy in that place. Black Hawk, in visiting the former residence of Governor Cass, remarked, "This is the old council ground. I have had much good counsel here; but my trail led to the opposite shore, and my ears were closed." Their visit to Detroit being over, they proceeded to Green Bay, and thence descended the Wisconsin to the Mississippi and down that river to Fort Armstrong, on Rock Island, which place they reached about the first of August. In passing by the site of the old Sac village, Black Hawk was deeply affected, and expressed much regret for the causes which compelled him to emigrate beyond the Mississippi. The return of the Prophet was also attended with melancholy associations. His village over which he had long presided, was entirely broken up—his *wigwam* in ashes—his family dispersed, and, he, a suppliant for a home in the village of some other chief.

Fort Armstrong, was chosen by Major Garland as the most appropriate spot for the ceremonies of the liberation of Black Hawk and his party; as its central position, would enable him to assemble, at a short notice, many Indians from the surrounding villages. This was the favourite island of the Indians; in former years abundant in fruits and flowers; and, from time immemorial the fancied abode of a good Spirit, which watched over their village, and protected their hunting grounds. No spot could have been selected, calculated to awaken so many painful associations in the mind of Black Hawk, as Rock Island. For half a century it had been the witness of his power and influence; it was now to become the scene of his disgrace, and reluctant submission to a rival.

Immediately after Major Garland's arrival at Fort Armstrong, he sent out runners for the purpose of assembling the neighbouring Indians. The messenger despatched for Keokuk and his chiefs, found them encamped about twenty miles below the island, having just returned from a buffalo hunt, and being on their way to Fort Armstrong, in expectation of meeting the returning captives. The runner

Treaty at Fort Armstrong.

returned that night, and reported to Major Garland, that on the morrow, Keokuk with a party of braves would reach Rock Island. About noon, on the following day, the sound of the Indian drum, and the shouts and wild songs of his people, announced the approach of the princely Keokuk. He ascended the Mississippi by water, and led the van with two large canoes, lashed side by side, handsomely decorated, with a canopy erected over them, beneath which sat the chief and his three wives, with the American flag waving over them.

More than twenty canoes followed the chieftain, each containing from four to eight of his warriors, whose shouts and songs, swept over the transparent waters of the Mississippi, and were echoed from shore to shore. This fleet of canoes, was rowed slowly up the stream, until it passed the camp of the captives; it then returned and the party landed on the bank of the river, opposite to the camp of Black Hawk. Here Keokuk and his party spent several hours in arranging their dress, painting their faces and equipping themselves with their implements of war. This duty of the toilet being finished, they returned to their canoes, resumed their songs, and proceeded directly across the river. Keokuk, very elegantly dressed, decorated with his medals and fully armed, was the first to land, and turning to his followers, said, "The Great Spirit has sent our brother back. Let us shake hands with him in friendship."

He then proceeded slowly, followed by his warriors, towards Black Hawk, who was seated, with his party, in front of his temporary lodge, leaning upon his staff, and deeply affected by the occasion. Keokuk kindly extended his hand to him, which the old man took with some cordiality. Having saluted the rest of the captives, he took a seat, his companions following his example. For some time all was silence— no one presuming to utter a word until the chief had spoken. At last, Keokuk inquired of Black Hawk how long he had been upon the road; and, remarked that he had been expecting his arrival, and was coming up the river to meet him, when met by the messenger of Major Garland. The pipe was now introduced and passed round among both parties, and an interchange of friendly civilities ensued. After an hour of alternate smoking and talking, Keokuk arose and shook hands with Black Hawk, saying he should return tomorrow; and then recrossed the river in silence. A considerable part of that night was spent by the chief and his party in singing and dancing.

The grand council, for the final liberation of the captives, was held, with all due solemnity, upon the ensuing day. It presented the novel spectacle of a chief, compelled by a third power, to acknowledge the authority of a rival, and formally descend from the rank which he had long sustained among his people. Fort Armstrong presented a commodious room, for the ceremonies of the day, and it was fitted up for the occasion. About ten o'clock in the forenoon, Keokuk and one hundred followers, recrossed the river, and proceeded in martial array to the garrison. They were conducted into the council room, and shown the seats which they were to occupy. Keokuk was seated with Pashepahow (the Stabber) on one side, Wapellar (the little Prince) on the other. The former a chief of the Sacs, the latter of the Foxes. The remainder of his band took their seats in the rear, and maintained throughout the ceremony, profound silence.

It was not long before Black Hawk and his associates, made their appearance. As they entered the room, Keokuk and the two chiefs by his side, arose and greeted them. They were seated directly opposite to Keokuk. Black Hawk, and his son, Nasinewiskuk, who seems to have been warmly attached to his father, appeared to be much dejected. They had the day previous made objections to this council, as unnecessary, and painful to their feelings. They now came into it with deep feelings of mortification. For a time profound silence reigned throughout the assembly. Major Garland at length arose and addressed the council. He was pleased to find so much good feeling existing among the Sacs and Foxes towards Black Hawk and his party; and he felt confident from what he had observed, since their arrival, that they would hereafter live in peace: He had but little further to add, as the president's speech, addressed to Black Hawk and his party, in Baltimore, contained the views of their great Father on the matters before them; and, this speech he should cause to be again interpreted to them.

Keokuk followed Major Garland, and after having shaken hands with those around him said,

I have listened to the talk of our great Father. It is true we pledged our honour with those of our young braves, for the liberation of our friends. We thought much of it—our councils were long—their wives and children were in our thoughts— when we talked of them our hearts were full. Their wives and children came to see us, which made us feel like women; but we were men. The words which we sent to our great Father were good: he spoke like the father of children. The Great

Spirit made his heart big in council. We receive our brothers in friendship—our hearts are good towards them. They once listened to bad counsel; now their ears are closed: I give my hand to them; when they shake it, they shake the hands of all. I will shake hands with them, and then I am done.

Major Garland rose a second time, and stated, that he wished it to be distinctly understood by all persons present, in the council, that their Great Father, the president, would hereafter receive and acknowledge Keokuk, as the principal chief of the Sac and Fox nation; that he wished and expected Black Hawk to listen and conform to his counsels; if any unkind feeling now existed, it must that day be buried, and, that the band of Black Hawk must be henceforth merged in that of Keokuk. The interpreter so reported the remarks of Major Garland, that Black Hawk understood the president to say that he *must* conform to the counsels of Keokuk; and, the old chief, losing all command of his feelings, became deeply and instantly excited. The spirit which had sustained him in earlier and better days, burst forth with uncontrollable violence. He sprung upon his feet, but so deeply excited as to be almost unable to utter a word. With the most indignant expression of countenance, and with a vehemence of manner characteristic of the savage when roused to action, he exclaimed,

I am a man—an old man—I will not conform to the counsels of anyone. I will act for myself—no one shall govern me. I am old—my hair is gray—I once gave counsels to my young men—Am I to conform to others? I shall soon go to the Great Spirit, when I shall be at rest. What I said to our great Father at Washington, I say again—I will always listen to him. I am done.

The speech of Black Hawk—the last struggle of a fallen chieftain, caused a momentary excitement throughout the council. When it had subsided, the interpreter was directed to explain to him, that the president had only *requested* him to listen to the counsels of Keokuk. He made no reply, but drawing his blanket around him, sat in moody silence. Keokuk approached him, and in a low but kind tone of voice said, "Why do you speak so before the white men? I will speak for you; you trembled—you did not mean what you said." Black Hawk gloomily assented, when Keokuk arose and remarked to the council,

Our brother who has again come to us, has spoken, but he spoke in wrath—his tongue was forked—he spoke not like a man, a Sac. He knew his words were bad: he trembled like the oak whose roots have been wasted away by many rains. He is old—what he said let us forget. He says he did not mean it—he wishes it forgotten. I have spoken for him. What I have said are his own words—not mine. Let us say he spoke in council today—that his words were good. I have spoken.

Colonel Davenport of the United States Army, then in command of Fort Armstrong, next arose, and taking Black Hawk by the hand, remarked that he was glad to meet him, that once he was his enemy, but now he met him as a friend; that he was there by the command of the president, and should always be glad to see him; and, would at all times be ready to give him any advice which he might need: that during his absence he had held frequent talks with the Sacs and Foxes, who were anxious for his return, and he felt authorized to say, that the nation entertained for him and his party, the most friendly feeling. Black Hawk listened with much apparent interest to the remarks of Colonel Davenport.

★★★★★★

Black Hawk seems to have entertained a warm friendship for Colonel Davenport. On another occasion, speaking of this council, he said, "I here met my old friend, a great war chief, (Colonel William Davenport) whom I had known for eighteen years. He is a good and a brave chief. He always treated me well, and gave me good advice. He made a speech to me on this occasion, very different from that of the other chief. It sounded like coming from a brave." He adds, "If our great father were to make such men our agents, he would much better subserve the interests of our people, as well as his own, than in any other way; and had the war chief alluded to, been our agent, we never should have had the difficulties with the whites which we have had."

Those who have the pleasure of a personal acquaintance with Colonel Davenport will join in Black Hawk's spontaneous tribute to his character as a brave, and a gentleman of humane and noble feelings.

★★★★★★

Major Garland now arose and told Black Hawk he was at liberty to go where he pleased;—that the people of the United States, as well as himself, were pleased with the uniform good conduct of all the captives while among them—that they were convinced their hearts were good, but they had listened to bad counsels: Having now seen the power of the white men, and taken their great father by the hand, who had restored them to their families, he hoped there would be no further difficulties; but that peace and harmony would long exist between them.

Black Hawk, rose in reply, cool and collected, and remarked, that having reflected upon what he had said, it was his wish that if his speech had been put upon paper, a line might be drawn over it—he did not mean it.

Wapellar, the chief of the Foxes, rose up to say that he had nothing to say.:

I am not in the habit of talking—I think—I have been thinking all day—Keokuk has spoken: am glad to see my brothers: I will shake hands with them. I am done.

The chiefs all arose, a general shaking of hands, followed by an interchange of civilities, ensued, and the council finally adjourned.

In the evening, Major Garland invited the principal chiefs, together with Black Hawk, to his quarters, as it would afford a good opportunity to ascertain explicitly, the feeling which existed among them towards their fallen foe. About seven o'clock they arrived. They took their seats in silence, passed the pipe for all to take a whiff, and in return, quaffed a glass of champagne, which seemed to have a peculiar relish. Pashepahow, shook hands with all present, and commenced:—

We met this morning: I am glad to meet again. That wine is very good; I never drank any before; I have thought much of our meeting today: it was one that told us we were brothers:—that we were Sacs. We had just returned from a buffalo hunt, we thought it was time for our brothers to be here, as our father at St. Louis told us this was the moon. We started before the rising sun to meet you; we have met, and taken our brothers by the hand in friendship. They always mistrusted our counsels, and went from the trail of the red men, where there was no hunting grounds nor friends; they returned and found the dogs howling around their *wigwams*, and wives looking for their husbands and children.

They said we counselled like women, but they have found our counsels were good. They have been through the country of our great Father. They have been to the *wigwams* of the white men, they received them in kindness, and made glad their hearts. We thank them: say to them that Keokuk and Pashepahow thank them. Our brother has promised to listen to the counsels of Keokuk. What he said in council today, was like the Mississippi fog—the sun has shone and the day is clear—let us forget it—he did not mean it. His heart is good, but his ears have been open to bad counsels. He has taken our great Father by the hand, whose words are good. He listened to them and has closed his ears to the voice that comes across the great waters. He now knows that he ought to listen to Keokuk. He counselled with us and our young braves, who listened to his talk. We told our great Father that all would be peace.

He opened his dark prison and let him see the sun once more, gave him to his wife and children, who were without a lodge. Our great Father made straight his path to his home. I once took the great chief of the Osages prisoner. I heard the cries of his women and children; I took him out by the rising sun, and put him upon the trail to his village; "there" said I, "is the trail to your village; go and tell your people, that I, Pashepahow, the chief of the Sacs, sent you." We thank our great Father—our hearts are good towards him; I will see him before I lay down in peace: may the Great Spirit be in his councils. What our brother said today let us forget; I am done.

Keokuk, after going through the usual ceremonies, said:

We feel proud that you have invited us here this evening, to drink a glass with you; the wine which we have drank, we never tasted before; it is the wine which the white men make, who know how to make anything: I will take another glass, as I have much to say; we feel proud that we can drink such wine: today we shook hands with our brothers, who you brought to us; we were glad to see them; we have often thought of our brothers; many of our nation said they would never return: their wives and children often came to our *wigwams*, which made us feel sad: what Pashepahow has said is true; I talked to our young men, who had the hearts of men; I told them that the Great Spirit was in our councils, they promised to live in peace: those who listened to bad counsels, and followed our brothers, have said their ears are closed, they will live in peace.

I sent their words to our great Father, whose ears were open,

193

whose heart was made sad by the conduct of our brothers; he has sent them to their *wigwams*. We thank him: say to him Keokuk thanks him. Our brothers have seen the great villages of the white men: they travelled a long road and found the Americans like grass; I will tell our young men to listen to what they shall tell them. Many years ago I went through the villages of our great Father—he had many—they were like the great prairies; but he has gone; another is our father; he is a great war chief; I want to see him; I shall be proud to take him by the hand; I have heard much of him, his head is gray, I must see him: tell him that as soon as the snow is off the prairie, I shall come. What I have said I wish spoken to him, before it is put upon paper, so that he shall hear it, as I have said it: tell him that Keokuk spoke it: What our brother said in council today, let us forget; he told me to speak; I spoke his words; I have spoken.

Black Hawk then said, in a calm and dejected manner,

I feel that I am an old man; once I could speak, but now I have but little to say; today we met many of our brothers; we were glad to see them. I have listened to what my brothers have said, their hearts are good; they have been like Sacs, since I left them; they have taken care of my wife and children, who had no *wigwam*; I thank them for it, the Great Spirit knows that I thank them; before the sun gets behind the hills tomorrow, I shall see them; I want to see them; when I left them, I expected soon to return; I told our great father when in Washington, that I would listen to the counsels of Keokuk. I shall soon be far away, I shall have no village, no band; I shall live alone. What I said in council today, I wish forgotten. If it has been put upon paper, I wish a mark to be drawn over it. I did not mean it. Now we are alone let us say, we will forget it. Say to our great father and Governor Cass, that I will listen to them.

Many years ago I met Governor Cass in councils, far across the prairies to the rising sun. His counsels were good. My ears were closed; I listened to the great father across the waters. My father listened to him whose band was large.—My band was once large. Now I have no band. I and my son and all the party, thank our great father for what he has done. He is old, I am old; we shall soon go to the great Spirit, where we shall rest. He sent us through his great villages. We saw many of the white men, who

194

treated us with kindness. We thank them. We thank you and Mr. Sprague for coming with us.

Your road was long and crooked. We never saw so many white men before. When you were with us, we felt as though we had some friends among them. We felt safe. You knew them all. When you come upon the Mississippi again, you shall come to my *wigwam*. I have none now. On your road home, you will pass where my village once was. No one lives there now; all are gone. I give you my hand; we may never meet again; I shall long remember you: The Great Spirit will be with you, and your wives and children. Before the sun rises, I shall go to my family. My son will be here to see you before we go. I will shake hands with my brothers here, then I am done.

Early on the following morning, the Indians crossed to the west side of the Mississippi, and returned to their villages.

In the autumn of 1837, deputations from several Indian tribes, residing upon the waters of the upper Mississippi, were invited to Washington city, by direction of the President of the United States. Among those represented were the united Sac and Fox tribe, and their ancient enemy the Sioux, between whom hostilities were then raging. For the purpose of effecting a peace between them, and also making a purchase of land of the Sioux, several councils were held under the direction of the Secretary at War, but without accomplishing the object in either case. Black Hawk, was connected with the delegation from the Sacs and Foxes, but not in the character of a delegate or chief. Keokuk, apprehensive, that if left at home, the old man might create some new difficulty, had prudently taken him along. He treated him, uniformly, with great respect, and invited him to sit with them in the councils.

After leaving Washington the delegation visited the principal eastern cities, and Black Hawk again attracted much attention. Public curiosity was still alive to see the renowned but fallen chieftain of the famous Black Hawk war. In Boston, which place he did not visit on his former tour, he was waited upon by a great concourse of citizens, and in common with the rest of the delegation, was publicly presented with some military weapons by the governor of the state, and made a brief speech upon the occasion.

Before the return of the deputation to the west, they remained a few hours in Cincinnati. Keokuk was sick and received but few visitors. "Which is Black Hawk," was the eager inquiry of almost every individual who succeeded in threading his way through the crowd, to the cabin of the steam boat. The old man manifested no interest in the passing scene. He was not inclined to conversation, but sat moody and silent, with an expression of countenance strongly indicative of wounded pride and disappointed ambition. He seemed to feel deeply the degradation of his situation. Shorn of power among his people, compelled to acknowledge the authority of his rival, and bending beneath the infirmities of age, it is not singular that he should shrink from the prying gaze of curiosity, and sigh for the deep seclusion of his wild hunting grounds.

In height Black Hawk is about five feet ten inches, with broad shoulders, but limbs not very muscular. His nose is sharp and slightly aquiline, and his eyes are of a dark hazel colour. The most striking peculiarity in his personal appearance is the head, which is singularly formed, and has been pronounced, by some observers, the envy of phrenologists. His countenance is mild and benevolent, having little if any of that dark and ferocious expression, not uncommon among the Indians; and which, during the late border war, was imagined to be eminently characteristic of Black Hawk. In tracing his history, few, if any incidents can be found, which bear out the charge of savage cruelty that has sometimes been preferred against him.

On the contrary, he seems to have an amiable disposition. He himself repels, with indignation, the charge of his ever having murdered women and children; and, declares the accusation made against him, on this point, to be wholly false. The character of Black Hawk for honesty in his dealings, and for general integrity, stands fair. In his domestic relations he appears to be kind and affectionate, and in one particular, is an exception to the chiefs and warriors of his tribe. He has never had but *one* wife. After his return from the campaign on the lakes, during the war with England, his first act was to visit his family.

> I then started to visit my wife and children. I found them well and my boys were growing finely. It is not customary for us to say much about our women, as they generally perform their part cheerfully, and never interfere with business belonging to the men. This is the only wife I ever had, or will ever have. She is a good woman and teaches my boys to be brave.

It is said, however, and upon pretty good authority, that on a certain occasion, Black Hawk's vow of exclusive devotion to *one* wife, had well nigh been broken. While visiting a respectable frontier settler, many years since, he became pleased with the comely daughter of his host; and having seriously contemplated the matter, decided in favour of the expediency of adding the pale faced beauty, to the domestic circle of his *wigwam*. He accordingly expressed his wishes to the father of the young lady, and proposed to give him a horse, in exchange for his daughter, but to his surprise the offer was declined. Some days afterwards he returned and tendered two fine horses, but still the father refused to make the arrangement. The old chief's love for the young lady, growing stronger, in proportion to the difficulty of gaining her father's assent, he, subsequently, offered five or six horses for her. But even this munificent price was rejected by the mercenary father. Black Hawk now gave up the negotiation, not a little surprised, at the high value which the white men place upon their daughters.

It is questionable whether Black Hawk possesses any marked military talents, although during his contest with the United States, it was common to represent him as an able warrior, who by the eloquence and fluency of his harangues, commanded the unlimited confidence of his band. He has, most probably, been overrated both for his eloquence and his skill in the battlefield. He is no doubt a man of courage, and seems, from early life, to have had a strong predisposition for war. Many of his measures as a leader, have been more influenced by a sense of what was right in the abstract, than expedient in practice. This circumstance has often placed him in situations, inimical to the permanent prosperity of his people.

Black Hawk never made any claims to the office of a peace chief. Even as a war chief, he was not recognised by all the tribe to which he belonged. A fragment of the Sacs and Foxes, however, followed his banner for more than twenty years, and acknowledged him in that capacity: and, over them, he certainly exercised, from their confidence in his judgment, his warlike talent, or some other cause, no small amount of influence. His age and kindness of disposition, probably, strengthened their attachment to him. In the campaign of 1832, although terminating in the defeat of Black Hawk, and the almost entire annihilation of his band, his military reputation did not suffer much, if the circumstances under which he was placed, be recollected.

During the operations of that period, General Atkinson estimated the warriors of Black Hawk at seven or eight hundred, but the better opinion is that it did not, at any time, exceed five hundred; and several persons, who had favourable opportunities for judging, place the estimate still lower. The commander of the United States troops, had with him, in the pursuit of Black Hawk, twenty seven hundred men, all of them well armed and most of them well mounted. This was independent of the militia in the different military posts and fortified stations. The entire number of the American forces, engaged in the campaign, is supposed to have approached to three thousand, five hundred.

Black Hawk was encumbered with the wives and children, the household property and travelling equipage of his whole band; and from the time of his recrossing the Mississippi to the Battle of the Bad-Axe, was constantly in want of provisions. Indeed, in the month of July, many of his party actually starved to death. Under such circumstances, the wonder is not, that he was finally defeated and captured, but that it should have required a campaign of three months in which to accomplish that object. The defeat of Stillman and the attack upon the fort at Buffalo Grove, may be claimed by Black Hawk and his band, to have been as honourable to their arms, as were the victories of the Wisconsin and the Bad-Axe to those of the United States.

But whatever may be the ultimate opinion in regard to him, either as a warrior or a man, his career for good and for evil, is now ended. The war-banner has passed from his hand—his seat in the council-house is vacant—the fire of his lodge is nearly extinguished: the autumn of life is upon him—and, in a little while the autumn leaves will rustle over the lone grave of Black Hawk.

CHAPTER 9

His Death and Burial

Since the three first editions of this work were published, the death of Black Hawk has occurred; and a few additional particulars of his life have been collected. These, it is proposed to embody in a new chapter.

In the course of the preceding pages, the difficulty of procuring full, and always exact information, in regard to the lives of a people having neither records nor historians, has been alluded to. This difficulty will be encountered by any one who may attempt to chronicle the annals of the aborigines in their aggregate condition, or to portray their individual history. In the compilation of this volume, much pains were taken to obtain all the prominent events in the life of Black Hawk, and, it is supposed, as much success attended the effort, as is usual in similar cases. Since its publication, however, it appears that all his military movements have not been narrated, and we proceed to supply the omission.

In chapter 3 of this volume, it is stated that Black Hawk was only in two engagements in the late war with Great Britain, and that the last of these was the assault upon Fort Stephenson, in August 1813, then under the command of Major Groghan. It is true that he and his band were with the British Army in the attack upon this post, but his connection with that army did not cease until after the capture of Fort Erie. The authority for this fact is to be found in the *Book of the Indians*. The author of that work, in narrating the incidents of Black Hawk's return to the north-west, in 1833, after his imprisonment at Fortress Monroe, says:

Having arrived at Buffalo, on Friday the 28th of June, they (the party returning with the old warrior) remained there until Sunday morning. The day after their arrival, they rode over to Black

Rock, where they viewed the union of the grand canal with the lake at that place. From this point they had a full view of the Canada shore, and Black Hawk immediately pointed out Fort Erie, and seemed well acquainted with the adjacent country; he having been there in the time of the last war with England, in the British service; and at the time 'when the Americans walked into Fort Erie,' as he expressed the capture of it.

Of the extent of his participation in the events attendant upon this capture, there is no satisfactory information.

Black Hawk was likewise in the Battle of the Thames, a fact not previously stated in this work, and which is now given on the authority of a writer in the Baltimore American, to whose respectability the editor of that paper bears testimony. We have, indeed, no reason to doubt the accuracy of this statement, which will be read with the more interest, from the circumstance that it embraces Black Hawk's account of the death of Tecumthe in regard to which much has been written and published. It is not proposed, on the present occasion, to compare the relation given by Black Hawk, of the fall of Tecumthe, with the testimony of others who have appeared as historians of this event, but shall content ourselves with simply quoting the article to which reference has been made. The writer professes to have been intimately acquainted with Black Hawk, and in the brief sketch which he has presented of the life of this warrior, we find corroborating evidence of the truth of many of the traits of character, which, in the course of this volume, has been assigned to him both as a man and a warrior. The article is in these words:

Messrs. Editors—Hearing of the death of the celebrated Sauk chieftain, Black Hawk, I am induced to make you the following communication, which may be interesting to some of your readers.

During a residence of several years in what is now the Territory of Iowa, I had many opportunities of seeing and conversing with this noted warrior, and often look back with feelings of great pleasure to the many tokens of good will and friendship that he has frequently bestowed upon me. His lodge was always open to a stranger, and he was ever ready to share that with him which he might most want, either his furs and blankets for a couch, or his corn and venison for a repast. He always spoke in terms of high regard of the whites, saying, that in war he fought like a brave man, but in peace he wished to forget that his hand had ever been raised against them. His career as a warrior commenced at a very early age; when he was but fourteen years old, his father, Pawheese, led a war party against the Osages, in which expedition he accompanied him. They succeeded in reaching the village of Osages, which they attacked, and after a very severe encounter, they routed their enemies and burnt their town.

In this battle Black Hawk's father was killed, but he revenged his death by killing and scalping the Osage who had slain him. He was fond of recounting his earlier exploits, and often boasted of his being at the right hand of Tecumthe, when the latter was killed at the Battle of the Thames. His account of the death of this distinguished warrior, was related to me by himself, during an evening that I spent in his lodge some winters ago. In the course of our talk, I asked him if he was with Tecumthe when he was killed. He replied—

'I was, and I will now tell you all about it.—Tecumthe, Shaubinne, and Caldwell, two Potawattimie chiefs, and myself, were seated on a log near our camp fire, filling our pipes for a smoke, on the morning of the battle, when word came from the British general, that he wished to speak with Tecumthe. He went immediately, and after staying some time rejoined us, taking his seat without saying a word, when Caldwell, who was one of his favorites, observed to him, 'my father, what are we to do? Shall we fight the Americans?'

'Yes, my son,' replied Tecumthe, '*We shall go into their very smoke*—but you are now wanted by the general. Go, my son, I never expect to see you again.' Shortly after this, (continued Black Hawk,) the Indian spies came in, and gave word of the near approach of the Americans. Tecumthe immediately posted his men in the edge of a swamp, which flanked the British line, placing himself at their head. I was a little to his right, with a small party of Sauks. It was not long before the Americans made their appearance; they did not perceive us at first, hid as we were by the undergrowth, but we soon let them know where we were by pouring in one or two volleys as they were forming into a line to oppose the British.

They faltered a little, but very soon we perceived a large body of horse (Colonel Johnson's regiment of mounted Kentuckians) preparing to charge upon us in the swamp. They came bravely on, yet we never stirred until they were so close that we could see the flints in their guns, when Tecumthe springing to his feet, gave the Shawnee war cry, and discharged his rifle. This was the signal for us to commence the fight; but it did not last long; the Americans answered the shout, returning our fire, and at the first discharge of their guns, I saw Tecumthe stagger forwards over a fallen tree near which he was standing, letting his rifle drop at his feet.

As soon as the Indians discovered he was killed, a sudden fear came over them, and thinking that the Great Spirit was displeased, they fought no longer, and were quickly put to flight. That night we returned to bury our dead, and search for the body of Tecumthe. He was found lying where he had first fallen; a bullet had struck him above the hip, and his skull had been broken by the butt end of the gun of some soldier, who had found him, perhaps, when life was not yet quite gone.

With the exception of these wounds, his body was untouched; lying near him, however, was a large, fine looking Potawattimie, who had been killed, decked off in his plumes and war paint, whom the Americans no doubt had taken for Tecumthe; for he was scalped, and every particle of skin flayed from his body. Tecumthe himself, had no ornaments about his person save a British medal. During the night we buried our dead, and brought off the body of Tecumthe, although we were within sight of the fires of the American camp.'

This is somewhat different from the account which is commonly given of Tecumthe's death, yet I believe it to be true; for after hearing Black Hawk relate it, I heard it corroborated by one of the Potawattimie chiefs, mentioned by him. I asked him if he had ever fought against the whites after the death of Tecumthe. He said not—that he returned home to his village on the Mississippi, at the mouth of Rock River, and there he remained until driven away by the whites, in the year 1832. The wish to hold possession of this village, was the cause of the war which he waged against the whites during that year.

He told me that he never wished to fight; that he was made to do so; that the whites killed his warriors when they went with a white flag to beg a *parley*, and that after this was done, he thought they intended to kill him at all events, and therefore he would die like a warrior.

In speaking of his defeat, he said it was what he expected; that he did not mind it; but what hurt him more than any thing else, was our government degrading him in the eyes of his own people, and setting another chief (Keokuk) over him. This degradation he appeared to feel very sensibly, still he continued to possess all his native pride. One instance that came under my observation, I recollect well, in which it was strongly displayed. He happened to be in a small town in Iowa, on the same day in which a party of dragoons, under Captain —— arrived: and in paying a visit to a friend with whom he always partook of a meal, whenever he stopped at the village, he met with the captain, who had been invited to dine.

 Black Hawk remained, also expecting the usual invitation to stay and eat with them: but when the dinner was ready, the host took him aside, and told him the captain, or rather the white man's chief, was to dine with him that day, and he must wait until they had finished. The old chief's eye glistened with anger as he answered him, raising the fore-finger of one hand to his breast, to represent the officer, 'I know the white man is a chief, but *I*,' elevating the finger of the other hand far above his head, 'was a chief, and led my warriors to the fight, long before his mother knew him. *Your meat,—my dogs should not eat it!*' Saying this, he gathered the folds of his blanket about him, and stalked off, looking as proudly as if he still walked over ground that he could call '*my own.*'

Black Hawk possessed, to a great degree, one fine trait which it is not usual for us to concede to the Indian—kindness and affection for his wife. He never had but one, and with her he lived for upwards of forty years; they had several children, three of whom still survive, two sons and a daughter. The eldest son is, (as at time of first publication), now one of the most promising young braves of the nation, and bids fair to be one of its most noble men. The daughter is still quite young, and is considered to be the most beautiful maiden belonging to her tribe.

He has now departed on his long journey, to join those of his people who have gone before him to their happy hunting grounds, far beyond the setting sun. May the Great Spirit grant him a clear sunshine, and a smooth path.

For the particulars, given below, of the last days and death of Black Hawk, we are indebted to a highly respectable gentleman, W. Henry Starr, Esq. of Burlington, Iowa Territory. His communication, under date of March 21st, 1839, is given entire, that the interest of the narrative may be preserved.

Your letter of the 2nd of January came to hand in due course of mail, in which you make some enquiries concerning the old chief of the Sac and Fox tribes—the venerable Black Hawk. I should have replied to it sooner, could I have done so satisfactorily either to you or myself. I knew much by report of the old chief, and something from personal acquaintance; but my knowledge was not so accurate as to be serviceable to a faithful biographer. I have, therefore, taken sometime to make the necessary enquiries, and satisfy myself of their accuracy.

After Black Hawk's last return from the eastern states, he passed the winter of 1837-8 in the county of Lee, in the south-eastern portion of this territory, on a small stream called Devil Creek. The white settlements extended for forty miles west of him, and the tribe to which he belonged, with the exception of a few old braves, and his family, resided on the frontier. From his tribe he was isolated in position and feeling. His family consisted of a wife, two sons, Nasheaskuk and Samesett, (as they are pronounced here,) a daughter and her husband. They passed their time principally in hunting deer, wild turkeys, and the prairie hen, which are abundant in that quarter of the territory. For hunting, Black Hawk is said to have displayed no fondness; but chose to spend his time in improving his place of residence, and exercising his ingenuity with mechanic tools. In the spring of 1838, they removed to the frontier, and settled upon the Des Moines River, about eighty or ninety miles from its mouth, near to a trading post, and in the immediate vicinity of the villages of the other chiefs of the tribe. Here he had a very comfortable bark cabin, which he furnished in imitation of the whites, with chairs, a table, a mirror, and mattrasses. His dress was that of the other chiefs, with the exception of a broad-brimmed black hat, which he usually wore. In the summer he cultivated a few acres of land in corn, melons, and various kinds of vegetables. He was frequently visited by the whites, and I have often heard his hospitality highly commended.

On the 4th of July last, he was present at Fort Madison, in Lee county, by special invitation, and was the most conspicuous guest of the citizens assembled in commemoration of that day. Among the toasts called forth by the occasion was the following:

'*Our illustrious guest, Black Hawk.*—May his declining years be as calm and serene as his previous life has been boisterous and full of warlike incidents. His attachment and present friendship to his white brethren, fully entitle him to a seat at our festive board.'

So soon as this sentiment was drank, Black Hawk arose and delivered the following speech, which was taken down at the time by two interpreters, and by them furnished for publication.

'It has pleased the Great Spirit that I am here today—I have eaten with my white friends. The earth is our mother—we are now on it—with the Great Spirit above us—It is good. I hope we are all friends here. A few winters ago I was fighting against you—I did wrong, perhaps; but that is past—it is buried—let it be forgotten.

'Rock River was a beautiful country—I liked my towns, my cornfields, and the home of my people. I fought for it. It is now yours—keep it as we did—it will produce you good crops.

'I thank the Great Spirit that I am now friendly with my white brethren—we are here together—we have eaten together—we are friends—it is his wish and mine. I thank you for your friendship.

'I was once a great warrior—I am now poor. Keokuk has been the cause of my present situation—but do not attach blame to him. I am now old. I have looked upon the Mississippi since I have been a child. I love the Great River. I have dwelt upon its banks from the time I was an infant. I look upon it now. I shake hands with you, and as it is my wish, I hope you are my friends.'

In the course of the day he was prevailed upon to drink several times, and became somewhat intoxicated, an uncommon circumstance, as he was generally temperate.

In the autumn of 1838, he was at the house of an Indian trader, in the vicinity of Burlington, when I became acquainted and frequently conversed with him, in broken English, and through the medium of gestures and pantomime. A deep seated melancholy was apparent in his countenance and conversation. He endeavoured to make me comprehend, on one occasion, his former greatness; and represented that he was once master of the country, east, north, and south of us—that he had been a very successful warrior,—called himself, smiting his breast, 'big Captain Black Hawk,' *'nesso Kaskaskias,'* (killed the Kaskaskias,) *'nesso Sioux a heap,'* (killed a great number of Sioux.) He then adverted to the ingratitude of his tribe, in permitting Keokuk to supersede him, who, he averred, excelled him in nothing but drinking whiskey.

Toward Keokuk he felt the most unrelenting hatred. Keokuk was, however, beyond his influence, being recognised as chief of the tribe, by the government of the United States. He unquestionably possesses talents of the first order, excels as an orator, but his authority will probably be short-lived on account of his dissipation, and his profligacy in spending the money paid him for the benefit of his tribe; and which he squanders upon himself and a few favourites, through whose influence he seeks to maintain his authority.

You enquire if Black Hawk was at the Battle of the Thames? On one occasion I mentioned Tecumthe to him, and he expressed the greatest joy that I had heard of him: and pointing away to the east, and making a feint, as if aiming a gun, said, *'Chemokaman* (white man) *nesso,'* (kill.) From which I had no doubt of his being personally acquainted with Tecumthe; and I have been since informed, on good authority, that he was in the battle of the Thames and in several other engagements with that distinguished chief.

Soon after this interview with Black Hawk, he set out for the frontier, where a payment was soon to be made to the tribe, of a portion of their annuity.

The weather was both hot and wet, and it is supposed, that, on this journey, he imbibed the seeds of the disease which soon after terminated his existence. This journey was in September. Early in October, the commissioner for adjusting claims with the Sac and Fox tribes, was to meet them at Rock Island, and most of the Indians were there on the first of that month. Black Hawk was taken sick and was unable to accompany them. A violent bilious fever had seized upon him, and on the 3rd of October, after an illness of seven days, he died. His only medical attendant was one of the tribe, who knew something of vegetable antidotes, and was called doctor. His wife, who was devotedly attached to him, mourned deeply during his illness. She seemed to have had a presentiment of his approaching death, and said, some days before it occurred, 'he is getting old—he must die—Monotah calls him home.'

After his death, he was dressed in the uniform presented to him at Washington, by the president or Secretary at War, and placed upon a rude bier, consisting of two poles with bark laid across, on which he was carried by four of his braves to the place of interment, followed by his family and about fifty of the tribe, (the chiefs being all absent.) They seemed deeply affected, and mourned in their usual way, shaking hands, and muttering in guttural tones, prayers to Monotah (their deity) for his safe passage to the land prepared for the reception of all Indians. The grave was six feet deep and of the usual length, situated upon a little eminence about fifty yards from his *wigwam*.

The body was placed in the middle of the grave, in a sitting posture, upon a seat, constructed for the purpose. On his left side the cane given him, as I am informed, by Mr. Henry Clay, was placed upright, with his right hand resting upon it. Many of the old warrior's trophies were placed in the grave, and some Indian garments, together with his favourite weapons. The grave was then covered with plank, and a mound of earth, several feet in height, was thrown up over it, and the whole enclosed with pickets twelve feet in height. At the head of the grave a flag staff was placed, bearing our national banner; and at the foot there stands a post, on which is inscribed, in Indian characters, his age. I do not know the exact age of Black Hawk, but understood from him, that he was seventy-two. His virtues commanded the respect of all the whites who knew him. He possessed much magnanimity of soul, and under all the mortifications to which he has been subjected, and the insults that have been heaped upon him by his tribe, and especially by the haughty Keokuk, he maintained, until the last years of his life, a uniform cheerfulness and resignation of mind, which bespoke a conscious superiority.

★★★★★★

With this sketch of the last days of Black Hawk, our narrative of his life is closed. After an eventful and restless career of "three score and ten years," this celebrated Sac has been "gathered to his fathers." His name cannot be forgotten, for his deeds are a part of the history of this country. If not distinguished for a high order of talent, or renowned for great warlike achievements, he has not often been surpassed in the history of his race, for those less dazzling virtues, humanity, courage, and love of country.

> He was an Indian who had a sense of honour, as well as policy; a man in whom those who know him confided. (Colonel Whittlesey, of the Geological Corps of Ohio.)

In the last speech which he made in the last year of his life, in alluding to his difficulties with the whites, he says, "Rock River was a beautiful country—I liked my towns, my cornfields, and the home of my people;—I fought for it,"—a declaration as creditable to the heart of the speaker, as it is important to a just estimate of his conduct, in resisting the removal of his tribe from their native land. The love of country is not confined to civilized life, but swells the heart and nerves the arm of the untutored man of the woods. "I liked my towns, my cornfields, and the home of my people;—I fought for it," should be inscribed over the humble grave of Black Hawk.

★★★★★★

Note.—Since writing that portion of the foregoing narrative which treats of the causes of the late war with the Sacs and Foxes, the following article, from the able pen of judge Hall, has met our observation. It was published in the *Western Monthly Magazine* in 1833, one year after the termination of that conflict. The writer was then a resident of Illinois, and intimately acquainted with the relations existing between the whites and Indians. His remarks are valuable. They embrace a graphic description of the region inhabited by the Sacs and Foxes, and fully sustain the position which we have taken in this volume, that the "Black Hawk War" was the result of unprovoked aggressions made by the American people upon the Indians.

> I have just returned from a delightful voyage. I have explored a portion of the exquisitely beautiful shores of the upper Mississippi; and am ready to confess that until now, I had little idea of the extent, the grandeur, or the resources of the west. The world cannot produce such another country as this great valley of ours. Yet to understand its value, one must ascend the Mississippi and the Illinois, and see the noble prairies of the two states which are destined to eclipse all others. I cannot convey to you in adequate language, my admiration of this attractive

region. The traveller who visits the western country, and fancies he has acquired *any* knowledge of it—I say *any*, by simply tracing the meanders of the Ohio, or spending weeks, or years, if you please, at Cincinnati or Louisville, is very much mistaken. There is much to admire in western Pennsylvania and Virginia; Kentucky and Ohio are full of attraction; but the man who is really an admirer of nature, and would witness the most splendid exhibitions of the creative power, must go to Illinois and Missouri.

I visited this region for the first time four years ago, while the Sacs and Foxes were at peace with the whites, and before Black Hawk had got to be a great man. They were friendly and well-disposed, and the white people residing near them, would almost as soon have distrusted or disturbed each other, as those peaceful red men. I took great interest in noticing their dwellings, and remarking their deportment, as it was the first occasion I had ever enjoyed of seeing the savage in his own wild home. I had embarked on board a steamboat at St. Louis, intending to take a pleasant excursion to the falls of St. Anthony. The weather was very delightful, only a little too warm; and the river was unfortunately so low, that on arriving at the *Des Moines* rapids, we found it difficult to ascend them, and above that point, our progress was continually impeded by the difficulty of the navigation.

This circumstance, though vexatious to such of the passengers as had business ahead, or families at home, was not disagreeable to one who, like myself, travelled only for amusement, as it afforded opportunities of exploring the romantic shores. We spent a day at the Lower Rapids, and I have seldom seen a more attractive country. The land is high on both sides, and rises gradually in beautiful swells. I saw hundreds of acres covered with the native buckeye, the most beautiful tree of the forest—if, indeed, any can be entitled to that distinction among so great a variety of noble and majestic trees. Beneath, was a rich undergrowth of wild gooseberry bushes.

Add to these the beautiful creeper, and the wild honeysuckle, which were occasionally seen, and it is impossible to imagine a vegetation more splendidly luxuriant and ornamental. The whole country is based on rock, and the springs which burst out from the hill sides are clear as crystal and delightfully cold.

The shores of the river are plentifully strewed with crystallizations and petrifactions. We picked up some fine specimens of cornelian, and saw a vast number of geodes of every size, from one inch in diameter to fifteen.

It was Sunday. Have you ever experienced the singular and pleasing associations connected with a Sabbath passed in the wilderness? I have often enjoyed these feelings, but never felt them with such force as on this day. It was calm and sultry. The brilliant sunbeams were brightly reflected from the broad bosom of the Mississippi, and the deep green outline of the forest was splendidly illumined, while the deep shadows underneath the foliage afforded an attractive appearance of coolness and seclusion. The passengers and crew were scattered about singly or in small parties, so that when I wandered but a small distance from the vessel, and seated myself on a hill which commanded a view of the river and its banks, I found myself perfectly alone. Not a living object was visible, not a sound was heard, not a leaf or a limb stirred.

How different from the streets of a city upon a Sabbath morn, when crowds of well-dressed persons are seen moving in every direction; when the cheerful bells are sounding, and the beautiful smiling children are hurrying in troops to Sunday school! Here I was in solitude. I saw not the labourer resting from toil, nor the smile of infancy, nor the Christian bowing before his God; but Nature proclaimed a Sabbath by the silence that reigned abroad, and the splendour with which she had adorned her works.

It is natural that these recollections of my first visit to the frontier should mingle with the observations made in my recent tour through the same scenes; I shall therefore not attempt to separate the remarks made on either occasion, but give some of the results of both voyages.

I can scarcely describe the sensations with which I first saw the solitary lodge of an Indian hunter, on the shore of the Mississippi. In my childhood I had read with thrilling interest, the tales of border warfare; but I had not learned to hate an Indian with mortal hatred. I verily believe they have souls. People may think differently in certain places, which shall be nameless, but I cannot be persuaded to the contrary. You cannot imagine any thing more frail than an Indian *wigwam*—a mere shelter of poles and mats, so small, so apparently inadequate to any purpose of security or comfort, that it is hardly possible to believe it to be intended for the residence of human beings.

In such habitations reside the Indian warrior, whose name is a terror to his enemies; and the dark maiden, whose story supplies the poet with rich materials, with which to embellish the page of fiction. In such wretched hovels reside the aboriginal lords of the soil.

I *have* seen in this region, evidences of persecution perpetrated by our people upon this unhappy race, such as the American people would scarcely believe; and I am satisfied that if the events of the late war could be traced to their true source, every real philanthropist in the nation would blush for his country.

★★★★★★

I could relate many anecdotes, to show the friendly feelings entertained towards our government and people by the Sacs— feelings which, whether of fear or of kindness, have rendered them wholly submissive, and which nothing but the most un-provoked aggression on our side, could have kindled into hostility. I will only, at this time, repeat one, which occurred during my first voyage, reserving others for a future letter.

One day, when the boat stopped to take in wood, some of us strolled up to the house of a Mr. D., a respectable farmer from Pennsylvania. He had been living here several years, at a spot distant from any settlements, and without a single neighbour. Upon our inquiring whether he felt no alarm in residing thus alone in the vicinity of the Indians, he replied that his family had formerly experienced much uneasiness, but that they had long since become satisfied that there was no ground for apprehension. He was convinced that the Sacs, their nearest neighbours, so far from being disposed to injure the whites, were cautious and timid of giving offence. In support of this opinion, he related the following anecdote.

His house stands on a high bank of the Mississippi, and the family were one day much alarmed by discovering a large number of Indians passing up the river in canoes. They passed along in a most disorderly manner, some paddling their little vessels, and others strolling along the shore, but the majority evidently intoxicated. It was the latter circumstance which caused alarm. The Indians had been to St. Louis to receive their annuities, and had procured a sufficient supply of whisky to render them unsafe visitors. They continued, however, straggling along in larger or smaller parties all day, without stopping. At night, one of them, a young warrior of prepossessing appearance, came to the house, and in the most respectful manner, asked permission to sleep upon the floor of the cabin. Mr. D., although by no means pleased with his guest, knew not how to refuse.

The Indian warrior was invited to supper. A plentiful meal, such as composed the ordinary repast of the family, was placed before him, and having satisfied his hunger, he wrapped himself in his blanket, threw himself on the floor before the fire, and went to sleep. In the course of the night, Mr. D. happening to go out, discovered some Indians lying in the bushes not far from the house; without disturbing them, he proceeded in a different direction, where he found another party; they were strewed, in short, entirely around his dwelling. The fact of being thus surrounded, the concealment, and the silence of the Indians, all conspired to awaken suspicion, and he passed the night in no small degree of uneasiness.

He rose early in the morning; his Indian guest also started up, gathered his blanket around him, and took leave; first, however, explaining to Mr. D. that he belonged to a party of Sacs who were returning from St. Louis, and that many of them being intoxicated, it had been thought proper to station a guard round Mr. D.'s house, to protect him and his property from injury. He added, that if any depredation should be discovered to have been committed by the Indians, the chiefs would pay Mr. D. the full amount. Such an example of the care taken by the chiefs of this tribe to avoid giving umbrage to the whites, affords the highest testimony, either of their friendship for our people, or their respect for our power.

The Sac and Fox tribe inhabited, at that time, a beautiful tract of country in Illinois, upon the borders of Rock River. These two tribes are usually mentioned in conjunction; because the Foxes, many years ago, having been nearly exterminated in a war with some of their neighbours, the remnant of the nation, too feeble to exist as a separate tribe, sought refuge in the Sac villages, and have remained ever since incorporated with the latter people. They are a fine looking race of people, and are well disposed towards the whites. They have long been divided, however, into two parties, one of which is friendly towards our government, while the other, called the *British band*, is under the influence of the British traders.

It has always been the policy of the latter, to keep the Indians upon the western frontier in a state of disaffection towards the American people, and by these means, to secure to themselves an undue proportion of the fur trade. So long as it should remain difficult upon our part to gain access to the tribes, and our intercourse with them be liable to interruption, jealousy, and distrust, so long would the British trader possess an advantage over us in relation to this traffic. The British fur companies, whose agents are numerous, intelligent, and enterprising, have always acted upon this policy, and the English officers in Canada, both civil and military, have given it their sanction.

Almost all the atrocities which have been committed on our frontiers by the Indians, within the last fifty years, have been directly or indirectly incited by the incendiary agents of that mercenary government. The *British band* of the Sacs and Foxes have been in the habit of visiting Malden annually, and receiving valuable presents—presents, which being made to a disaffected portion of a tribe residing not only within the United States, but within the limits of a state, could be viewed in no other light than as bribes,—the wages of disaffection. Black Hawk, though not a chief, is one of the most influential individuals of the *British band*.

★★★★★★

In a late number of the *American Museum,* we find the following article. It bears intrinsic evidence of coming from the same pen, and presents in a striking point of view the rapid extension of our settlements, and the consequent recession of the Indians.

Most of our readers have become familiarly acquainted with the name of the redoubted Black Hawk, whose adventures are detailed in this volume and whose fame has been spread from Maine to Florida. There was a time when he shared the eager attention of the public with Fanny Kemble and the cholera, and was one of the lions of the day; and as regularly talked about as the weather, the last new novel, or the candidates for the presidency. The war in Illinois, though of brief duration, and not marked by any stirring events, came suddenly upon us after a long series of peaceful years upon the north-western border. The savages, weary of fruitless conflicts, or quelled by the superior

213

numbers of a gigantic and growing foe, seemed to have submitted to their fate, and the pioneer had ceased to number the war-whoop among the inquietudes of the border life.

The plains of Illinois and Missouri were rapidly becoming peopled by civilized men. A race less hardy than the backwoodsmen were tempted by the calm to migrate to those delightful solitudes, that bloomed with more than Arcadian fascinations of fruitfulness and beauty. The smoke of the settler's cabin began to ascend from the margin of every stream in that wide region, and the cattle strayed through rich pastures, of which the buffalo, the elk, and the deer, had long enjoyed a monopoly—an unchartered monopoly—wondering, no doubt, at their good luck in having their lives cast in such pleasant places.

It was the writer's lot to ramble over that beautiful country while these interesting scenes were presented; while the wilderness still glowed in its pristine luxuriance: while the prairie-grass and the wild flowers still covered the plain, and the deer continued to frequent his ancient haunts, and while the habitations of the new settlers were so widely and so thinly scattered, that the nearest neighbours could scarcely have exchanged the courtesy of an annual visit without the aid of the seven-leagued boots of ancient story. But though in solitude, they lived without fear. There were none to molest nor make them afraid. If they had few friends, they had no enemies. If the Indian halted at the settler's door, it was to solicit hospitality, not to offer violence.

But more frequently he stalked silently by, timid of giving offence to the white man, whom he doubtless regarded as an intruder upon his own ancient heritage, but whose possession he had been taught to respect, because he had ever found it guarded by a strong and swift arm, that had never failed to repay aggression with ten-fold vengeance. Suddenly, however, a change came over this cheering scene. The misconduct of a few white men disturbed the harmony of a wide region. The Indians were oppressed and insulted to the last point of forbearance, and a small but restless band, regarded as insubordinate and troublesome even by their own nation, seized upon the occasion to rush to war.

It is wonderful to look back upon this eventful history. The country over which Black Hawk, with a handful of followers, badly armed, and destitute of stores or munitions of war, roamed for hundreds of miles, driving off the scattered inhabitants, is now covered with flourishing settlements, with substantial houses, and large farms—not with the cabins and clearings of bordermen—but with the comfortable dwellings and the well-tilled fields of independent farmers. Organized counties and all the subordination of social life are there; and there are the noisy school-house, the decent church, the mill, the country store, the fat ox, and the sleek plough-horse.

The Yankee is there with his notions and his patent-rights, and the travelling agent with his subscription book; there are merchandise from India and from England, and, in short, all the luxuries of life, from Bulwer's last novel down to Brandreth's pills. And all this has been done in six years—in less than half the time of Jacob's courtship. In 1832 the Saukie warriors ranged over that fertile region, which is now (1838) covered with an industrious population; while the Territories of Wisconsin and Iowa, and vast settlements in Missouri, have since grown up, beyond the region which was then the frontier and the seat of war.

Appendix

The Sioux or Dacotas, are a numerous, powerful and warlike nation of Indians, who have been appropriately called the Arabs of the west. Between them and the Sacs and Foxes, there has existed, from the settlement of the two latter tribes on the waters of the Mississippi, a hostility of feeling that has kept them embroiled in a constant warfare. The efforts of government to break down their prejudices and make peace between them, have failed in accomplishing that benevolent end. It is not, however, against the Sacs and Foxes alone, that their arms are turned. From time immemorial they have been at war with the Chippeways, and are also constantly making hostile incursions upon other neighbouring tribes. They usually fight on horseback, and being very superior horsemen, they are generally more than a match for their antagonists. In Schoolcraft's *Narrative*, we find the following account of their numbers, habits and peculiarities of character.

The numerical strength of the Sioux nation was stated by the late General Pike at 21,675, three thousand eight hundred of whom are warriors. This is the most powerful Indian tribe in North America. It consists of seven bands, namely the Minokantongs, the Yengetongs, the Sissitongs, the Wahpetongs, the Titongs, the Mendewacantongs and the Washpecontongs. These are independent bands under their own chiefs, but united in a confederacy for the protection of their territories; and send deputies to a general council of the chiefs and warriors, whenever the concerns of their nation require it. If one of the tribes is attacked, the others are expected to assist in the repulsion of the enemy.

They inhabit all the country, between the Mississippi and Missouri Rivers, from north latitude about 46° to the junction of these rivers near St. Louis, with trifling exceptions in favour of some scattered bands of Foxes, Sacs and Kickapoos. Their country also extends south of the Missouri, where the principal part of the Titongs reside, and east of the Mississippi to the territories of the Chippeways—the Winnebagoes and the Menominies. The greatest chief of the nation at present (1820) is Talangamane, or the Red Wing.

The Minocantongs, or people of the waters, are located at St. Peters, and along the banks of the Mississippi towards Prairie du Chien. They reside in four principal villages.

The Yengetongs and the Sessitongs inhabit the upper parts of the river St. Peters, and are sometimes called the Sioux of the plains. Their traffic is principally in Buffalo robes. The Wahpetongs, or people of the leaves are the most erratic in their dispositions of all the Sioux; they inhabit the St. Peters between the Prairie de Francois and the White Rock, during a part of the year, and generally go out to hunt above the falls of St. Anthony towards the sources of the River De Corbeau, and upon the plains which give origin to the Crow, Sac and Elk Rivers.

The Titongs inhabit both banks of the Missouri, and rove in quest of game over an immense extent of country. They are said to be related to the Mahas, and some other bands south of the Missouri.

The Mendewacantongs, or people of the Medicine Lake, the Washpecontongs, or people of the Leaves, who have run away, and some other scattered bands, whose names are unknown, inhabit the country generally, from St. Peters south to the mouth of the Missouri, and are chiefly located upon the sources of the Rivers Ocano, Iowa, and Desmoines.

The Sioux are generally represented as a brave, generous and spirited people, with proud notions of their origin as a tribe, and their superiority as hunters and warriors, and with a predominant passion for war. They speak the Narcotah language, which is peculiar to themselves, and appears to have little affinity with any other Indian tongue. It is not so soft and sonorous as the Algonquin which abounds in labials, but more so than the Winnebago, which is the most harsh and guttural language in America. The Narcotah sounds to an English ear, like the Chinese, and both in this, and in other respects, the Sioux are

217

thought to present many points of coincidence.

It is certain that their manners and customs differ essentially from those of any other tribe, and their physiognomy, as well as their language, and opinions, mark them a distinct race of people. Their sacrifices and their supplications to the unknown God—their feasts after any signal deliverance from danger—their meat, and their burnt offerings—the preparation of incense, and certain customs of their females, offer too striking a coincidence, with the manners of the Asiatic tribes, before the commencement of the Christian era, to escape observation, while their paintings and hieroglyphics bear so much analogy to those of the Asteeks of Mexico, as to render it probable that the latter are of Naudowessian origin.

Lieutenant Pike observes:

From my knowledge of the Sioux nation I do not hesitate to pronounce them the most warlike and independent nation of Indians, within the boundaries of the United States, their every passion being subservient to that of war. Their guttural pronunciation, high cheek bones, their visages, and distinct manners, together with their own traditions, supported by the testimony of neighbouring nations, put it in my mind beyond a shadow of doubt, that they have emigrated from the north west point of America, to which they had come across the narrow straights, which in that quarter divide the two continents; and are absolutely descendants of a Tartarean tribe.

The following anecdote of a Sioux chief, and of a council held by Governor Cass, some years since, for the purpose of making peace between the Sioux and Chippeways, is drawn from a letter from that officer, to the war department. (See *Traits of Indian Character*, by G. Turner.)

Some years since, mutually weary of hostilities, the chiefs of both nations met, and agreed upon a truce. But the Sioux disregarding the solemn compact they had formed, and actuated by some sudden impulse attacked and murdered a number of Chippeways. The old Chippeway chief was present at the time, and his life was saved by the intrepidity and self-devotion of a Sioux chief. This man entreated, remonstrated, threatened. He adjured his countrymen, by every motive, to abstain from any violation of their faith: and finding his remonstrances useless, he attached himself to the Chippeway chief, and avowed his determination to save him or perish. Awed by such intrepidity, the Sioux finally agreed that he should ransom the Chippewa. This he did at the expense of all the property he possessed. The Sioux chief now accompanied him on his journey, until he considered him safe from any of the parties of the Sioux, who might be disposed to pursue him.

Believing it equally inconsistent with humanity and sound policy, that these border contests should be suffered to continue; and feeling that the Indians have a full portion of moral and physical evils, without adding to them the calamities of a war, which had no definite object, Governor Cass being at Sandy Lake, offered his mediation to the Chippeway chiefs, to which they readily acceded. In consequence, a deputation of ten of their men descended the Mississippi with him.

The Chippeways landed occasionally, to examine whether any of the Sioux had recently visited that quarter. In one of these excursions, there was found, suspended to a tree, in an exposed situation, a piece of birch-bark, made flat, by being fastened between two sticks, about eighteen inches long by fifteen broad. This bark contained the answer of the Sioux nation, to overtures which the Chippeways had made, on Governor Cass' offer of mediation:—which overtures had been found and taken off by a party of the Sioux. So revengeful and sanguinary had the contest been between these tribes, that no personal communication could take place. Neither the sanctity of the office, nor the importance of the message, could protect the ambassador of either party from the vengeance of the other.

The preliminaries to a peace being thus settled, the Sioux and Chippeways met in joint council—smoked the pipe of peace together, and then in their own figurative language, 'buried the tomahawk so deep, that it could never be dug up again.'

Another anecdote is related by Mr. Schoolcraft which we quote as illustrative of the character, in some degree, of this "singular and warlike race."

Le Petit Corbeau, a chief of a small band of Sioux, located upon the banks of the Mississippi, towards the confines of the Chippeway territory, going out one morning to examine his beaver trap, found a Sauteur in the act of stealing it. He had approached without exciting alarm, and while the Sauteur was engaged in taking the trap from the water, he stood maturely surveying him with a loaded rifle in his hands. As the two nations were at war, and the offence was in itself one of the most heinous nature, he would have been justified in killing him on the spot, and the thief looked for nothing else, on finding himself detected. But the Sioux chief walking up to him discovered a nobleness of disposition which would have done honour to the most enlightened of men.

'Take no alarm,' said he, 'at my approach; I only come to present to you the trap of which I see you stand in need. You are entirely welcome to it. Take my gun also, as I perceive you have none of your own, and depart with it to the land of your countrymen, but linger not here, lest some of my young men, who are panting for the blood of their enemies, should discover your footsteps in our country, and fall upon you.' So saying he delivered him his gun and accoutrements, and returned unarmed to the village of which he is so deservedly the chief.

COLONISATION OF THE INDIANS.

The plan, now in progress of execution, for the removal of all the Indians, within the limits of the United States, to a region of country west of Missouri and Arkansas, will of course, when carried out, greatly modify our relations with them. New laws must be enacted by Congress, and new treaties formed between the Indians and the United States.

From the organisation of the federal government to the present time, our relations with the Indians have been the subject of frequent legislation, and the statute book bears many evidences of benevolent action towards this ill-fated race. If the laws enacted by Congress for the protection and civilization of the aborigines of this country, had been regularly and rigidly enforced, and a more impartial interpretation of the treaties made with them, had been observed, their condition would have been far better than it now is—they would have passed from the hunter to the pastoral state, and have grown in numbers, virtue and intelligence. But these laws and these treaties, have been year after year violated by our own people, and the result has been a constant deterioration of the Indians. This is especially true of those laws intended to prevent our citizens from hunting on the

Indian lands, residing in their country, and trading with them without a license from the United States.

These have generally been a dead letter upon the national statute book, and the encroachments of the lawless frontiers-men, the trader, the land speculator, and the vender of spirituous liquors, have impoverished degraded, and vitiated, more or less, every tribe within the limits of the United States. It is to this intercourse, with these classes of persons, that the bad faith, the savage barbarities, and border-wars, of which so much complaint is made against the Indians, are to be mainly attributed. The rapacity of our people, for their peltries and their land, the feeble execution of laws made for their protection, and the loose morality which has governed our general intercourse with them, have wasted their numbers, debased their character, and tarnished the honour of that nation, which, from the very organisation of its government, has claimed to be their benevolent protector.

The plan of removing the Indians beyond the limits of the United States is not new. If not original with Mr. Jefferson, it was commended by him, and has been approved, we believe, by each successive administration since his day. It looked of course to a peaceable not a forcible removal of them. Whether the details of the original plan corresponded with those of the law, under which this removal is going on, we do not know.

The substance of the present plan may be gathered from the following provisions:

1st. To secure the lands on which they are placed to the several tribes by patent, with only such restrictions as are necessary to prevent white men from purchasing them, or encroaching upon them.

2nd. To establish a territorial government, all the offices of which, (except those of the governor and secretary,) are to be filled with Indians, wherever competent natives can be obtained.

3rd. To provide for a general council of delegates, chosen by and from the tribes, with legislative powers; their enactments not to be valid till they have been approved by the President of the United States.

4th. To have a delegate, always a native, remain at Washington, during the sessions of Congress, to attend to the affairs of the territory, who shall be allowed the pay and emoluments of a member of Congress.

5th. To encourage, by liberal annual payments of money provided for in treaties, the establishment of schools and colleges; in which competent native teachers are always to be preferred when they can be had.

The power and influence of the United States are to be directed in protecting them from the whites; in preserving peace among the different tribes, and in stimulating them, by rewards and emoluments, in acquiring the habits of civilized life. The efforts of the benevolent to carry Christianity among them, if made in conformity with the regulations of the territory, are to be cherished. These are the leading features of the new system of Indian regulations, established by government for the civilization of the Indians. The territory set apart for this object, lies west of the states of Arkansas and Missouri, running north from the Red River about six hundred miles, and west from the western boundaries of these states about two hundred miles. The number of Indians within the territory of the United States is estimated to approach to near half a million of souls.

It must be obvious to every one familiar with the Indian character, and with the history of our past relations with this people, that the success of this plan, will depend, in a very great degree, upon the manner in which its details shall be executed by the government. A failure will inevitably ensue, if white men are permitted to come in contact with the Indians. The strong arm of the military power of the United States, will be requisite to stay the encroachments of our people, whose love of adventure and whose thirst for gain, will carry them among the Indians, unless arrested by more cogent considerations than a sense of duty, or the prohibitions of the statute book.

Instead of attempting to supply them with goods by licensing traders to reside among them, they should be encouraged to sell their furs and peltries and to make their purchases in the United States. On the former system they are liable to constant imposition, and the very articles which the traders carry among them, are worthless in kind and poor in quality; but if the Indians traded with us, within the limits of the United States, they would have the competition arising from a number of buyers and sellers, they would obtain better prices for their furs and procure more valuable articles, upon fairer terms, in exchange. They would also be benefitted by observing our manners and customs, adopting our style of dress, learning the value of property, and gaining some knowledge of agriculture and the use of mechanical tools, and implements of husbandry. But the most important advantage to be gained by their trading within the United States, would be in their protection from imposition. It has been truly and forcibly remarked:

> Humanity shudders at the recital of the nefarious acts practised by the white traders upon the Indians.

Yet not half of them are known or dreamed of by the American people. We refer again, to Mr. Tanner's narrative, which every man who has a vote on this subject ought to read. Here we find the traders sometimes taking *by force*, from an Indian, the produce of a whole year's hunt, without making him any return, sometimes pilfering a portion while buying the remainder, and still oftener wresting from the poor wretches, while in a state of intoxication, a valuable property, for an inadequate remuneration. In one place, our author tells of an Indian woman, his adopted mother, who:

> In the course of a single day, sold one hundred and twenty beaver skins, with a large quantity of buffalo robes, dressed and smoked skins, and other articles, *for rum*.

He pathetically adds:

> Of all our large load of peltries, the produce of so many days of toil, so many long and difficult journeys, one blanket and three kegs of rum, only remained, besides the poor and almost worn out clothing on our bodies.

> The sending of missionaries, to labour by the side of the miscreants who thus swindle and debauch the ignorant savage, is a mockery of the office, and a waste of the time of these valuable men. If the Indians traded within our states, with our regular traders, the same laws and the same public sentiment which protects us, would protect them.

This is no exaggerated picture. Fraud, oppression and violence, have characterized our intercourse with the Indians, and it is in vain to hope for any amelioration of their savage condition, so long as an intercourse of this kind is permitted. In the very nature of things, the plan of civilizing the Indians, by forming a confederacy of them, beyond the limits of the United States, will prove unsuccessful, unless they are surrounded by a cordon of military posts, and the whites are stayed, by physical force, from entering their territories for any purpose whatever.

It is to this intercourse that the Indian wars, which have so frequently caused the blood of the white and the red man to flow in torrents, upon our frontier, are mainly to be attributed. It has been asserted, even by those who claim to be the grave historians of this unfortunate people, that these wars are almost without exception, the result of that cruelty and insatiable thirst for blood which belong to the Indian character. One of these writers, the Rev. Timothy Flint, in his *Indian Wars of the West*, says:

> We affirm an undoubting belief, from no infrequent, nor in-considerable means of observation, that aggression has com-menced, in the account current of mutual crime, as a hundred to one, on the part of the Indians.

We do not question the sincerity of this belief, but we do question, entirely, the correctness of the conclusion to which the writer brings his mind: we affirm without hesitation, that it is a conclusion that can-not be sustained by testimony. If the individual making it, had looked less superficially at the case, and had gone to the primary causes that have produced the bloody collisions between his countrymen and the Indians, he could never have made so great a mistake as the one he has committed in the paragraph quoted above. If kindness, good faith and honesty of dealing, had marked our social, political and commercial intercourse with the Indians, few, if any of these bloody wars would have occurred; and these people, instead of being debased by our in-tercourse with them, would have been improved and elevated in the scale of civilization.

The history of the early settlement of Pennsylvania and its illustri-ous founder, affords the strongest testimony on this point. The jus-tice, benevolence and kindness which marked the conduct of Penn towards the Indians, shielded his infant colony from aggression, and won for him personally, a generous affection, that would have been creditable to any race of people.

Upon this point it has been well and forcibly remarked by a phil-anthropic writer, of our country, (Job R. Tyson, Esq. of Philadelphia. *Discourse on the Surviving Remnant of the Indian Race in the United States*):

> The American Indian is sometimes regarded as a being who is prone to all that is revolting and cruel. He is cherished in excited imaginations, as a demoniac phantasm, delighting in bloodshed, without a spark of generous sentiment or native be-nevolence. The philosophy of man should teach us, that the

Indian is nothing less than a human being, in whom the animal tendencies predominate over the spiritual. His morals and intellect having received neither culture nor development, he possesses on the one hand, the infirmities of humanity; while on the other the divine spark in his heart, if not blown into a genial warmth, has not been extinguished by an artificial polish. His affections are strong, because they are confined to a few objects; his enmities are deep and permanent, because they are nursed in secret, without a religion to control them.

Friendship is with him a sacred sentiment. He undertakes long and toilsome journeys to do justice to its object; he exposes himself, for its sake, to every species of privation; he fights for it; and often dies in its defence. He appoints no *fecial* messenger to proclaim, by an empty formality, the commencement of war. Whilst the European seeks advantages in the subtle finesse of negotiation, the American pursues them according to the instincts of a less refined nature, and the dictates of a less sublimated policy. He seeks his enemy before he expects him, and thus renders him his prey.

No better evidence need be adduced of his capacity for a lively and lasting friendship, than the history of Pennsylvania, during the life time of the founder. It is refreshing and delightful to see one fair page, in the dark volume of injustice and crime, which American annals, on this subject present. While this page reflects upon the past an accumulated odium, it furnishes lessons for the guide and edification of the future. Let me invite the philanthropist to this affecting story.

A chief object of Penn, in the settlement of his province, was neither land, gold nor dominion, but "the glory of God, by the civilization of the poor Indian." Upon his arrival in Pennsylvania, the pledge contained in his charter was redeemed by a friendly compact with the "poor Indian" which was never to be violated, and by a uniform and scrupulous devotion to his rights and interests. Oldmixon and Clarkson inform us, that he expended "thousands of pounds" for the physical and social improvement of these untutored and houseless tenants of the woods. His estate became impaired by the munificence of his bounty. In return for benevolence so generous and pure, the Indians showed a reality of affection and an ardour of gratitude, which they had on no previous occasion professed.

The colony was exempted from those calamities of war and desolation, which form so prominent a picture in the early annals of American settlements. During a period of forty years, the settlers and natives lived harmoniously together, neither party complaining of a single act of violence or the infliction of an injury unredressed. The memory of Penn lived green and fresh in their esteem, gratitude, and reverence, a century after.

The tribe thus subdued by the pacific and philanthropic principles of Penn, have been untruly described as a cowardly and broken down race. They were a branch of the great family of Indians, who, for so many years, carried on a fierce and bloody strife with the Alligewi on the Mississippi, and waged a determined hostility with the Mengwe. At one period they were the undisputed masters of the large tract of country, now known as the territory of the middle states. On the arrival of the English, their number in Pennsylvania was computed at thirty or forty thousand souls.

Their history spoke only of conquest. They were a brave, proud and warlike race, who gloried in the preservation of a character for valour, descended from the remotest times. The confederacy of the Six Nations, by whom they were finally vanquished, was not formed until 1712, and their defeat, as evidenced by their peculiar subjugation occurred within a few months antecedent to the demise of the proprietary. The same people annihilated the colony of Des Vries, in 1632, formed a conspiracy to exterminate the Swedes, under Printz, in 1646; and were the authors of the subsequent murders which afflicted the settlements, before the accession of the English colonists.

Such an example furnishes some insight into the elements of Indian character. Little doubt can exist, if the subject were fairly examined, that most of those sanguinary wars, of which history speaks with a shudder, would be found to have arisen less from the blood-thirsty Indian, than from the aggressions of the gold-thirsty and land-thirsty defamer.

INDIAN DANCING CEREMONIES.

In a historical memoir of the Indians, published in the North American Review and attributed to the able pen of our present minister to France, there is a description of a war-dance, from which the following extract is made.

An Indian War Dance is an important occurrence in the passing events of a village. The whole population is assembled, and a feast provided for all. The warriors are painted and prepared as for battle. A post is firmly planted in the ground, and the sing-ers, the drummers and other musicians, are seated within the circle formed by the dancers and spectators. The music and the dancers begin. The warriors exert themselves, with great energy. Every muscle is in action: and there is the most perfect concord between the music and their movements. They brandish their weapons, and with such apparent fury, that fatal accidents seem unavoidable. Presently a warrior leaves the circle, and with his tomahawk or *casse-tete*, strikes the post. The music and dancing cease, and profound silence ensues. He then recounts, with a loud voice, his military achievements.

He describes the battles he has fought—the prisoners he has captured—the scalps he has taken. He points to his wounds, and produces his trophies. He accompanies his narrative with the actual representation of his exploits; and the mimic en-gagement, the advance and the retreat, are all exhibited to his nation as they really occurred. There is no exaggeration, no misrepresentation. It would be infamous for a warrior to boast of deeds he never performed. If the attempt were made, some one would approach and throw dirt in his face saying, "I do this to cover your shame; for the first time you see an enemy, you will tremble."

But such an indignity is rarely necessary: and, as the war parties generally, contain many individuals, the character and conduct of every warrior are well known. Shouts of applause accom-pany the narration, proportioned in duration and intensity to the interest it excites. His station in the circle is then resumed by the actor, and the dance proceeds, till it is interrupted in a similar manner.

In the poem of Ontwa, a scene like this is so well described, that we cannot resist the temptation to transfer it to our pages. Of all who have attempted to embody in song, the "living manners" of the Indians, the anonymous author of that poem has been the most successful. His characters, and traditions and descrip-tions, have the spirit and bearing of life; and the whole work, is not less true to nature than to poetry.

A hundred warriors now advance,
All dressed and painted for the dance;
And sounding club and hollow skin

A slow and measured time begin:
With rigid limb and sliding foot,
And murmurs low the time to suit;
Forever varying with the sound,
The circling band moves round and round.
Now slowly rise the swelling notes
When every crest more lively floats;
Now tossed on high with gesture proud,
Then lowly mid the circle bow'd;
While clanging arms grow louder still,
And every voice becomes more shrill;
Till fierce and strong the clamour grows,
And the wild war whoop bids it close.
Then starts Skunktonga forth, whose band
Came from far Huron's storm-beat strand,
And thus recounts his battle feats,
While his dark club the measure beats.

Major Long of the U.S. Army, in his expedition up the Missouri, gives an account of a council which he held, at Council Bluff, with a party of one hundred Ottoes, seventy Missouries, and fifty or sixty Soways. The Otto nation is known by the name of Wah-toh-ta-na. Their principal village is situated on the River Platte, about forty miles above its junction with the Missouri. At the period of this visit, these Indians had held little if any intercourse with the whites. After the council was over, they performed a dance, in honour of their visitors, the description of which will convey to the reader a very vivid picture of this ceremony. We give it, in Major Long's own words.

The amusement of dancing was commenced by striking up their rude instrumental and vocal music; the former consisting of a gong made of a large keg, over one of the ends of which, a skin was stretched, which was struck by a small stick, and another instrument, consisting of a stick of firm wood, notched like a saw, over the teeth of which a small stick was rubbed forcibly backward and forward. With these, rude as they were, very good time was preserved with the vocal performers, who sat around them, and by all the natives as they sat, in the inflection of their bodies, or the movements of their limbs.

After the lapse of a little time, three individuals leaped up, and danced around for a few minutes; then, at a concerted signal of

228

the master of ceremonies, the music ceased and they retired to their seats, uttering a loud noise, which, by patting the mouth rapidly with the hand, was broken into a succession of similar sounds, somewhat like the hurried barking of a dog. Several sets of dancers succeeded, each terminating as the first. In the intervals of the dances, a warrior would step forward, and strike a flag-staff they had erected, with a stick, whip, or other weapon, and recount his martial deeds.

This ceremony is termed *striking the post*, and whatever is then said, may be relied upon as rigid truth, being delivered in the presence of many a jealous warrior and witness, who could easily detect, and would immediately disgrace the *striker* for exaggeration or falsehood. This is called the *beggar's dance*—during which, some presents are always expected by the performers; as tobacco, whiskey, or trinkets. But on this occasion, as none of these articles were immediately offered, the amusement was not, at first, distinguished by much activity.

The master of the ceremonies continually called aloud to them to exert themselves, but still they were somewhat dull and backward. Iëtan now stepped forward, and lashed a post with his whip, declaring that he would punish those that did not dance. This threat, from one whom they had vested with authority for this occasion, had a manifest effect upon his auditors, who were presently highly wrought up, by the sight of two or three little mounds of tobacco twist, which were now laid before them, and appeared to infuse new life.

After lashing the post, and making his threat, Iëtan went on to narrate his martial exploits. He had stolen horses seven or eight times from the Kanzas; he had first struck the bodies of three of that nation slain in battle. He had stolen horses from the Iëtan nation, and had struck one of their dead. He had stolen horses from the Pawnees, and struck the body of one Pawnee Loup. He had stolen horses several times from the Omawhahs, and once from the Puncas. He had struck the bodies of two Sioux. On a war party, in company with the Pawnees, he had attacked the Spaniards, and penetrated into one of their camps; the Spaniards—excepting a man and a boy—fled, himself being at a distance before his party; he was shot at and missed by the man, whom he immediately shot down and struck. 'This, my father,' said he, 'is the only material act of my life that I am ashamed of.'

After several rounds of dancing, and of striking at the post, by the warriors, Mi-a-ke-ta, or *The Little Soldier*, a war-worn veteran, took his turn to strike the post. He leaped actively about, and strained his voice to its utmost pitch, whilst he portrayed some of the scenes of blood in which he had acted. He had struck dead bodies of individuals of all the Red nations around; Osages, Konzas, Pawnee Loups, Pawnee Republicans, Grand Pawnees, Puncas, Omawhaws, Sioux, Padoucas, La Plain, or Bald heads, Iëtans, Sacs, Foxes, and Ioways. He had struck eight of one nation, seven of another, &c.

He was proceeding with his account, when Iëtan ran up to him, put his hand upon his mouth, and respectfully led him to his seat. This act was no trifling compliment to the well-known brave; it indicated, that he had so many glorious achievements to speak of, that he would occupy so much time, as to prevent others from speaking; and, moreover, put to shame the other warriors, by the contrast of his actions with theirs.

Their physical action in dancing is principally confined to leaping a small distance from the ground, with both feet, the body being slightly inclined, and, upon alighting, an additional slight but sudden inclination of the body is made, so as to appear like a succession of jerks; or the feet are raised alternately, the motion of the body being the same. Such are the movements in which the whole party correspond; but, in the figures—as they are termed in our assembly rooms—each individual performs a separate part, and each part is a significant pantomimic narrative. In all their variety of action, they are careful to observe the musical cadences.

In this dance, Iëtan represented one who was in the act of stealing horses; he carried a whip in his hand as did a considerable number of the Indians, and around his neck were thrown several leathern thongs, for bridles and halters, the ends of which trailed upon the ground behind him. After many preparatory manoeuvres, he stooped down, and with his knife, represented the act of cutting the hopples of horses. He then rode his tomahawk, as children ride their broomsticks, making use of his whip, as to indicate the necessity of rapid movement, lest his foes should overtake him. Wa-sa-ha-jing-ga, or *Little Black Bear*, after a variety of gestures, threw several arrows in succession, over his own head—thereby indicating his familiarity with the flight of such missiles. He, at the same time, covered his eyes with his hand, to indicate that he was blind to danger. Others represented their manoeuvres in battles, seeking their enemy, discharging at him their guns or arrows, &c. &c.

Most of the dancers were the principal warriors of the nation—men who had not condescended to amuse themselves or others, in this manner, for years before. But they now appeared in honour of the occasion, and to conciliate, in their best manner, the good will of the representative of the government of the *Big Knives*. Amongst these veteran warriors, Iëtan, or *Sha-mon-e-kus-see*, *Ha-she-a* (the Broken Arm), commonly called Cut Nose, and *Wa-sa-ha-zing-ga* (or Little Black Bear), three youthful leaders, in particular, attracted our attention.

In consequence of having been appointed soldiers on this occasion, to preserve order, they were painted entirely black. The countenance of the first indicated much wit, and had, in its expression, something of the character of that of Voltaire. He frequently excited the mirth of those about him, by his remarks and gestures. *Ha-she-a*, (called Cut Nose, in consequence of having lost the tip of his nose, in a quarrel with Iëtan,) wore a handsome robe of white wolf skin, with an appendage behind him, called a *crow*. This singular decoration is a large cushion, made of the skin of a crow, stuffed with any light material, and variously ornamented. It has two decorated sticks, projecting from it upward, and a pendent one beneath; this apparatus is secured upon the buttocks by a girdle passing round the body. The other actors in the scene were decorated with paints of several colours, fantastically disposed upon their persons.

Several were painted with white clay, which had the appearance of being grooved in many places. This grooved appearance is given by drawing the finger-nails over the part, so as to remove the pigment from thence in parallel lines. These lines are either rectilinear, undulated, or zigzag; sometimes passing over the forehead transversely, or vertically; sometimes in the same direction, or obliquely over the whole visage, or upon the breast, arms, &c. Many were painted with red clay, in which the same lines appeared. A number of them had the representation of a black hand, with outspread fingers, on different parts of the body, strongly contrasting with the principal colour with which the body was overspread; the hand was depicted in different positions upon the face, breast, and back. The face of others was coloured, one half black, and one half white, or red and white, &c. Many coloured their hair with red clay, but the eye-lids and base of the ears were generally tinged with vermilion.

At the conclusion of the ceremony, whiskey—which they always expect on similar occasions—was produced, and a small portion was given to each. The principal chiefs of the different nations who had remained passive spectators of the scene, now directed their people to return to their camp. The word of the chiefs was obeyed, excepting by a few of the Ioways, who appeared to be determined to keep their places, notwithstanding the reiterated command of the chiefs. Ïetan now sprang towards them, with an expression of much ferocity in his countenance, and it is probable a tragic scene would have been displayed, had not the chiefs requested him to use gentle means; and thus he succeeded; after which, the chiefs withdrew.

SALE OF WHISKEY TO THE INDIANS.

In tracing out the causes which led to the late war with the Sac and Fox Indians of Rock River, reference was made to the violations of the laws of Congress in the introduction of whiskey among them by the white traders. The opinion, moreover, was expressed that the licensed traders of the United States, among these tribes, were in the habit of selling this article to them, and under circumstances which must have brought home the fact to the knowledge of our Indian agents. Black Hawk with other chiefs of the band to which he belonged, earnestly remonstrated against the introduction of whiskey among his people, because of its debasing effect upon their morals, and the danger of its provoking them to acts of aggression upon the whites, while in a state of intoxication.

One of the facts, set forth in the memorial which the white settlers on Rock River, presented to Governor Reynolds, in 1831, and upon which he declared the state to be actually invaded by the Sac and Fox Indians, and ordered out the militia to repel it, was the destruction, by Black Hawk, of a barrel of whiskey, which the owner was retailing to the Indians. The violation of the laws of Congress and of express treaty provisions, in the sale of ardent spirits to the Indians, winked at, as they undoubtedly were, by the public agents, mainly contributed to bring about a war, which resulted in the destruction of a great part of the band of Black Hawk. That the allegations, in regard to the sale

232

of intoxicating liquors, to the Indians, by the regularly licensed traders of the United States, may not be supposed to rest upon gratuitous assumptions, the following letter, is quoted, which places the matter beyond all question.

St. Peters, July 25, 1832

General Joseph M. Street,
Indian Agent, Prairie du Chien.
Sir—I arrived at this place yesterday from the sources of the Mississippi, having visited the Chippewa bands and trading-posts in that quarter. Much complaint is made respecting the conduct of the persons licensed by you last year, who located themselves at the Granite Rocks, and on the St. Croix. No doubt can exist that each of them took in, and used in their trade, a considerable quantity of whiskey. And I am now enabled to say, that they each located themselves at points within the limits of my agency, where there are no trading-posts established.

My lowest trading-post on the Mississippi, is the Pierced Prairie, eighteen miles below the mouth of the De Corbeau. It embraces one mile square upon which traders are required to be located. On the St. Croix, the posts established and confirmed by the Department are Snake River and Yellow River, and embrace each, as the permanent place of location, one mile square. I report these facts for your information, and not to enable you to grant licenses for these posts, as the instructions of the Department give to each agent the exclusive control of the subject of granting licenses for the respective agencies.

Much solicitude is felt by me to exclude ardent spirits wholly from the Chippewas and Ottowas, the latter of whom have, by a recent order, been placed under my charge. I am fully satisfied that ardent spirits are not necessary to the successful prosecution of the trade, that they are deeply pernicious to the Indians, and that both their use and abuse is derogatory to the character of a wise and sober government. Their exclusion in every shape, and every quantity, is an object of primary moment; and it is an object which I feel it a duty to persevere in the attainment of, however traders may bluster. I feel a reasonable confidence in stating, that no whiskey has been used in my agency during the last two years, except the limited quantity taken by special permission of the Secretary of War, for the trade of the Hudson's Bay lines; and saving also the quantity clandestinely introduced from Prairie du Chien and St. Peters.

I know, sir, that an appeal to you on this subject cannot be lost, and that your feelings and judgment fully approve of temperance measures. But it requires active, persevering, unyielding efforts. And in all such efforts, judiciously urged, I am satisfied that the government will sustain the agents in a dignified discharge of their duties. Let us proceed in the accomplishment of this object with firmness, and with a determination never to relinquish it, until ardent spirits are entirely excluded from the Indian country.

I am sir,

Very respectfully,

Your obedient servant,

Henry R. Schoolcraft.

P.S. Capt. Jouett, commanding at this post, has recently seized sixteen kegs of high-wines. His prompt, decisive, and correct conduct in this, and other transactions relating to Indian affairs, merits the approbation of government.

The Petite Corbeau has requested that no trader may be located at the mouth of the St. Croix.

The following picture of the present condition of the Winnebagoes, given in the St. Louis Bulletin, shows the deplorable results of the intercourse of the whites with the Indians—the baneful effects of spirituous liquors upon their morals and habits. The Winnebagoes were neighbours of the Sacs and Foxes, and long intimately associated with them. Twenty years ago, all of these tribes, raised annually more corn, beans and other vegetables, than were needed for their own consumption. Now they are miserable, squalid beggars, without the means of subsistence. The faithlessness of the government, the perfidy and avarice of its agents and citizens, have brought this race of people to the horrible condition, in which they are represented in the statement that follows.

An agent of the Temperance Society, in a journal of a late tour to the region of the Upper Mississippi, presents a picture, melancholy indeed, of the present condition of the Indian tribes in that quarter, which must deeply rouse the commiseration of every benevolent man. From our own personal observation one year since, we would corroborate the assertion, that were the world ransacked for a subject in which should be concentrated and personified injustice, oppression, drunkenness, squalid filth, and degradation, one would point to the straggling Indian on the banks of the Upper Mississippi for the aptest exemplification.

There were some two or three hundred of these stragglers—Winnebagoes, chiefly, about Prairie du Chien—men, women, and children, many of whom had scarcely the fragments of a filthy blanket to hide their nakedness or screen them from the cold—strolling and straggling about in squads of from two to a half dozen each, begging for whiskey, or cold potatoes, or crusts of bread. One old female, doubtless turned of threescore and ten, half naked, was gathering up from the dirt and ashes about the boiler of the steam boat, a few pieces of dried apples that had been dropped and trodden under foot, which, with her toothless gums, she attempted to masticate with all the eagerness of a starving swine.

Little children, from one to four years old, were crawling about in a state of nudity, and almost of starvation, while their own mothers and fathers, were staggering, and fighting, and *swearing*. It is a fact, that while these poor creatures cannot articulate a word of anything else in English, the most awfully profane expressions will drop from their lips in English, as fluently as if it had been their vernacular tongue. When the whites first settled in that neighbourhood, the Indians raised corn and other provisions enough, not only for their own use, but also for the fur-traders and settlers.

Now they are altogether dependent for even the scanty subsistence by which they are dragging out the remnant of a miserable life, upon the whites. And what has been the cause of so great a change in a few years in the circumstances and habits of a whole people! The answer is plain to every one at all acquainted with Indian history. It is the perfidy and avarice of the whites, and whiskey, whiskey has been the all potent *agent* by which it has been effected. By selling and giving them whiskey till they become drunk, they are soon filched of the little annuities received from government; and then treated the rest of the year like so many dogs.—As an illustration of the feeling towards them, a merchant at Prairie du Chien expressed the very humane wish, that there might soon be another Indian war to kill them all off.

235

Narrative of the Capture and
Providential Escape of
Misses Frances and Almira Hall

Contents

Narrative, &c.

The preceding year (1832) will be long remembered as a year of much human distress, and a peculiarly unfortunate one for the American nation—for while many of her most populous cities have been visited by that dreadful disease, the cholera, and to which thousands have fallen victims, the merciless savages have been as industriously and fatally engaged in the work of human butchery on the frontiers.

In the month of May last, a considerable body of Indians (principally of the tribes of the Sacs and Foxes) having, as they professed, become dissatisfied with the encroachments of the whites, invaded and made a furious and unexpected attack upon the defenceless inhabitants of the frontier towns of Illinois. The first and most fatal was upon a small settlement on Indian Creek, running into Fox River, where were settled about twenty families, who, not being apprised of their approach, became an easy prey to their savage enemies—indeed so sudden and unexpected was the attack, that they were unalarmed until the savages with their tomahawks in hand, had entered their houses, and began the perpetration of the most inhuman barbarities! No language can express the cruelties that were committed; in less than half an hour more than one half of the inhabitants were inhumanly butchered—they horribly mutilated both young and old, male and female, without distinction of age or sex, among the few whose lives were spared, and of whom they made prisoners, were two highly respectable young women (sisters) of the ages of 16 and 18.

As soon as the melancholy tidings of the horrid massacre were made known to the white inhabitants of the neighbouring settlements, a company of volunteers of about 270 in number, were hastily collected and sent in pursuit of the savages, whom they overtook near Sycamore Creek, and resolutely attacked, but were unfortunately repulsed by a force far superior to their own, and were compelled to retreat with the loss of 50 of their number—many of the Indians were killed, but as they carried off their dead, the exact number could not be ascertained; one only was found on the ground the succeeding day; he had received a mortal wound, and in the agonies of death, had tomahawked one of the whites and cut his head half off, dying in the very act; his last convulsive struggle being an embrace of his enemy even in death! The bodies of the slain whites were cut and mangled in the most cruel manner that savage barbarity could devise; their hearts taken out and their heads cut off!

Immediately on the receipt of the melancholy news of the defeat of the volunteers, Governor Reynolds issued his proclamation, and a very formidable force (comprised of about 1400 men) were speedily raised, and under command of the governor and General Atkinson, marched forthwith in pursuit of the murderous foe, but were unable to overtake them, as it appears by the reports of the captives, who have since been ransomed, that after their engagement with the volunteers (the better to evade the pursuit of the whites) they separated into small parties, and fled in different directions. The two unfortunates females, whom they retained as prisoners, and whose unfortunate parents were among those who were inhumanly butchered at Indian Creek, were providentially (by the aid of the Winebagoes) rescued from the hands of the savage monsters, after having been ten days in their power; in which time they were compelled to travel many miles, either on horseback or on foot, through almost impenetrable forests, and subjected to great privations and hardships, and in the expectation at every step in having their heads severed from their bodies, by the bloody tomahawk.

The third day after their engagement with the volunteers, and while on their return to their settlement, they fell in with a Kentuckian hunter, a young man of about 24 years of age, whom, after a consultation among themselves, whether they would dispatch him on the spot, or reserve him for other purposes, it was finally decided that his life should be spared until they reached the place of their destination, when and where (agreeable to his own statement) he was for 22 days made the subject of the most cruel treatment.

The report of the unfortunate young women (Misses Frances and Almira Hall) communicated to their friends and relatives, on their return from captivity, although treated with less severity, cannot fail to be read with much interest—they state, that after being compelled to witness, not only the savage butchery of their beloved parents, but to hear the heart-piercing screeches and dying groans of their expiring friends and neighbours, and the hideous yells of the furious assaulting savages, they were seized and mounted upon horses, to which they were secured by ropes, when the savages with an exulting shout, took up their line of march in Indian file, bending their course west; the horses on which the females were mounted, being each led by one of their number, while two more walked on each side with their blood-stained scalping knives and tomahawks, to support and to guard them—they thus travelled for many hours, with as much speed as possible, through a dark and almost impenetrable wood; when reaching a still more dark and gloomy swamp, they came to a halt.

A division of the plunder which they had brought from the ill-fated settlement, and with which their stolen horses (nine in number) were loaded, here took place, each savage stowing away in his pack his proportionable share as he received it; but on nothing did they seem to set so great a value, or view with so much satisfaction, as the bleeding scalps which they had, ere life had become extinct, torn from the mangled heads of the expiring victims, the feelings of the unhappy prisoners at this moment, can be better judged than described, when they could not be insensible that among these scalps, these shocking proofs of savage cannibalism, were those of their beloved parents, but, their moans and bitter lamentations had no effect in moving or diverting for a moment, the savages from the business in which they had engaged, until it was completed; when, with as little delay as possible, and without giving themselves time to partake of any refreshment, (as the prisoners could perceive) they again set forward, and travelled with precipitancy until sunset, when they again halted, and prepared a temporary lodging for the night.

The poor unfortunate females, whose feelings as may be supposed, could be no other than such as bordered on distraction, and who had not ceased for a moment to weep most bitterly during the whole day, could not but believe that they were here destined to become the victims of savage outrage and abuse; and that their sufferings would soon terminate, as they would not (as they imagined) be permitted to live to see the light of another day, such were their impressions, and such their dreadful forebodings—human imagination can hardly picture to itself a more deplorable situation; but, in their conjectures, they happily found themselves mistaken, as on the approach of night, instead of being made the subjects of brutal outrage, as they had fearfully apprehended, a place separate from that occupied by the main body of the savages, was allotted them; where blankets were spread for them to lodge upon, guarded only by two aged squaws, who slept on each side of them.

With minds agitated with the most fearful apprehensions, as regarded their personal safety, and as solemnly impressed with the recollection of the awful scene which they had witnessed the morning previous, in the tragical death of their parents, they spent, as might be expected, a sleepless night; although the savages exhibited no disposition to harm or disturb them—early the morning ensuing, food was offered them, but in consequence of the disturbed state of their minds and almost constant weeping, they had become too weak and indisposed to partake of it, although nearly twenty hours had passed without their having received any sustenance.

The second day they passed much as the first, the Indians travelling with the same speed as on the former one; but nearly at its close, the two unfortunate females had become, through great fatigue and long fasting, too weak to support themselves longer on their horses, and were consequently dismounted and compelled to travel many miles on foot; and not until it was perceived by the savages that they were about to sink under the weight of their miseries, did they consent to come to a halt, and prepare quarters for a second night's lodging—a fire was kindled and some venison broth made, of which the unhappy prisoners were compelled by hunger to partake, and were then permitted to retire and spend the night as they had the preceding one, (as regarded any insult being offered them;) and being unable longer to resist the calls of nature, they the morning ensuing felt much relieved by the undisturbed repose which they had been permitted to enjoy.

During the long travel, or rather flight of the Indians the two preceding days, although they had in two or three instances met with small squads of armed savages, bound as was supposed to commit further depredations on the defenceless inhabitants of the frontier settlements, yet they had not until this the third day of their captivity, met with or beheld the face of any white inhabitant; when, at about noon, a Kentuckian hunter unfortunately fell into their hands; he was immediately seized and pinioned; and after nearly half an hour's consultation among those who appeared to be, chiefs, devising, as the prisoner concluded, the best plan to dispose of him, they again put forward, and a few hours before sunset, arrived at one of their Indian settlements, where, in consequence of their enfeebled and emaciated state, it was concluded that the two female captives should remain until recruited;

and it was here that it was first communicated to them why their lives had been spared, and why they had been protected from insult, to wit: for the reason that they were to become the adopted wives of the two young chiefs by whom they were first seized!

If there was anything calculated to add more horror to their feelings, it was this, which was indeed calculated to produce a greater shock than the intelligence that they were doomed to become the victims of the most savage torture! Yet however great their afflictions, it was evident that they were supported and protected by that Supreme Being, who has power alone to soften the savage heart—*"to break the chains of bondage, and bid the captive go free,"*—for, although now completely in the power of the savages, and by everyone acknowledged the rightful property of two of their young and distinguished chiefs, yet for the seven days that they passed with them, they received none other but kind and civil treatment—the two young chiefs, to whom it was intended that they should be espoused, manifesting that regard for, and protecting them with as much interest, and apparent good feeling, as if they had been actually their lawfully wedded companions!

On the mornings of the 10th day from that of their capture, about fifty of the Winebagoes, (of a neighbouring tribe so called) who had been dispatched by the friends of the two young women, in quest of them, with means to ransom them if found alive, arrived—although the prisoners could not but feel overjoyed at this sudden and unexpected prospect of a deliverance, and to hail the tawny messengers as beings commissioned by Heaven, to rescue them from their perilous situation, yet they could not but discover, that on the minds of the two whose companions it was intended they should be, it had quite a different effect; and more particularly with one, who for some time manifested an unwillingness to receive anything that could be named, in exchange for his highly prized captive, the ransom was however finally effected by adding ten horses more to the number already offered.

On parting with her, he insisted upon exercising the right of cutting from her head a lock of her hair, not as a relic which he was desirous to retain in remembrance of one, for whom he felt any uncommon degree of friendship and affection, but to be retained and interwoven into his belt, as an invaluable trophy of his warlike exploits, such indeed is the Indian character—such their love of fame! The price paid in consideration of the ransom of the two female captives, was forty horses, together with a specified quantity of *wampum* and trinkets—the bargain closed, the prisoners were taken under the protection of the Winebagoes, and conveyed in safely to Galena (Illinois) and although they appear not insensible of the gratitude they owe to God, for their wonderful preservation and final deliverance from the hands of a merciless enemy, yet it is to be expected that they will long remember in sorrow, that fatal day, and the melancholy event, which not only deprived them of their liberty, but of their beloved parents, forever.

While the two females (for whose safety so much was apprehended) appear to have providentially escaped unharmed, a different fate appears to have attended the unfortunate Kentuckian—who states, that after his separation from the other captives, he was compelled to travel on foot with a heavy burden, and was conducted by the savages to one of their settlements still further west; where on his arrival, he was beset by a throng of the natives, of both sexes and of all ages, armed with sticks and bludgeons, and who commenced beating him to a degree almost to deprive him of life, and after having undergone this introductory discipline, he was (with the exception of his shirt and pantaloons) stripped of his clothing, and bound hand and foot to a tree, and where he concluded they intended to leave him to perish, as he was suffered there to remain for more than ten hours, without food, exposed to the heat of the sun, and enduring much bodily pain from the many bruises and deep wounds produced by the blows inflicted upon him.

He was however finally removed from thence, to an old deserted booth, or *wigwam*, which contained nothing but a few rotten mats covered with vermin, and on which he was given to understand he would be permitted to repose himself, until otherways disposed of. The only food allowed him during his captivity was the offal of wild animals, some of which it was apparent had been slain many days. While confined in the hut, he was constantly guarded night and day by two young savages, and from whom he received the most brutal treatment; whenever they had occasion to leave him, if even but for a few moments, they never failed to bind him with withes to a log of his miserable habitation; and in one instance, he was so left bound for the space of twenty-four hours, without food or a single drop of water to allay his thirst.

During the 22 days of his captivity, he witnessed the departure of many of the savages, in small bodies, of from 15 to 20 in number, bound as he supposed to depredate on the frontier settlements; as they were frightfully painted, and well provided with fire arms, tomahawks, and other instruments of death; and while some were thus departing, others in still smaller squads were almost constantly arriving, with valuable horses, laden with various articles plundered from the whites; and what was still more melancholy to view, in some instances, with human scalps, among which would be not only those of the hoary headed, but of tender infants, apparently not exceeding two years of age! All of which, after being sufficiently dried or cured in the sun, were hung up in their *wigwams*, as the highly prized trophies of their bravery!

Whenever a very considerable body of the savages were on the point of departing, for the purpose before mentioned, preparatory to the event, the war dance was performed, which was most frightful in view of one in the situation of the unfortunate prisoner, who was in two or three instances an involuntary spectator of the whole performance. It was (as he states) performed in the midst of a circle of warriors, and commenced by a chief, moving from the right to the left, singing at the same time both his own exploits, and those of his ancestors—and when he had concluded his account of some memorable action, he gives a violent blow with his war-club, against a post that was fixed in the ground near the centre of the circle.

His example was followed by every warrior who was to engage in the expedition, each recapitulating the wondrous deeds performed by his family, till all finally joined in the dance; when, to the unfortunate captive, it became truly alarming, as the savages (to frighten him as he supposed) threw themselves into every horrible and terrifying posture that can be imagined; at the same time hurling their tomahawks and brandishing their long and sharp knives, within a few inches of his body, he was fearful every moment of receiving a fatal blow! By these motions it is supposed that they intend to represent the manner in which they kill, scalp and take their prisoners. To heighten the scene, they set up the same hideous yells, cries, and war-whoops they use in the time of action!

In the twenty-two days in which the narrator remained a prisoner with them, many horses and a number of human scalps were brought in, but not a single prisoner; which rendered it very probable that all the unfortunate whites who fell into their hands, of whatever sex or age, were murdered—which, indeed, appears to have been in obedience to the commands of Black Hawk, the blood-thirsty chief, who was the prime mover and instigator of the war; and who, to encourage the neighbouring tribes to unite with him for the purpose, had pledged himself either to compel the whites to recede to their older settlements, or totally to exterminate them.

Never did the unfortunate Brigdon feel (as he expressed himself) more afraid of becoming the victim of savage torture, than when they in an engagement with the whites, were so unfortunate as to meet with a repulse, and to return lamenting the loss of either some favourite chief, or some of their best warriors.—So exasperated were they on such occasions, that nothing but an immediate opportunity to revenge themselves, seemed calculated to pacify them; nor does he doubt but that they would have selected him, as a proper subject on whom to retaliate, had they not been so confident that as soon as his situation should be made known to his friends, a sum equal to that paid for the ransom of the two female captives (of which they had been advised) would be offered for his release!

To this alone he imputes the preservation of his life; and in confirmation of which, on the very day of his providential escape, the savages having ascertained that the Winebagoes were neither authorised or disposed to negotiate for his release, after a short consultation, he believes that it was their conclusion to put him to death, in the awful manner as described—preparatory to which, two posts were set firmly and perpendicularly in the ground, to which two cross pieces were fastened horizontally, with withes, one about two and the other about six feet from the ground, to which it is probable that his hands and feet were to be bound. Around the whole were piled dry fagots, and other combustibles—the whole construction being within a short distance of the place where the prisoner was confined, he witnessed the preparations making for a dreadful scene of torture, (and of which he doubted not he was to be the subject) with feelings that may be better imagined than described!

Nor did he fail at the important moment to send up a petition to Heaven, that his sufferings might not be of long duration, and that the Almighty, in his infinite mercy, might be pleased to have compassion on and cause provision to made for his bereaved family!—Indeed dreadful as he viewed his own situation, his greatest concern was for their welfare—for while precluded from the sweet hope of ever beholding them again in this world, his thoughts were ultimately fixed on a happier state of existence, beyond, the tortures which he doubted not he was about to endure!

For nearly two hours after the savages had completed their work (preparatory to the commencement of the work of death) was the un-happy prisoner suffered to remain in a state of awful suspense—when, suddenly, a state of the utmost tumult and confusion, attended with the most terrific whoops and yells, appeared to prevail throughout the whole village. A party of the savages who had the morning previous left for the purpose of depredating on the whites, had returned in great haste, and communicated something to their Indian brethren, evidently of a very alarming nature; what, the prisoner was not able to determine, but it has since been ascertained that they had been, and probably still supposed themselves closely pursued by an armed and very considerable body of the whites.

On the receipt of this alarming intelligence, every visage seemed to wear the gloom of despair, and but one principle seemed to govern them, which was, each to seek his own safety, and to hasten with, their squaws and papooses from their invaded village; which, the prisoner believes, was totally deserted by the savages in less than 25 minutes, and that he might without opposition easily have reduced the whole to ashes, had not the thought of self-preservation (at this unexpected opportunity to escape from captivity and death) alone occupied his mind—and fortunate indeed was it for him, that so great was the pan-ic of the savages, and their anxiety to remove their wives and children, that he was probably forgotten by them, for had it been otherways, without causing them but a moment's delay, they might (and agree-ably to their barbarous custom, certainly would) have dispatched him by a single blow of the tomahawk, as they have been seldom known to fail to scalp and cut the throats of their prisoners, when hard pushed by an enemy.

As soon as the natives had totally disappeared, the prisoner having with some difficulty succeeded in unbinding himself, he hastily seizing an old musket, the only weapon which the hut contained, (and with-out a moment's reflection that without ammunition it would prove but a useless burden) he set out with light feet through a pathless wilderness, in a direction as he supposed leading to the nearest white settlement—and which, after much hard travelling, he succeeded in reaching; but, in a truly pitiful condition—his only clothing, a pair of tattered, dirty pantaloons, and a shirt in no better condition—his beard long, and legs and feet blistered and torn by thorns and briars.

Since the commencement of hostilities by the disaffected Indi-ans, in May last, their depredations and shocking barbarities exercised upon the defenceless inhabitants of the frontiers, are some of them of a nature too shocking to be presented to the public—it is sufficient to observe, that the scalping knife and tomahawk, were in some cases the mildest instruments of death! One, of many remarkable instances of whole families having been inhumanly murdered, by the merciless barbarians (of which we have been credibly informed) is that of the truly unfortunate family of Captain Joseph Naper, near Fort Chicago, comprised of himself, wife, wife's sister, and four children—when the alarm became general, Naper with many others fled with his family to the fort; but after remaining there a short time, being a bold and daring man, and doubting the hostile views of the savages, he imprudently returned with his family to his log cabin, but, a fatal remove it proved to him, for two days after, every member of his family with himself, were found murdered, and their bodies mangled in the most brutal manner—however shocking the spectacle, the scene of human slaughter afforded a proof that the ill-fated Naper, although single handed, had bravely defended himself and friends—nine of the Indians were found dead near his house, who unquestionably fell before his intrepid arm!

Indian Depredations

The continual fears and apprehensions of the defenceless inhabitants of the west, since the savage warfare commenced, have been great in the extreme; while some have been driven from their homes, in the most destitute condition, others have retired to and fortified themselves in blockhouses, with the determination to defend themselves therein so long as a single man remained alive—in two or three instances these have been attacked, and nobly defended, and in which defence the women took a distinguished part. A very considerable body of the troops of the United States (united with more than two thousand of the militia, of Kentucky, Illinois, &c.) under command of the brave General Atkinson, have done and are still continuing to do all, (as at time of first publication), in their power to check the savage foe, in his murderous career, and prevent the further effusion of innocent blood, but their crafty and distinguished chief. Black Hawk, by cunningly dividing his men into small bodies, with advice to scout in different directions and to act independently of each other, has thereby avoided a general engagement with the whites—with some of these detached parties of the enemy, the troops have had several severe engagements, and in most instances much to the disadvantage of the savages.

Since the commencement of hostilities by the Sacs and Foxes, and in the many depredations committed upon the defenceless inhabitants of the frontier settlements, the lives of but few, who have been so unfortunate as to fall into their hands, have been spared. Their tomahawks have, literally, been made drunk with innocent blood! the virgin's shriek, the mother's wail, and infant's trembling cry, has proved music in their ears! Mothers while entreating for the lives of their poor children, have themselves fallen victims to the bloody tomahawk, no language can express the cruelties which have been committed—and the distressing scene is not infrequently presented, of whole families lying murdered and scalped presenting a spectacle too horrid for description. These shocking barbarities have called up the spirit of more than two thousand of the brave and patriotic citizens of Kentucky and Illinois, who have volunteered their services, and have marched against the savages, determined to revenge the cruelties perpetrated on the infant, the mother and the defenceless. As soon as the horrid massacre of the inhabitants of the white settlement was made known at St. Louis, (Kentucky) the following appeal was published in the form of a hand bill, and generally and expeditiously circulated throughout the state.

War! War!! War!!!
Women and Children Butchered!

Two young ladies taken by the Savages. Authentic information has been received from the most inhumanly butchered, and the women in a most shocking manner mangled and exposed. Two highly respectable young women of 16 and 18 years of age, are in the hands of the Indians, and if not already murdered, are perhaps reserved for a more cruel and savage fate. Whole families are driven from their homes, actually starving; and without a day's provision before them.

Shall we, fellow citizens, quietly look upon these transactions? Can we look upon them without feelings of revenge—without knowing that our assistance is necessary? How soon may it be before our frontiers are in the same way invaded, and our own brothers and sisters scalped? Shall we allow these brutes to dull their tomahawks on the bones of our friends, in order that they may only re-sharpen them for our relations? Allow these murderers further success, and they will be joined by bands from every quarter, and their "border warfare" will be terrible. Rise, fellow citizens of this city and county—let us no longer delay—talk no more, but act.

To arms—unloose the spirit of revenge— each one raise a horse, gun, and a few days rations, and put himself under the guidance of some respectable members of the community, (one of experience, and well acquainted with the Indian character, and their mode of warfare) resolved to revenge or die in defence of his relatives and friends. Let us convince our brethren of our neighbour State, that we are willing and able to assist them—and in assisting them to protect ourselves. Let us, as has been already suggested, meet at 5 o'clock this afternoon—form ourselves on the spot, in companies of fifty men each—and the *St. Louis Corps* will march to the seat of war.

Customs of the Western Savages

There are but two tribes (the Sacs and Foxes) who have as yet, (as at time of first publication), engaged in the war—they are powerful tribes, inhabiting the country bordering on Sandy Bay and Rocky River; by historians they were formerly denominated the "Saux of the Wood," and now boast that they can bring more than 5000 warriors into the field! They are of a cruel and revengeful disposition, and avow themselves the natural enemies of the whites, with whose encroachments they have ever been highly displeased, and prefer the savage customs and habits of their ancestors, to civilization.

Their military appearance is very odd and terrible—they paint themselves with a red pigment down to the eyebrows, which they sprinkle over with white down—a single lock left to grow upon the crown of their heads, is divided into several parcels, each of which is stiffened and intermixed with beads and feathers of various shapes and colours, the whole twisted and connected together—on their breasts are a gorget or medal of brass, copper, or some other metal; and by a string which goes round their necks, is suspended that horrid weapon the scalping knife—thus equipped, they set out for some frontier settlement of the whites, singing the war-song, till they lose sight of their village.

The weapons now used by them are commonly a firelock, a tomahawk and scalping knife. As the commander in chief governs only by advice, and can neither reward or punish, every private may return home when he pleases, without assigning any reason for it; or any number may leave the main body and carry on a private expedition, in whatever manner they please, without being called to an account for their conduct. The scalps of their enemies (those dreadful proofs of savage barbarity) are valued and hung up in their houses as the trophies of their bravery; and they have certain days when the young men gain a new name or title of honour, according to the qualities of the persons to whom these scalps belonged—this name they think a sufficient reward for the dangers and fatigues of many campaigns, as it renders them respected by their countrymen, and terrible to their enemies.

Their houses or *wigwams* are at best but miserable cells; they are constructed generally like arbours or small young trees bent and twisted together, and so curiously covered with mats or bark, that they are tolerably dry and warm— their household furniture is of but small value, a few mats or skins compose their beds—they have a method of lighting up their huts with torches, made of the splinters cut from the pine or birch tree.

They have generally one commander for ten men; and if the number amounts to one hundred, a general is appointed over the others, not properly to command, but to give his opinion. They have no stated rules of discipline, or fixed methods of carrying on a war, but make their attacks in as many different ways as there are occasions, but generally in flying parties, equipped for that purpose.

When the Indians return from a successful campaign, they contrive their march so as not to approach their village till toward the evening. They then send two or three forward to acquaint their chief, and the whole village with the most material circumstances of their campaign At daylight next morning, they give their prisoners new clothes, paint their faces with various colours, and put into their hands a white staff, tasselled round with the tails of deer. This being done, the war captain sets up a cry, and gives as many yells as he has taken prisoners and scalps, and the whole village assemble at the water side. As soon as the warriors appear, four or five of their young men, well clothed, get into a canoe, if they come by water, or otherwise march by land; the two first carrying each a calumet, go out singing to search the prisoners, whom they lead in triumph to the cabin where they are to receive their doom.

The owner of this cabin has the power of determining their fate, though it is often left to some who has lost her husband, brother or son in the war; and when this is the case, she generally adopts him into the place of the deceased. The prisoner has victuals immediately given him, and while he is at his repast, a consultation is held; and if it be resolved to save his life, two young men untie him, and taking him by the hands, lead him to the cabin of the person into whose family he is to be adopted, and there he is received with all imaginable marks of kindness. He is treated as a friend, as a brother, or as a husband, and they soon love them with the same tenderness as if he stood in the place of one of their friends. In short, he has no other marks of captivity, but his not being suffered to return to his own nation, for his attempting this would be punished with certain death.

But if the sentence be death, how different their conduct! These people, who behave with such disinterested affection to each other, with such tenderness to those whom they adopt, here shew that they are truly savages; the dreadful sentence is no sooner passed, than the whole village set up the death-cry; and, as if there were no medium between the most generous friendship and the most inhuman cruelty; for the execution of him whom they had just before deliberated upon admitting into their tribe, is no longer deferred, than whilst they can make the necessary preparations for rioting in the most diabolical cruelty.

They first strip him and fixing two posts in the ground, fasten to them two pieces from one to the other; one about two feet from the ground, the other about five or six feet higher: then obliging the unhappy victim to mount upon the lower cross piece, they tie his legs to it a little asunder: his hands are extended and tied to the angles formed by the upper piece. In this posture they burn him all over the body, sometimes first daubing him with pitch. The whole village, men, women and children, assemble round him, everyone torturing him in what manner they please, each striving to exceed the other in cruelty, as long as he has life.

But if none of the bystanders are inclined to lengthen out his torments, he is either shot to death, or enclosed with dry bark, to which they set fire; they then leave him on the frame, and in the evening run from cabin to cabin, superstitiously striking with small twigs, the furniture, walls and roofs, to prevent his spirit from remaining there to take vengeance for the evils committed on his body. The remainder of the day and night following is spent in rejoicing.

This is the most usual mode of murdering their prisoners; but sometimes they fasten them to a single stake, and build a fire around them; at other times they cruelly mangle their limbs, cut off their fingers and toes joint by joint, and sometimes scald them to death.

What is most extraordinary, if the sufferer be an Indian, there seems during the whole time of his execution, a contest between him and his tormenters, which shall outdo the other, they in inflicting the most horrid pains, or he in enduring them—not a groan, nor a sigh, not a distortion of countenance escapes him in the midst of his torments. It is even said, that he recounts his own exploits, informs them what cruelties he has inflicted upon his countrymen, and threatens with the revenge that will attend his death—that he even reproaches them for their ignorance of the art of tormenting; paints out methods of more exquisite torture, and more sensible parts of the body to be afflicted.

The savages of the West are high spirited and soon irritated, the most trifling provocations frequently rouse them to arms and prove the occasion of bloodshed and murder.—Their petty private quarrels are often decided this way, and expeditions undertaken without the knowledge or consent of a general council. These private expeditions are winked at, and excused as a means of keeping their young men in action, and inuring them to the exertions of war.

When war becomes a national affair, it is entered upon with great deliberation—they first call an assemblage of their sachems or chief warriors to deliberate upon the affair—when they are thus assembled, the head sachem or leader, proposes the affair they have met to consult upon, and taking up the tomahawk, which lies by him, enquires "who among you will go and fight against such a nation ?"—"Who among you will bring captives from thence to feed our fires, that we may be revenged for the wrongs that they have done us?—then one of the principal warriors rising, harangues the whole assembly, and afterward, addressing himself to the young men, enquires who will go along with him and fight the whites, their natural enemies? when they generally rise, one after another and fall in behind him, while he walks round the circle till he is joined by a sufficient number.

It has been remarked that such is the influence of their women in these consultations, that the issue depends much upon them—if any one of them, in conjunction with the chiefs, has a mind to excite one who does not immediately depend upon them, to take an active part in the war, she presents, by the hands of some trusty young warrior, a string of *wampum*, to the person whose help she solicits, which seldom fails of producing the effect. But, when they solicit an offensive or defensive alliance with a whole nation, they send an embassy with a large belt of *wampum* and a bloody hatchet, inviting them to come and drink the blood of their enemies.

In time of peace they are kind and hospitable to all who visit them, with manifested tokens of friendship—but to those who intentionally offend them, the western savage is implacable! he never indeed makes use of oaths, or indecent expressions, but cruelly conceals his sentiments, till by treachery or surprise he can gratify his revenge. No length of time is sufficient to allay his resentment; no distance of place is great enough to protect the object; he crosses the steepest mountains, pierces impervious forests, and traverses the most hideous deserts; bearing the inclemency of the season, the fatigue of the expedition, the extremes of hunger and thirst, with patience and cheerfulness, in hopes of surprising the enemy, and exercising upon him the most shocking barbarities!

Then these cannot be effected, the revenge is left as a legacy, transferred from generation to generation, from father to son, till an opportunity offers of taking what they think ample satisfaction!

It is a characteristic of the aboriginals of the west, to testify great indifference for the productions of art—but, such however, is not their behaviour when they are told of a person, who distinguishes himself by agility in running; is well skilled in hunting; can take a most exact aim; work a canoe along a rapid, with great dexterity; is skilled in all the arts which their stealthy mode of carrying on a war is capable of; or is acute in discerning the situation of a country, and can, without a guide pursue his proper course through a vast forest, and support hunger, thirst, and fatigue with invincible firmness; at such a relation their attention is aroused—they listen to the interesting tale with delight, and express in the strongest terms their esteem for so great and so wonderful a man.

www.ingramcontent.com/pod-product-compliance
Lightning Source LLC
Chambersburg PA
CBHW032039080426
42733CB00006B/136